D0315116

DATE DUE			

STUDIES IN
TUDOR AND STUART POLITICS
AND GOVERNMENT

VOLUME TWO

The Tudor Revolution in Government (C.U.P. 1953)

England under the Tudors, History of England, vol. 4 (Methuen 1955)

(ed.) *The Reformation*, New Cambridge Modern History, vol. 2 (C.U.P. 1958)

Star Chamber Stories (Methuen 1958)

The Tudor Constitution (C.U.P. 1960)

(ed.) *Renaissance and Reformation, 1300-1648*, Ideas and Institutions in Western Civilization (Macmillan, N.Y. 1963)

Reformation Europe, 1517-59 (Collins 1963)

The Practice of History (Sydney U.P. 1967)

England, 1200-1640, The Sources of History (Hodder & Stoughton 1969)

The Future of the Past, Inaugural Lecture (C.U.P. 1968)

Modern Historians on British History, 1485-1945 (Methuen 1970)

Political History: Principles and Practice (Basic Books 1970)

Policy and Police: Enforcement of the Reformation in the Age of Thomas Cromwell (C.U.P. 1972)

Reform and Renewal: Thomas Cromwell and the Common Weal (C.U.P. 1973)

STUDIES IN
TUDOR AND STUART POLITICS
AND GOVERNMENT

PAPERS AND REVIEWS 1946-1972

G. R. ELTON

VOLUME TWO

PARLIAMENT/POLITICAL THOUGHT

CAMBRIDGE UNIVERSITY PRESS

Published by the Syndics of the Cambridge University Press
Bentley House, 200 Euston Road, London NW1 2DB
American Branch: 32 East 57th Street, New York, N.Y.10022

© Cambridge University Press 1974

Library of Congress Catalogue Card Number: 73-79305

ISBNs
0 521 20282 5 vol. I
0 521 20288 4 vol. II
0 521 20388 0 set of two volumes

First published 1974

Printed in Great Britain
at the University Printing House, Cambridge
(Brooke Crutchley, University Printer)

CONTENTS

VOLUME ONE

v

Contents

Contents

VOLUME TWO

ACKNOWLEDGMENTS

The author and publisher are grateful to the following for permission to reproduce material first published by them:

The English Historical Review, and Longman Ltd. (for Nos. 24 and 25)
The Bulletin of the Institute of Historical Research (for No. 23)
The Economic History Review (for No. 26)
The Royal Historical Society (for No. 31)
The British Academy (for No. 32)
Encounter (for No. 29)
Annali della Fondazione italiana per la storia amministrativa (for No. 27)
The British Studies Monitor (for No. 21)
The University Press of Virginia (for No. 22)
Random House Inc. (for No. 28)
Harper & Row Inc. (for No. 30)

ABBREVIATIONS

Allen *Opus Epistolarum Desiderii Erasmi Roterodami*, ed. P. S. Allen et al. 12 vols. (Oxford, 1906–58)

APC *Acts of the Privy Council of England*, ed. J. R. Dasent

BIHR *Bulletin of the Institute of Historical Research*

BM British Museum

CHJ *Cambridge Historical Journal*

CPR *Calendar of Patent Rolls*

DNB *Dictionary of National Biography*

EHR *English Historical Review*

HJ *The Historical Journal*

LJ *Journal of the House of Lords*

LP *Letters and Papers, Foreign and Domestic, of the Reign of Henry VIII*, ed. J. S. Brewer, J. Gairdner, R. H. Brodie, 21 vols. (1862–1932)

Merriman R. B. Merriman, *The Life and Letters of Thomas Cromwell*, 2 vols. (Oxford, 1902)

Policy and Police G. R. Elton, *Policy and Police: the enforcement of the Reformation in the age of Thomas Cromwell* (Cambridge, 1972)

PRO Public Record Office, London

Reform and Renewal G. R. Elton, *Reform and Renewal: Thomas Cromwell and the Commonweal* (Cambridge, 1973)

Rogers *The Correspondence of Sir Thomas More*, ed. E. F. Rogers (Princeton, 1947)

Roper W. Roper, *The Life of Sir Thomas More, Knight*, in *Two Early Tudor Lives*, ed. R. S. Sylvester and D. P. Harding (New Haven, 1962)

StP *State Papers of Henry VIII*, 11 vols. (1830–52)

Abbreviations

TRHS   *Transactions of the Royal Historical Society*

Tudor Constitution   The Tudor Constitution: Documents and Comment-
ary, ed. G. R. Elton (Cambridge, 1960)

Tudor Revolution   G. R. Elton, *The Tudor Revolution: administrative
changes in the reign of Henry VIII* (Cambridge, 1953)

References to *LP* are to numbers of documents, elsewhere to pages.
Books for which no place of publication is noted were published in
London.

III

PARLIAMENT

21

(A)

STUDYING THE HISTORY
OF PARLIAMENT*

There are, of course, good reasons for the amount of attention which historians have given to the English Parliament. So much has been written about it, one way or another, that the uninitiate might suppose the subject exhausted; and for some time a good deal of the labour available has been directed into other channels. Nevertheless, the magnetic field of parliamentary studies continues to operate, so much so that even historians looking at social structure or economic reform keep returning helplessly to the small number of people who made up that institution. The central position of Parliament in all English history is virtually axiomatic, and like all axioms it ought to be more often questioned than it is; but whatever one may think of that point, so long as historians will devote themselves to Parliament it is desirable that their labours should now and again be put under the lens. Several major and many lesser works have appeared in the last twenty-five years; two major 'projects' are in hand; it is not improper to enquire whether all that energy is being put to the best possible uses.

There is no need to do more than mention the achievements of recent years; they are familiar to all concerned. Nearly every century of parliamentary history has had its devotees. Sir Goronwy Edwards and J. S. Roskell have enlarged our knowledge of the late-medieval Commons; a fairly solid orthodoxy has been established which returns the lower House almost to the central position assigned to it by Stubbs but recognizes the influential weight of the Lords as well.[1] Though I remain less than perfectly convinced that everything that mattered about Parliament was clearly present before the battle of Bosworth, I agree that the representative institution experienced in medieval

---

* [*British Studies Monitor,* ii. 1 (1971), 4–14. This paper called forth an attack from Professor J. H. Hexter, to which I replied in 21 (B) below: ibid. iii. 1. 16–22.]

[1] J. G. Edwards, *The Commons in Medieval English Parliaments* (1958); J. S. Roskell, *The Commons in the Parliament of 1422* (Manchester, 1954); *The Commons and Their Speakers in English Parliaments, 1376–1523* (Manchester, 1965); 'Perspectives in Parliamentary History,' *Bulletin of the John Rylands Library,* 46 (1963–4), 448–75.

England a unique political and social development; I would only continue to maintain that what happened under Henry VIII amounted to a further transformation into the 'modern' institution – the consolidation of a self-consciously sovereign legislature.[1] The early-Tudor period has so far yielded only one book on Parliament, but this, especially because of the attention it gives to the often neglected House of Lords, is notable.[2] The reign of Elizabeth, on the other hand, the stamping ground of Sir John Neale, stands out as one of the major areas of parliamentary research.[3] Curiously enough, the century in which Parliament at last really became the obvious centre of politics has produced hardly any specifically parliamentary studies of weight, perhaps just because Parliament is bound to come into every treatment of seventeenth-century politics.[4] One Parliament has received specific study;[5] some attempts have been made to unravel the inner history of the Commons during the Interregnum;[6] biographical analysis has twice been applied to the Long Parliament.[7] Things change with a bang after 1689 when a whole series of solid works following in the wake of Namier's revolution (sometimes obediently and sometimes rebelliously) wrestle with the reality of political behaviour in those now regular sittings at Westminster. From this point the history of Parliament becomes (so far as historians are concerned) increasingly the history of parties, a story continued in the 'new manner' into the nineteenth century.[8] A lesser, but no less significant, chord has been

[1] Cf. below, no. 22.

[2] S. E. Lehmberg, *The Reformation Parliament* (Cambridge, 1970).

[3] J. E. Neale, *The Elizabethan House of Commons* (1949); *Elizabeth I and Her Parliaments*, 2 vols. (1953, 1957).

[4] P. Zagorin, *The Court and the Country* (1970) deals really with neither court nor country but with the behaviour of groups in Parliament. But it does not mean to be parliamentary history.

[5] T. L. Moir, *The Addled Parliament of 1614* (Oxford, 1958).

[6] E.g. articles by Lotte Glow (Mrs Mulligan) in *Journal of Modern History*, 36 (1964), 373–97; *EHR* 80 (1965), 289–313; *HJ* 8 (1965), 1–15; *BIHR* 38 (1965), 48–70; *Journal of British Studies*, 5 (November 1965), 31–52; *HJ* 12 (1969), 3–22. Also, H. R. Trevor-Roper, 'The Fast Sermons in the Long Parliament' and 'Oliver Cromwell and His Parliaments' in *Religion, the Reformation, and Social Change* (London, 1967).

[7] D. Brunton and D. H. Pennington, *The Members of the Long Parliament* (1954); Mary F. Keeler, *The Long Parliament, 1640–1641* (Philadelphia, 1954).

[8] E.g. Denis Rubini, *Court and Country, 1688–1702* (1968); Robert Walcott, *English Politics in the Early Eighteenth Century* (Oxford, 1956); Geoffrey S. Holmes, *British Politics in the Age of Anne* (1967); John Owen, *The Rise of the Pelhams* (1957); John Brooke, *The Chatham Administration* (1956); Bernard Donoughue, *British Politics and the American Revolution* (1964); Ian R. Christie, *The End of North's Ministry* (1958); J. Cannon, *The Fox–North Coalition* (Cambridge, 1969); L. G. Mitchell, *Charles James Fox and the Disintegration of the Whig Party* (1971); Norman Gash, *Politics in the Age of*

struck by students of the franchise and of elections.[1] By themselves stand, so far unfinished, W. O. Aydelotte's quantifying researches into the 1840s.[2]

So much – too briefly – for the past; what of the present and the future? There are at the moment two major enterprises in hand which belong entirely to this one historical theme: the History of Parliament Trust in London and the project at Yale to publish unprinted seventeenth-century parliamentary diaries. Both are organized, both rely on co-operative labours, both deserve credit as well as respectful criticism.

The History of Parliament Trust is the child of Sir Lewis Namier's old age. It was planned to produce a complete biographical dictionary of all persons ever elected to sit in the House of Commons; and although it now seems that the resistance to this approach among specialists on the nineteenth century will succeed in removing that area from the operation, the scheme still runs from Edward I to George III, a fairly awesome undertaking. Though some parts of this timespan remain unallocated, others are well advanced. One sector has reached the term of its gestation: the three volumes in which Namier and John Brooke cover the years 1754–90;[3] and the preceding section from 1715 (in Romney Sedgwick's charge) has just appeared. The Elizabethan volumes, naturally handed over to Neale, await their editor's introduction: the biographies appear to be completed. S. T. Bindoff has for some time been at work on the years 1485–1558, and the biographies accumulate. Roskell is sorting things from 1377 to the end of the Middle Ages, and Basil Duke Henning (loosely connected with the Trust) is taking care of the Restoration period. The Trust has existed for over twenty years; many young people's time has been absorbed by its detailed labours; results have certainly been slow in coming, but the prospects now look quite bright.

Has it all been worth it? In itself, of course, all new information is always welcome, and the staff of the Trust have worked diligently and

Peel (1953); H. J. Hanham, *Elections and Party Management* (1959). For more bibliographical details on this and other work, see my *Modern Historians on British History, 1485–1945* (1970), under index-entries 'Parliament' and 'Party'.

[1] E.g. J. H. Plumb, 'The Growth of the Electorate of England from 1600 to 1715,' *Past and Present*, 45 (1969), 90–116; John R. Vincent, *Poll Books: How the Victorians Voted* (Cambridge, 1967); Henry Pelling, *The Second Geography of British Elections, 1885–1910* (1967).

[2] Of his many articles, see esp. 'Voting Patterns in the House of Commons in the 1840s,' *Comparative Studies in Society and History*, 5 (1962–3), 134–63, and 'Parties and Issues in Early-Victorian England,' *Journal of British Studies*, 5 (May 1966), 95–114.

[3] 1964.

widely in many archives that might otherwise have remained untouched. Not only a body of fact but a satisfactory body of skilled techniques has been built up, despite the rapid turnover among assistants, of whom only one or two have given really prolonged service. True, one hears at times of errors and deficiencies in the files, but that is in the nature of things when so much is taken in hand. More seriously, it looks as though the work has been done with such single-mindedness that matters not directly relevant to the enterprise have been ignored, including even details of parliamentary history and procedure not bearing immediately on the questions of elections, patronage, and members. This constitutes a distressing missing of opportunities, for those scattered searches will not be repeated soon. The main doubt, however, must attach to the larger purposes of the scheme. What is really being learned about the history of the Commons (History of *Parliament* Trust being something of a misnomer) from that patchwork of biographies? Any final judgment must clearly await a larger body of published work; it is hard to know the answer when all one has to go on is the sector which had already been so thoroughly 'namierized' that surprises or new insights could hardly have been expected. The same problem afflicts the other well-advanced section, the age of Elizabeth, since Neale's massive work rests on precisely the sort of analysis which the Trust has been doing again, perhaps rather more solidly and extensively.

If Namier was the father of this biographical factory, the Yale diaries project acknowledges the paternity of Wallace Notestein. So far nothing has appeared, but one may express a hope that the work will improve on that produced by Notestein himself. One looks for rather more rigorous scholarship in the description of the manuscripts printed, the exposition of material included or omitted, and the ordering of highly confusing particles than went, for instance, to the seven large and frustrating volumes in which Notestein and Frances Relf collected the diaries of the 1621 Parliament. The new editors need to remember that their task (to make all recourse to the originals superfluous) involves a good deal more than putting together an adequate text and identifying names and events, but a good deal less than writing parliamentary history. The project – which has made marked progress on the Parliament of 1628 – will, one hopes, remember that its proper purpose is to make historical evidence not only accessible but also manageable and comprehensible, but that the exploitation of that evidence should be left to other historians or at least other occasions.

However, rather more is at stake than the quality of these labours on biographies and diaries. The very fact that both schemes took their inspiration from eminent scholars now dead sounds a note of warning. These are the methods pioneered in an earlier generation. The point does not abate their usefulness but it does suggest that fundamental questions might be asked about the supposition that parliamentary studies are best pursued in these ways. As a matter of fact, the Namier method has been showing very clear signs of diminishing returns. Not every age has proved equally amenable to those techniques, and scholars' desire to know what went on in Parliament has once again been shouldering aside a preoccupation with the kind of men who sat there. In view of the deficiencies of official parliamentary records before the nineteenth century, additional information from possibly progressively less distinguished private notes will always have its uses, though it is a little disconcerting to find how often treasured manuscripts merely repeat what has long been available in the much underrated *Parliamentary History*. At any rate, I feel quite strongly that these established methods are no longer enough and, moreover, that they will fail to satisfy because they evade the asking of some highly pertinent questions. They do so because they are still dominated by a traditional and very partial view of the nature of the institution which they study.

Historians of Parliament have almost always concerned themselves with politics; they have treated the assembly as a political arena in which political conflicts were fought out and major political changes carried through. Before the age of Walpole, historians of Parliament have almost always (unconsciously) confined themselves to one theme – the battles between Crown and 'nation'; thereafter, they almost exclusively regard Parliament as the meeting ground of parties. This is obvious among the historians of the seventeenth century and later, but it is also true of Neale's narrative volumes, with their interest concentrated on 'conflict', and dominates both the descriptions and the debates of medievalists who are forever trying to do curious things like 'measuring' the power of the Commons. Historians still effectively live under the signs embodied in the titles of Pollard's famous *Evolution of Parliament* and Notestein's even more famous *Winning of the Initiative by the House of Commons*, titles which urge us to seek nothing but the 'growth' of the Commons' independence and political ascendancy, in a constant struggle against the power of the Crown. Yet quite a few question marks must stand against this whiggish conviction, not least the last hundred years during which the institution's lack of political initiative and control has become a commonplace of the commentators.[1] Parliamentary history has traditionally been treated as though all that mattered was the ambition of elected representatives to limit the power of the executive, a tradition the more strongly maintained because of the considerable influence that American scholars, who perhaps cannot be expected to know better, have exercised in this field. Now of course I do not deny that one side of that history is rightly seen in that light, but I gravely doubt whether it deserves to be treated as the sole, or even as the main, aspect.

Against what I may call the constitutional historian's preferred purpose, I should like to advocate the administrative historian's questions. Not that I really believe in the virtues of such categorization, but the term may help to explain what I have in mind. From first to last, Parliament has been an instrument of action, a body which *does* things and achieves ends; and these ends have regularly become apparent in the legislation passed. It thus comes as a surprise to find that parliamentary historians regularly ignore the statutes passed,[2] interest in which is, in the main, left to historians of the economy, the Church, and other concerns which in this context are extraneous. No one has systematically used the acts of Parliament – their planning, passage, and achievement – as an instrument for the study of the institution which produced them. A few sixteenth-century historians have made a small beginning by investigating the inner history of some statutes,[3] but they, too, have so far confined themselves to particular occasions only. Neale's three volumes on Elizabethan parliamentary history ignore the better part of the legislation passed or frustrated, confining themselves to what is politically 'significant', and Notestein's seven volumes of diaries attend to a Parliament which succeeded in passing two subsidy acts – no more. This slanting of

---

[1] A small start has been made for the nineteenth century with studies of governmental control, a hitherto neglected aspect of the same theme: Peter Fraser, 'The Growth of Ministerial Control in the Nineteenth Century House of Commons,' *EHR* 75 (1960), 444–63; Valerie Cromwell, 'The Losing of the Initiative of the House of Commons, 1790–1914,' *TRHS*, 1968, 1–23.

[2] In the Introduction to the Namier and Brooke volumes in the *History of Parliament*, two out of 545 pages attend to legislation.

[3] Articles by Neale on the Elizabethan act of uniformity in *EHR* 45 (1950), 304–32; by S. T. Bindoff on the statute of artificers in *Elizabethan Government and Society*, ed. S. T. Bindoff, J. Hurstfield, and C. H. Williams (1961); by G. R. Elton on the act of appeals (below, no. 24), on the act of proclamations (above, no. 19), and on the treasons act (*Policy and Police*, ch. 6); and by E. W. Ives on the statute of uses in *EHR* 82 (1967), 673–97. Lehmberg (see p. 4, n. 2 above) does study legislation.

interest seems almost perverse, but so ingrained is the habit of ignoring the making of laws – the chief purpose of parliamentary meetings – that no one to my knowledge has even commented on it.

What would be gained if historians looked at Parliament from the angle of legislative procedure and achievement rather than from the specialized viewpoint of political debate? In the first place, they might come to realize that the normal condition of sessions was agreement, even harmony, and not conflict. Legislation (a vast flow of statutes) always represents the co-operation, however obtained, of all those present. Conflict thus becomes far from normal but rather a symptom of disease, and unresolved conflict becomes a sign of genuine failure on the part of all concerned. This does not mean leaving out the great debates and quarrels; but it does mean placing them properly and understanding their occurrence more correctly. We should hear less about packing and corruption and more about management and political competence, a marked gain in reality. With luck we may even be able to expose for the illusion it is the conviction that only opposition entitles a man to respect. The period of parliamentary history likely to profit most is the early seventeenth century, which badly needs liberating from the bonds of doctrine: it would really be nice to know what actually happened in the Parliaments of James I and Charles I instead of continuing to think in terms of 'constitutional conflicts'.

Secondly, a different set of records will become the object of attack, namely, the records in which the institution itself embodied its work. On the face of it, this seems too obvious a point to make, but most parliamentary historians do not, in fact, study these. They rely on letters and diaries. The *Journals* they regard essentially as providing information on debates. But the *Journals* are, in the first place, records of business done; they are the clerks' record and not the members', and remain so to the present day. This – their basic – character has never yet been systematically exploited. For the years down to about 1550, the Rolls of Parliament similarly provide the record of business and should likewise be used to discover how and by whom business was done. Historians, one hopes, will at last discover the road to the Record Office of the House of Lords where the original acts (the physical product of business) are preserved almost complete from 1497 onwards, and other materials become plentiful from about the middle of the seventeenth century onwards. These pieces of evidence were produced by what was actually done, and they should therefore be used to discover what was done in both Houses, how and when and by whom and possibly for what reasons, how days were organized and who profited, all sorts of questions which continuously fail to be asked and which unanswered leave all our understanding of parliamentary history poised in midair.

If this different approach is consciously adopted – if people come to look upon Parliament as a working institution rather than as an arena of political and party conflict – certain consequences can be predicted. Editorial labours will switch from diaries to two neglected sets of materials: treatises on procedure and the *Journals* themselves. A first look at especially the earlier volumes of the *Journals* in manuscript is likely to astonish anyone familiar only with the printed versions, and a really searching look will assuredly produce much valuable new knowledge as well as a good deal of instructive bewilderment. That the only treatise edited in recent years (leaving aside the worth of that edition) should be the so-called *Liverpool Tractate* of the later eighteenth century (ed. C. Strateman, 1937) is a pity: where are the professional editions of Hooker, Lambarde, Hakewill, Elsynge, Scobell which would incorporate important manuscript material and greatly illumine the inner history of both Houses?[1] Until we know the practices governing the conduct of business we cannot understand the business that went on: a point so obvious that one is almost ashamed of making it, were it not for the willingness of so many generations of historians to labour confidently without such knowledge. To cite one example: very often one cannot properly assess the meaning of a debate until one understands what information was available to members, in what form it reached them, and how it was obtained. A start has at least been made on this important problem,[2] but conventional parliamentary historians not only do not do this work themselves but do not even read what more original scholars produce. The lure of conflict, of faction, of social structure proves too strong. Real hopes of finding out the truth rest on studies of procedure.

Procedure, and the men responsible for it, is one of the questions awaiting attention. Pollard showed his sound instincts when in his last years he devoted himself so unreadably to the history of the clerks, and Neale's analysis of procedure in his *Elizabethan House of Commons* is the

---

[1] Mrs Elizabeth Read Foster is reported to be at work on Elsynge, but there is a lot more to be done besides.

[2] Sheila Lambert, *List of House of Commons Sessional Papers, 1700–1750* (List and Index Society, spec. ser. i, 1968); 'Printing for the House of Commons in the Eighteenth Century,' *Library*, 5th ser., 23 (1968), 25–46.

most remarkable part of his work. O. C. Williams' *Clerical Organization of the House of Commons* (Oxford, 1954) should not be regarded as exhausting the theme.[1] Happily, there are signs of improvement in the situation for the eighteenth century,[2] but (despite Neale) gaps in our knowledge for the sixteenth are very large, while no one has yet devoted himself seriously to these fundamental questions in the most crucial of all parliamentary ages, the seventeenth century. We do not even know for sure how committees were appointed – by whom, at whose nomination, whether in public or upon lists privately submitted. How can we suppose that we understand the politics of Parliament when we are ignorant of the devices which gave politicians their opportunities?

Another topic which needs much more attention than it has received – and which it will not receive until the change of heart here suggested has taken place – is private bills and private acts. The importance of private bill legislation – or rather, the importance of the use of Parliament by private individuals and interests to arrange their own affairs – has been consistently overlooked; yet the quantity of work involved, the financial outlays, the benefits to clerks and Speakers, and the organization developed for the purpose make private bill matters a major item of parliamentary business. Clearly Parliament mattered (at least to the propertied classes) because people not in politics needed its services as much as king and politicians needed it for their different purposes. In this fact lie unsuspected reasons for the endurance of the institution through all sorts of political troubles: it is worth wondering whether the absence of Parliament in the 1630s was not, perhaps, resented as much because no one could get private acts passed as because of the lapse of 'constitutional government'.

Thus there is a really sizable programme of parliamentary studies waiting to be undertaken, work which neither the standard writings of the past nor the main current enterprises have had in view at all. I am willing to suppose that if this kind of study is really taken in hand the

[1] E.g., Sheila Lambert, 'The Clerks and Records of the House of Commons,' *BIHR*, 43 (1970), 215–31.

[2] Two books are in the press: one which gives a general description of procedure, while another deals with the machinery which produced acts of Parliament. The second also illumines the question of private legislation, on which subject see also the massive but far from exhaustive treatise by O. C. Williams, *The Historical Development of Private Bill Procedure and Standing Orders in the House of Commons*, 2 vols. (1948).

[The two books are now out: P. G. D. Thomas, *The House of Commons in the Eighteenth Century* (Oxford, 1971), and Sheila Lambert, *Bills and Acts: Legislative procedure in eighteenth-century England* (Cambridge, 1971).]

history of Parliament will be transformed and that of the realm will have to be considerably rewritten. Tempting though it might be to forecast the sort of revisions that may result, I must not engage in premature speculation. For the moment I can only say that four students of mine are now engaged in looking at Parliament in the manner here proposed, tackling the periods 1484–1504, 1536–47, 1589–1601, and 1604–21. We shall see what may emerge.

(B)

A REPLY

My lord, after hearty commendations, I cannot but both much marvel that you, whom I have taken to be mine earnest friend, should judge me as I may perceive by your letter you do, and also be glad that ye so frankly utter your stomach to me – Thomas Cromwell to Bishop Shaxton, 1538.

Controversies among historians commonly arise from misunderstandings. One man fails to make his meaning clear; or the other fails to read with sufficient attention; or, as in this case, both things happen. I am sorry to have casually used a metaphor ('putting under a lens') which suggested to Professor Hexter an exhaustiveness of treatment I should hardly have thought he expected to find in an article of nine pages. I am sorry not to have explained that when I referred to manuscripts repeating what is found in the *Parliamentary History*, I had mainly the eighteenth century in mind. Of course, the Yale Project will add considerably to our information on the early-Stuart Parliaments. And I am sorry to have employed a phrase, 'the statute book', which over here is understood to mean all the legislative business of Parliament, including private acts and failed bills, but which could be read as referring only to a limited source, the *Statutes of the Realm*. On the other hand, it is not reasonable of Professor Hexter to demand a complete bibliography of parliamentary studies; my obvious omissions, readily understood especially when they touch parties rather than Parliaments, were more numerous for other centuries than the seventeenth. No doubt the good historian can look into the future but it is simply true that when I despatched my piece early in 1971, I was still unaware of those forthcoming studies on Stuart Parliaments.[1] And Professor Hexter should not blame me for omitting Mrs Foster's two volumes from a list expressly concerned with secondary writings, not with edited texts.

[1] Professor Hexter should know that even news of the products of American university presses rarely penetrates to these backwoods *less than a year after publication*. Only review copies become available within a reasonable time, and not everybody gets those. (Perhaps the *British Studies Monitor* could find some way to help here?) I have now read the works in question and reviewed three of them in the *Historical Journal* (during 1972) where I give my reasons for doubting whether we now really have sufficient histories of the Parliaments of James I.

13

If I had done this either upon affection or intending prejudice to your estimation, you might have expostulated with me; and yet, if ye had then done it after a gentler sort I had both sooner have amended that I did amiss, and also have had better cause to judge your writing to come of a friendly heart towards me.

The remarks to which so much exception has been taken were concerned with a larger question than that which exercises my critic. I was writing about the whole history of Parliament; it is Professor Hexter who refers all I say to one-twelfth of that history. He is wrong in supposing that my view of Parliament is determined by Thomas Cromwell. If he will glance over the essay I wrote on Parliament (a copy of which was sent to him, in accordance with his standing orders to myself),[1] he will, I think, recognize that I wish to emphasize the early and continuous efficiency of the English Parliament as an active business organization, especially as distinguishing it from representative institutions elsewhere. The origins of that organization are found even in those early and undeveloped meetings, one of whose chief purposes it was to make possible the settlement of petitions by royal or conciliar response, a practice from which the legislative machinery of Parliament was to descend. The constant flow of statutes, the constant preoccupation with getting acts passed, extends from Edward I to the present day.

I therefore repeat that the *normal* condition of parliamentary meetings has always involved not conflict, but a high degree of ultimate co-operation. Set against the prevalent behaviour of centuries, the early-Stuart period does indeed depart from 'normalcy', just because, as Professor Hexter is right to point out, the flow then ceased, rendering the whole purpose and function of Parliament problematical. Professor Hexter's remarks on this, emphasizing the particular character of his particular period, seem to me exactly to prove the virtue of looking at legislation, as he has done. There is nothing censorious in drawing attention to this deviation from the norm. It ought not to be necessary even to mention it, nor would it be if it were not for the long-standing habit of historians to treat the reigns of the early Stuarts as typical, to transfer the primacy of conflict to other ages where at best it played a secondary role, and to wax censorious about Parliaments which, because in them co-operation proved possible, are so often called corrupt or subservient. In studying eleven-twelfths of the history of Parliament, we go astray if we concentrate on strife; trying to under-

[1] See no. 22 below.

stand an institution through that main part of its existence when it functioned for business, we shall greatly profit by approaching it through the technical study of its processes.

I seem to have given Professor Hexter the impression that I would wish to abolish the enterprise over which he presides. Of course not.

I assure you I am right glad ye are in the place ye are in and will do what shall lie in me to aid you in your office.

Perhaps the study even of the early-Stuart Parliaments can gain something from methods which appear so profitable for other periods. I have, it seems, offended in three particulars: in offering foolish advice on the editing of diaries, in casting doubt on conflict as the sole event in Parliament, and in suggesting that what my critic disparagingly calls 'the administrative historian's insight' might contribute significantly even to his special area of parliamentary history. I will explain myself a little more fully.

I need say nothing further on the inadequacies of the Notestein, Relf, Simpson edition: no one could improve on Professor Hexter's description of them. The principles of sound editing are neither so esoteric nor (thanks to the labours of ancient historians and medievalists) so unsettled as some editors would seem to believe. Editions which do not provide a clear listing of the manuscripts used, do not give precise references to what has been omitted, and do not describe what the manuscripts look like in their unprinted form, are not, by those established canons, adequate editions. An editor needs to establish the descent and relationship of manuscripts, an important task for early-seventeenth-century materials when so many people copied one another's extracts and treatises. One would expect him to debate the exact meaning of his materials, a task which in this case includes such questions as the date and reliability of the text, the diarist's relations to the events described, problems of religious and political bias, and a consideration of what proportion of the event we may have record of. Professor Hexter misunderstands my hope that a good edition would both make 'recourse to the originals superfluous' and render evidence properly accessible. Editions of materials which for the second purpose have to be rearranged achieve the first when they preface the information with a full technical description of the sources used. There are many editions of materials at least as difficult as these parliamentary diaries which have solved these problems, but the editions so far produced of the diaries have not done so.

To turn to conflict. Agreed it was painfully 'normal' between 1604 and 1640, but even so the traditional historical investigation, which concentrates on debates and issues while it ignores bills and acts, seems to miss significant points. Some of the notes printed as proceedings are in fact collections of precedents intended to illumine bill procedure, and the period produced important treatises on procedure, such as Elsynge's and Hakewill's writings. These matters are assuredly no nearer my heart than they were to theirs, and Professor Hexter might like to pause before allowing his contempt for me to carry him into neglect of men like Cotton and Selden. Procedure, it is true, could play its part in equipping the Commons for resistance to the king, although this is one of the points that has always been taken for granted rather than proved. In any case, the treatises and precedents make it perfectly plain that what concerned those parliamentarians was the manner in which Parliament went about the production of laws. These men witnessed Parliaments that passed few or no laws, but they do not seem to have been persuaded that this was a 'normal' state of affairs. They were not even sure that a non-legislating Parliament deserved the institutional title at all. In dissolving the Addled Parliament James I explicitly declared that assembly no Parliament on the grounds that he had not been called upon to assent to any bills; this interpretation was formally endorsed by all the judges in 1623 and accepted by Coke in his *Institutes*.[1] The reason had nothing to do with politics: if 1614 were reckoned a Parliament, a number of statutes, due for renewal in that session, would have lapsed. What mattered were the technicalities of legislation; on their account the law of England regarded such meetings as conventions, not Parliaments – hardly an acceptance of 'normalcy'. The same principle still influenced parliamentary practice in the eighteenth century. In 1754 and 1768, when, exceptionally, Parliament assembled briefly after a spring election with a prolonged recess in prospect, it was thought necessary to pass an act and thus make Parliaments of those assemblies, in order that upon a possible demise of the Crown a Parliament should be in being, as required by the Regency Acts.[2] Of course, historians are quite right in treating

---

[1] *LJ* ii. 717: '...pro eo quod nullus Regalis Assensus aut Responsio per Nos praestitus fuit, nullum Parliamentum, nec aliqua Sessio Parliamenti, habita aut tenta extitit'; W. J. Jones, *Politics and the Bench* (1971), 80–2, 157–9. And cf. T. L. Moir, *The Addled Parliament of 1614* (Oxford, 1958), 145–6.

[2] J. Hatsell, *Precedents and Proceedings in the House of Commons* (1818), ii. 298–301; *LJ* xxviii. 272 ff. and xxxii 145 ff. In 1754, one private naturalization act was thought sufficient for the purpose.

those non-legislating Stuart Parliaments as real Parliaments, but it is quite evident that well-informed and influential people thought sessions without legislation less normal than Professor Hexter will allow. Recognition of the essential character of the English Parliament throughout its history would thus seem to help to a better view of it at its time of crisis.

Lastly, let us see whether by starting from the fact that Parliaments were supposedly called to make laws something important may not be learned even about Parliaments that made few or none. For James's first Parliament, which did pass acts and discussed many more bills, the usefulness of the method is at present being proved by work in progress, but we need not confine ourselves to that relatively legislative Parliament. We ought to beware of the tendency of so many historians to grade statutes in an order designed to suit their own tastes; Professor Hexter's remarks do just that. Private acts especially get regularly forgotten. Their number shot up from 1604. In the one Parliament of the 1620s which saw enough peace to achieve legislation, they amounted to thirty-eight out of seventy-three acts passed. Professor Hexter says that Charles I's first Parliament passed only seven acts. Well, seven were printed. In 1626, as in 1624, the King's Printer did not list the private acts at the end of his collection of public acts, and in 1624 he thus concealed the existence of thirty-eight acts. In 1628, when he did print a list of titles, he added eighteen more to the eight public acts printed.[1] Since in 1626 the Original Acts are missing, only a careful analysis of the Journals could discover whether there really were only seven acts that session – a session in which the Upper House alone received thirty-seven bills (public and private) of which not one appears among the acts printed.[2] Evidently, even in these Parliaments the history of bills and acts poses problems central to an understanding of events.

Moreover, are not those failures to achieve legislation in themselves of concern to the historian of Parliament? What of the people who, increasingly used to settling their private affairs by statute, found the source run dry? Important people could not get their interests served in Parliament: what effect did this have upon attitudes toward both Parliament and Crown? The point was familiar in those products of political revolution, Oliver's Parliaments, when 'private business jostles all out' and 'if you have not private business you will have no house'.[3] As so often, one gathers a feeling that the politics of early-

---

[1] Strictly seven acts and the Petition of Right.   [2] *LJ* iii. 683.
[3] Thomas Burton, *Diary*, ed. J. T. Rutt (1828), i. 190; ii. 133.

Stuart England are somehow supposed to be totally different from everybody else's politics. It does not seem altogether probable. But reliance on traditional sources and questions is not likely to alter traditional answers, however improbable.

What I do not seem to have got across to Professor Hexter is really very simple. I am not proposing that we should study the history of Parliament as though it equalled the history of parliamentary legislation. I am proposing that we should use the business activity and organization of Parliament (productive or not) in order to understand the history of Parliament. This is what Parliaments did or were supposed to do – what people even in the seventeenth century still thought they might get from Parliament. No historian of the Stuart Parliaments will ignore conflict, and Professor Hexter has no right to accuse me of wishing to do so. But even those Parliaments cannot necessarily be fully understood as occasions of conflict alone; and the rest of the breed, the vast majority, must on no account be studied as though political dispute had been their main concern.

You might have provoked some other in my place that would have used less patience with you, finding so little in you.

'THE BODY OF THE WHOLE REALM': PARLIAMENT AND REPRESENTATION IN MEDIEVAL AND TUDOR ENGLAND*

ORIGINS OF PARLIAMENT

When the first assembly of the colony of Virginia met in 1619, it inherited the achievements of a very ancient tradition. Indeed, the whole history of representative institutions in the New World since that date covers only about the same length of time as that which separates 1619 from the beginnings of the English Parliament. Ever since the middle of the thirteenth century, kings of England had called various gatherings of nobles and sometimes of commons to meet in conclave, to debate the affairs of the realm, and to assist in the tasks of government; in those 350 years just about every conceivable parliamentary event had occurred. The one inconceivable event lay in the not very distant future. So far, no Parliament of England had tried to govern without the king, though when from 1642 it came to do so, it was in turn to set an example which the young daughter assembly in Virginia was in time to find useful.

In 1619, however, if any of those who assembled at Jamestown had kept in touch with affairs in the mother country, they might have had some doubts about the future of the model which they were copying. There had then been no effective meeting of the English Parliament for nine years, easily the longest break in the history of the institution. That last session of 1610 had left a great many unresolved conflicts behind, and the one attempt since at a Parliament, in 1614, had produced total deadlock, with not one achievement to the credit of king, Lords, or Commons. All over Europe, representative assemblies were not doing very well, and the men at Jamestown showed some resistance to dominant trends by assembling at all. Yet the Parliament of England survived, and its transatlantic offspring flourished. Even in 1619 that Parliament was radically different from similar assemblies in other parts of Europe, a difference not so much of age as of maturity.

* [*Jamestown Essays on Representation*, ed. A. E. Dick Howard (Charlottesville, University Press of Virginia, 1969).]

The long history of the medieval and Tudor Parliaments is shot through with obscurities and surrounded by controversy. This is particularly true of the origins of Parliament, a point perhaps too remote from 1619 to call for detailed consideration here. And yet, since some of the peculiarities of the English Parliament derive directly from its origins, a word is necessary, however foolhardy one may be in straying into the preserves of the most learned and most jealous of specialists.[1] The debate has in the main turned on the question whether the early Parliament was essentially a representative assembly called to discuss the affairs of the kingdom and vote taxes, or an enlarged session of the king's ordinary Council, mainly occupied with deciding pleas brought by petition. Not surprisingly, the truth of the matter would seem to be that it was both – both a political and a judicial body, or rather an occasion (frequent in the reign of Edward I when some fifty-two parliamentary meetings in thirty-five years have been identified) on which all the activities of government came together to be exercised in a meeting of the realm.[2] This is not just the habitual historian's compromise between conflicting theories based on insufficient data, but a conclusion which takes account of the double root from which these meetings stemmed.

This double root was not, in fact, anything out of the way; it was the same as that which gave to the Angevin institution of the 'king's court', the *curia regis*, its similar double meaning. On the one hand, the king held his court for his honour of England, a body to which all his tenants-in-chief were suitors and at which matters touching all were dealt with; on the other, the court constituted sittings of professional judges (his Council) to hear the pleas of the subject and do the justice which it was one of the chief functions of kingship to dispense. In the reign of Henry III, the notion of the feudal honour of England was being replaced by the notion of the realm, the *universitas* or *communitas Anglie*, in which not only the king's feudal tenants but all men with an 'interest' in the kingdom could claim a voice. This development reflected major social changes: the feudal knighthood was turning into the landed gentry, wealth and political weight were coming to be distributed more widely, and the old baronial class was dividing into great men (magnates) and lesser but still influential men.

[1] For two good recent summaries, see Edward Miller, *The Origins of Parliament* (Historical Association Pamphlet G44, 1960), and Peter Spufford, *Origins of the English Parliament*, (1967).
[2] J. G. Edwards, 'Justice in Early English Parliaments,' *BIHR* 27 (1954), 35–53, especially 53.

At the same time, the establishment of regular courts out of the *curia regis* divided pleas at law into those properly cognizable by the settled courts and those so novel or peculiar as to require attention by the residue of the king's power to do justice. The English Parliament resulted from the necessity to find a new opportunity to amalgamate the political and judicial tasks once discharged by the *curia regis*. It was for this reason that writs of summons (to individuals and occasionally for representatives from shires and boroughs) called men to 'treat' (discuss) with the king, while the surviving records of what was done in Parliament suggest that almost all the business of the meeting consisted of the hearing of private pleas. Though assemblies summoned for various purposes had met before 1272, it was really in the reign of Edward I, the king who found in these meetings a useful instrument for governing his realm, that the practice became habitual.

Nevertheless, when Edward I died, the Parliament was a good way from being a real or a defined institution. Even its membership remained entirely variable, at the pleasure of the Crown; it had become quite usual to call for elected men from the 'communities', but many more meetings attended only by magnates, or even by some such sectional interest as the merchants, were also thought of as Parliaments. Of Edward I's fifty-two Parliaments – 'afforced' (enlarged) sessions of his Council, summoned by special writs – only thirteen included representatives of shires and boroughs. In session, a full Parliament was unicameral, and it existed even after the better part of those summoned had gone home. There would seem to have been little in the way of regular procedure, and there was certainly no regular form of record. The early 'rolls of Parliament' were registers of pleas – at best, quite well-kept plea rolls, and at worst, mere files of private petitions for redress at law. At this point, the question whether these occasions would become political assemblies primarily concerned to debate and approve *quod omnes tangit* or plenary judicial sessions really still remained open; the frequency of meetings, and the call for more, rather suggest that an established law court was more likely to emerge than a representative assembly. In France, indeed, the name 'Parliament' came to be attached to the supreme court, but in fourteenth-century England, the Parliament, while acquiring institutional status and (using the conventional language of the day) the title of high court, in actual fact lost the character of a court for private suits. The king's Council in ordinary session, and more particularly the king's chancellor in his nascent court of Chancery, took over the function of filling the gaps in the law and helping the distressed. Though private matters never entirely vanished from the agenda of Parliament – where they survived as private bills subjected to a formally legislative rather than judicial process – the Parliament became a predominantly political institution. The circumstances which helped to settle the fate of the institution were the events of Edward II's reign on the one hand and the demands of Edward III's wars in France on the other.

Two facts stand out about Parliament in 1307. It was essentially a royal instrument of government, called by the king for purposes of his own, though naturally this did not exclude seeking advice and comment on actions which might be critical and even hostile. Secondly, the permanent Council formed the operative and animating element within it. In these facts, the institution reflected the purposeful strength and relative popularity of Edward I's rule. His son's reign, on the other hand, turned out to be the most conflict-ridden and unhappy period of English history since the anarchy of Stephen's reign, worse even than the troubles of Henry III, and it is of the utmost importance that the king's enemies found in the king's Parliament a proper and useful arena for political opposition. In effect, the baronial opposition to Edward II took over the Parliament: the essential core of the Parliament transferred from the permanent Council (soon summoned only to advise, not to resolve) to the Great Council of magnates, the Lords of the Parliament. At the same time, the magnates' need for support lower down the social scale led them to call in the representatives of the communities with greater regularity, a policy copied in turn by the king, who bid for the commons' support in fruitful rivalry. Whatever the precise implication of the famous statement in the Statute of York (1322) may have been,[1] there was a meaningful propaganda appeal in its insistence that matters touching the estate of the king and the estate of the kingdom shall be 'treated, granted and established in Parliament by our lord the king and with the consent of the prelates, earls, barons, and of the commonalty of the kingdom'.[2] As a result of the faction battles of Edward II's reign, Parliament had come to follow one road of development rather than the other. It was now in the main a political assembly of the great men of the realm, and representatives of

---

[1] For the lively debate, see Bertie Wilkinson, *Constitutional History of Medieval England, 1216–1399* (1952), ii. 134–56; to the bibliography there cited add Dionna Clementi, 'That the Statute of York of 1322 is no longer Ambiguous', in *Album, Helen Maud Cam* (Louvain–Paris, 1961), ii. 93–100.

[2] Wilkinson, *Const. Hist.* ii. 136.

shires, boroughs and the lower clergy were commonly called to attend and assist at meetings.

The consequences of these changes were still working themselves out in the first decade of Edward III's reign,[1] but it would appear that a truly formative period came to an end about the year 1340. In that year, the representatives of the lower clergy ceased to attend Parliaments and withdrew to the ecclesiastical Convocations, while the representatives of shires and boroughs came together in a common body, not unfairly (though anachronistically) to be called the House of Commons. At this point, the earlier structure by estates of the realm (spirituality, nobility, commonalty, with possible subdivisions), which continued to characterize most European assemblies, became quite impossible in England, with the result that natural sectional interests were given no chance of acting exclusively on their own behalf. Before this, the regular description of the great men as 'the prelates, earls and barons', the notion of an estate of merchants, the separate treatment accorded to the knights of the shire, the presence of the spiritual proctors (elected by the lesser clergy), as well as the fancies of the *Modus Tenendi Parliamentum*,[2] make it plain that the elements of an 'estates' organization were strong in the early days of the English Parliament. After 1340, they could appear in theories of the Parliament but remained forever excluded from its practice.[3] But while this well-known division into the embryos of the two 'houses' may strike the student as the most significant thing in marking the emergence of the characteristic Parliament of England, it has been shown that the change was neither so unprecedented, nor so final, nor so entirely unlike all Continental practice, as to deserve the concentration which analysis has bestowed on it. It is therefore worth stressing that the records of Parliament, reflecting (as records always do) genuine changes of practice, also call attention to the year 1340. In that year, the rolls acquired regularity of form and became a proper continuous record.[4] It would seem that to the Chancery clerks who kept the roll the fact of institu-

---

[1] See T. F. T. Plucknett, 'Parliament,' in James F. Willard and William A. Morris, eds., *The English Government at Work, 1327–1336* (Cambridge, Mass., 1940), i. 82–128.

[2] For the *Modus*, a radical reform programme rather than an administrative treatise, see V. H. Galbraith in *Journal of the Warburg and Courtauld Institutes*, 16 (1953), 81 ff.

[3] For the growing theoretical use of a three-estates doctrine in the fifteenth century, see S. B. Chrimes, *English Constitutional Ideas in the Fifteenth Century* (Cambridge, 1936), especially pp. 115–26.

[4] Down to *c*. 1339, the extant records are a mingle-mangle, not a series; from 1340 a standard form emerges which remained almost unaltered until 1483 (*Rotuli Parliamentorum*, ii. 103 ff.).

tional perfection had become clear; from 1340, but not really before that, they had no doubt that a new record class existed, to be distinguished not only from the plea rolls of the king's courts of law but also from the archives of the king's Council.

Very probably, these changes of about 1340 should be linked with the general reorganization of the government which Edward III attempted when he first embarked on his French adventures. The serious crisis of 1341, which effectively consolidated the new regularity and significance of a Parliament of Lords invariably accompanied by a 'house' of Commons,[1] was certainly the outcome of the war and the weakness of the organization which tried to run it. In 1341 Edward learned that he could not rely on a domestic system headed by his Chamber[2] or on the resources available to the king as of right. The lesson was driven home in the prolonged struggle over grants of taxation which ended only when it was finally conceded (in 1350 or 1362, according to one's reading of the situation) that not only 'aids' but the customs duties too must be consented to in Parliament, and nowhere else.[3] Edward's need for military support and money increasingly forced him into alliance with the Lords of the Parliament and dependence on the Commons; his reign, in fact, witnessed the achievement of the characteristic bases of parliamentary power. Not only was that body recognized as the only proper source of consent to taxation, but by about 1350 it was also becoming doctrine that ordinances made in response to petitions in Parliament were superior to all other forms of legislation; in 1376, in the Good Parliament, the role of the institution as the effective weapon against misgovernment was consolidated in the processes against Edward's ministers. The events of Richard II's reign, when once again both the king and his baronial enemies used Parliament to conduct their battles for power, maintained the momentum gained. Notoriously, under Henry IV both Parliament in general and the Commons in particular asserted claims to the right to interfere in the king's government which led earlier historians to refer to a period of 'Lancastrian constitutionalism'.

In the revolution of 1399, meetings of 'estates' and of 'the people',

---

[1] Wilkinson, *Const. Hist.* ii. 176–203. The crisis produced this effect, even though its most radical triumph, a statute subjecting the king's ministers to accountability in Parliament, was revoked in 1343.

[2] T. F. Tout, *Chapters in the Administrative History of Medieval England* (Manchester, 1920–8), iii. 69–142.

[3] Bertie Wilkinson, *Studies in the Constitutional History of the Thirteenth and Fourteenth Centuries* (Manchester, 1937), 55–80.

as well as a more properly constituted parliamentary assembly, provided stages for political action, but Henry IV was careful to avoid any suggestion that he owed his title to any such body. Nevertheless, since the presence of faction and his own ill health made him relatively weak, the reign witnessed much apparent activity. The Parliament he inherited now consisted of the Lords and Commons, but these partners were still very unequal. It was still strictly the case that the Commons, though necessary to make a true Parliament, nevertheless stood formally outside it; they were petitioners whose demands the king submitted to the Lords of the Parliament so that they might advise him how to answer. The history of Parliament in the fifteenth century consists largely in the disappearance of these differences, till by the time the Tudors came to rule the characteristic bicameral institution had arrived.[1] In 1399, the Commons explicitly denied any notion that in addition to being petitioners they also had the right to assent to what was done; in 1414 they claimed to be assentors but found Henry V unsympathetic; by 1460 their assent was coming to be regularly recorded. The full acceptance of a Parliament consisting of two equipollent Houses was delayed by the minority of Henry VI; from 1422 to about 1440, government was in the hands of a regency Council, dominated by magnates, which called relatively few Parliaments and which, when it did, paid little heed to the Commons.[2] But the crises of the mid-century caused the breakup of the Council and returned the battle to Parliament, until civil war ended all recourse to constitutional machinery. By the 1450s references to a lower and a higher House of Parliament were so casual as to show them to be commonplace;[3] and Edward IV, who deliberately wooed non-aristocratic opinion, from the first treated the House of Commons as effectively comparable to the Lords in constitutional standing.

Once again, the records indicate the point of change. Until 1482, the rolls of Parliament adhered to the pattern begun in 1340. An account of the opening procedures was followed by matters touching the king and private individuals; by the fifteenth century, these appeared in the form of petitions reciting the desired remedy. Lastly, the public bills were grouped under one head; they constituted a series of petitions not reciting the remedy and annotated with the royal response. (The

---

[1] See Bertie Wilkinson, *Constitutional History of England in the Fifteenth Century* (1964), 277-320.

[2] The 23 years of Henry IV's and Henry V's reign produced 21 Parliaments; the 16 years of Henry VI's minority, 11.

[3] Chrimes, *Constitutional Ideas*, 128-9.

resultant statutes, really produced in Parliament, were enrolled on the statute roll.) From 1 Richard III (1484), this last part, the really weighty business of Parliament, no longer formed a list of petitions including those refused, but simply a list of statutes passed.[1] The king's Parliament, of Lords and Commons equally engaged in the task of law-making and the remedying of grievances, had seemingly arrived. The clearest indication of this was provided in the Acts of Attainder with which victorious parties rid themselves of their enemies or appropriated their enemies' property. After the middle of the century, no impeachment took place in which the Lords of the Parliament sat as a high court and listened to the Commons acting as prosecutors; instead, state trials were superseded by the joint legislative action of the attainder. In 1489 the judges declared an attainder invalid because 'the Lords assented and nothing was said of the Commons'.[2]

By the time the Tudors came to the throne, the English Parliament had thus passed through three distinguishable phases. Its formative years – during which its composition was variable, its sittings mostly unicameral, and its occasions filled with whatever business of the realm seemed called for but very much preoccupied with the dispensation of justice by the Council – had clearly ended in 1340. For the next sixty years or so, no meeting was a Parliament unless it included not only the individually summoned Lords but also the representative Commons. Yet these last were formally not members of the Parliament and regarded themselves as the voice of the nation, bringing grievances before the king and his Great Council in Parliament and granting money for extraordinary purposes. The experience and influence gained in those years assisted the Commons to a somewhat precocious prominence in the reign of Henry IV, but it took the third phase, and especially the policy of the Yorkist kings, to make them more equal partners with the Lords who, at the same time, were being reduced to the position of one of two Houses. This Parliament controlled taxation and assented, in all its parts, to legislation. It almost looks as though nothing further could have happened to it to produce the assemblies

[1] *Rotuli Parliamentorum*, vi. 220 ff. This form continued through the reign of Henry VIII, with the exception that the roll for the first session of the Reformation Parliament (1529) recorded public acts before private (*LJ*, i). By the later fifteenth century the Lords seem to have kept another record, leaving the rolls with purely formal statements of business (see, e.g., William Huse Dunham, Jr, ed., *The Fane Fragment of the 1461 Lords' Journal* [New Haven, 1935]), but this alone does not account for the changing form of the purely formal record in 1484.

[2] *The Reign of Henry VII from Contemporary Sources*, ed. A. F. Pollard (1914), ii. 19.

which faced the early Stuarts, and the sixteenth century might thus be regarded as marking an interlude before the revival of parliamentary effectiveness. Indeed, such a view, at one time current, has lately been persuasively reasserted, against the opinion of recent Tudor scholars that in the sixteenth century Parliament underwent a transformation which produced the 'true' modern institution.[1]

Though Professor Roskell's revival of the notion that the medieval Parliament was a much more effective and important part of the constitution than whatever Parliaments met under the Tudors rests on some sound enough points, it also runs into some manifest difficulties both of the evidence and of interpretation. By the seventeenth century, the English Parliament looked and acted very differently from what survived of its Continental counterparts. Earlier, it may have differed from them in details of composition and procedure, but it had differed far less in powers and purposes; indeed, in influence and weight it stood well behind some. The various Cortes of the Spanish kingdoms, the estates of Brabant or Flanders, the estates of Languedoc or Brittany, even occasionally the Estates General of France, all at times or regularly restrained the liberties of monarchs, reserved the right to grant taxation, and took part in the processes of lawmaking. The Estates General of Tours in 1484, in particular, showed much maturity of judgment and a high institutional development; and the Cortes of Aragon, as is very well known, played a much larger part in the affairs of that kingdom than did any medieval English Parliament. Yet it was in England that the institution adapted itself to changing conditions and survived as the only powerful representative assembly to exist in any of the centralized monarchies of early modern Europe. Either the events making for ultimate differences in fate happened only after 1485, or essential differences existed even before this behind the seeming likeness; or both. It has still to be established both what the distinguishing features of the English medieval Parliament really were and what happened to it in the sixteenth century.

PLACE AND FUNCTION

What view did the fifteenth century hold of its Parliament? The answer to this question is complicated by the fact that the fifteenth century rarely spoke of such things, in marked contrast to the increasing con-

[1] J. S. Roskell, 'Perspectives in English Parliamentary History,' *Bulletin of the John Rylands Library*, 46 (1964), 448 ff.

centration upon Parliament as the special possession of Englishmen which one finds from the 1530s onwards. When it did, the words were usually a lawyer's, and lawyers – common lawyers in particular – tend to think in very circumscribed ways. When called upon to consider the body politic, they found both their cast of mind and their vocabulary confining them to applying terms of the private law to very unprivate matters. In 1441, a chief baron of the Exchequer could call parliamentary taxation a profit of court, of the same order as fines levied in a manorial court baron, and even though a more intelligent judge denied the comparison, the idea proved acceptable to the minds of those present.[1] In 1492, it was held that Parliament was simply a court; its acts were regarded as judgments different from other judgments merely because Parliament was the court in which remedies unobtainable elsewhere were provided.[2] This obtuse doctrine had a long life; as late as 1550, a chief justice of Common Pleas called Parliament 'nothing but a court' and treated the Statute of Uses as equivalent to a conveyance.[3] However, these men were not really trying to express themselves in terms of political theory. The one man among them who tried was curiously reticent about Parliament. Sir John Fortescue wrote his *Governance of England* to prove the superiority of constitutional rule (*dominium politicum et regale*) to autocracy, yet his only reference to Parliament occurred when he noted that the Three Estates of France were like the English Parliament.[4] Given his purpose and his conviction that France suffered from having no constitutional limitations on its government, this is singularly significant and contrasts markedly with sixteenth-century attitudes. Fortescue was just a trifle more revealing in his *De Laudibus Legum Anglie* where he explained that English statutes must be of a more general benefit because the king cannot make them without assent,[5] and where he did provide a brief statement of one essential fact:

Neque rex ibidem per se, aut ministros suos, tallagia, subsidia, aut quevis onera alia imponit legiis suis, aut leges eorum mutat, vel novas condit, sine concessione vel assensu tocius regni sui in parliamento suo expresso.

[1] Cf. T. F. T. Plucknett, 'The Lancastrian Constitution,' in *Tudor Studies Presented to A. F. Pollard*, ed. R. W. Seton-Watson (1924), 161 ff., for this and other cases.

[2] Chrimes, *Constitutional Ideas*, 74–5.

[3] Cited in Charles Howard McIlwain, *Constitutionalism Ancient and Modern* (Ithaca, N.Y., 1947), 116. But see my remarks in 'The Tudor Revolution: A Reply,' *Past and Present*, 29 (1964), 26, 39: the same judge on another occasion clearly thought of Parliament as a legislature.

[4] *The Governance of England*, ed. Charles Plummer (Oxford, 1885), 113.

[5] *De Laudibus Legum Anglie*, ed. S. B. Chrimes (Cambridge, 1942), 40.

In both taxation and legislation, the king requires the consent of the realm in Parliament.[1]

This is accurate enough, but not at all developed. The question is: who makes the law? Fortescue's words clearly show his opinion that the only lawmaker was the king, though his laws were not valid without consent in Parliament. In this view he may be thought already a little out of date – significantly so. It is important to establish on what authority English statutes rested. Of course, from the reign of Edward I they were often, and from about 1350 always, promulgated in Parliament. Frequently they claimed to be in response to requests from others or made with the agreement of given parties. But those qualifications, while politically important, do not touch the legal essence; to a much later date than seems usually to be realized, the power to *make* law continued to be vested in the Crown alone. There is a reminder to this very day in the words of the royal assent to legislation: *le roi le veult*, the king so wills it. This sits much closer to the civil law doctrine that the prince's will (*quod principi placuit*) makes law than to the concept of the whole Parliament as legislator. For the first 150 years or so of parliamentary history, the conventional words spoke nothing but the truth. Statute rested on the king's will. Down to 1432, the sanctioning clause of each session's statutes never, except once, placed the lawmaking power in anyone but the king. The other parties present – lords spiritual and temporal, great men and nobles, the Parliament, Lords and Commons, in various permutations – were stated to be requiring, advising, and nearly always assenting.[2] The one exception occurred in 1381, during Richard II's minority and in the year of the Peasants' Rebellion, when the statutes were said to be made by the king, prelates, lords, and commons.

The critical issue is the addition of the phrase 'by authority of Parliament'; this occurred first in 1432. It was used off and on, till from 1455 it became customary.[3] Even then, the formula had not become standardized. As late as 1485, in Henry VII's first Parliament, the Commons were stated to have 'requested', even though on many previous occasions they had been described as having 'assented'. Throughout Henry VII's reign, enacting clauses could still vary almost freakishly, so much so that on some occasions the king was accidentally

---

[1] Ibid. 86. Nevertheless, I think the editor went further than the facts warrant when he glossed this to show that to Fortescue Parliament is a 'legislative body as well as an assembly assenting to fiscal business'. Fortescue speaks of assent, not authority.

[2] The sanctioning clauses from 1377 to 1485 are usefully listed in Chrimes, *Constitutional Ideas*, 101–4. [3] It was inexplicably omitted once, in 1468.

omitted.[1] The full formula – 'by the king's most excellent majesty, with the advice and assent of the Lords spiritual and temporal and the Commons in this present Parliament assembled, and by authority of the same' – did not become general until the 1530s. Thus we are once again driven to seek a moment of significance in the resumption, under Edward IV, of parliamentary activity after the collapse of conciliar and royal rule in the 1450s. From that time on, though the king remained the formal maker of law (as Fortescue still held him to be), the statutes he made rested as a rule on the authority of the Parliament. This effectively made Parliament a legislative body, though the history of the enacting clause shows that the concept took a long time to establish itself.

The reason for this difficulty lies in a transformation of Parliament which historians have failed to notice because they have been preoccupied with one side of parliamentary history.[2] The long tradition of 'whig' historiography has concentrated attention upon the so-called constitutional conflicts of English history, with their theme of resistance to arbitrary government and the ultimate triumph of political liberty in 1688. Parliament has nearly always been treated as a restraint upon the royal power, as an opposition to rulership; its performance has been judged by the degree to which it approximated to the ideal stereotype of a counterbalance. A Parliament unwilling to oppose the Crown has been too readily suspected of being 'packed' or 'subservient'. There is, to be sure, sufficient warrant in history for this point of view, but that it is totally inadequate is shown by the difficulties consequently encountered in explaining both the triumph of parliamentary government in England and the differences between England and other countries in this respect. Explanations have had to fall back on circumstantial and largely external details which are often easily shown to be nonexistent or at least hardly of weight.[3]

The clue to the true explanation seems to me to lie in the answer to two questions: why did Parliament come into existence in the first place, and what were its ultimate fate and purpose? The original reason

---

[1] See my remarks in no. 15 above, vol. 1 p. 289.

[2] This is particularly true of Roskell, 'Perspectives,' *Bull. J. Rylands Lib.* 1964.

[3] As for instance the emphasis on the joint sittings of knights and burgesses (found in France) or the peculiar position of the gentry (found in Poland and Hungary). The criticism applies even to parts of A. R. Myers 'The English Parliament and the French Estates-General in the Middle Ages,' in *Album, Helen Maud Cam*, ii. 139–53, an article which rightly stresses the greater regionalism of France and the greater frequency of English Parliaments, but still overemphasizes details of composition and ignores the very advanced claims of, for instance, the 1484 assembly at Tours.

for calling Parliaments was not to call into being a 'counterbalance' or restraint, but simply that the king wanted assistance in the tasks of government. The purposes of the sitting were produced by him – to consider the nation's affairs (the *grosses besoignes* of Edward I's writs of summons), to consent to aids and tallages, to see justice done. Discussion is always liable to lead to argument and even opposition, a risk which sensible rulers will take and which Edward I did take. It is also perfectly true that once an opportunity for opposition is provided, the occasion may come to be regularly used. Though the frequent demands for more regular Parliaments laid the stress on justice, the history of Parliament in the fourteenth century is certainly the history of various bodies and interests pressing their claims against the exercise of unfettered royal power. Of course, Parliament was, by the later middle ages, an instrument of opposition and a 'constitutional' (limiting) force in the body politic, but it had not begun as such, nor was this the whole of its being.

Neither did it, at the last, end as such. The constitutional monarchy which emerged from the troubles of the Stuart era was parliamentary in the fullest sense; that is to say, Parliament was in every way part of the government, so much so that in loose parlance today many people identify the two terms. To many the word government *means* Parliament. This, of course, is wrong, but it is revealing. Even as it was in the year 1307, so in the year 1969 the Parliament of England includes the government of England; the two are not now, any more than they were then, opposed to each other or parts of a system of checks and balances. But the Parliament of conventional historical interpretation hardly qualified for such a role, any more than did the Cortes of Castile or the Estates General of France. How can a body be said to be part of the national government when, like the French Estates in Bodin's opinion, that body had the sole function of presenting petitions to the king, *sans avoir aucune puissance de rien commander, ni décerner, ni voix délibérative*?[1] The law of France was that which it pleased the king *consentir ou assentir, commander ou défendre* – an accurate description of monarchic autocracy, despite all those fundamental laws and conventional restraints which much expert opinion today uses to deny the absolutism of French monarchy in the sixteenth century. The bodies that survived the sixteenth-century reconstruction of monarchy were those that shared in the work of governing, not those that regarded themselves as counterweights to government, at best consenting to

---

[1] Cited ibid. 153.

what was done. Thus surviving were the various estates of the Low
Countries, some provincial estates in France (Languedoc), some of the
active assemblies in German principalities (especially Württemberg),
and, above all, the English Parliament.

But the Parliament briefly alluded to by Fortescue was in no condition to be any such participant because it was treated as a restraint, a
check, fundamentally an opposition. As we have seen, he was being
blind to developments: even in his own day, the doctrine embodied
in the record regarded the Parliament as sharing to the full in the
authority behind lawmaking. Indeed, Fortescue was perhaps the first
writer to mislead opinion by the use of whiggish blinkers. The Yorkist
kings seem to have seen the truth more precisely: all their actions
proclaim them to have been aware of how useful to the monarchy the
co-operation of a body supposedly representing the realm could be.
The Tudors on the whole saw more clearly still, or at any rate Henry
VIII did, under the tutelage of Thomas Cromwell, when in 1543 he
stated unequivocally that

we be informed by our judges that we at no time stand so highly in our estate
royal as in the time of Parliament, wherein we as head and you as members are
conjoined and knit together into one body politic.[1]

Henry had never used such language before (in 1520 he had told the
Irish that 'of our absolute power we be above the laws');[2] that he
probably learned the doctrine of his 1543 speech from Cromwell as
much as from anyone may be inferred from the fact that the earliest
official statement which included the king within the Parliament
occurred in the Dispensations Act of 1534. There legislative sovereignty
was described as being vested in 'your royal majesty and your Lords
spiritual and temporal and Commons, representing the whole state of
your realm in this your most High Court of Parliament'.[3] Implicit in
that statement from the most wilful king ever to sit on the throne of
England is a profoundly different doctrine of Parliament from that
which prevailed even in the later fifteenth century; and this is true
even though there is also so explicit an assertion of the royal superiority
in the joint 'body politic'.

To the fifteenth century, influenced by the doctrine of the three
estates, it was in fact obvious that Parliament consisted of the lords
spiritual, the lords temporal, and the commons. The king formed no

[1] *Tudor Constitution*, 270.
[2] Cited by David B. Quinn, 'Historical Revision, Henry VIII and Ireland, 1509–34,'
in *Irish Historical Studies*, 12 (1961), 325. [3] 25 Henry VIII, c. 21 (1534).

part of Parliament, which was his court; they stood to each other as
the king stood to the court of Common Pleas or the King's Bench. A
parliamentary sermon of 1467 stated this plainly enough when it spoke
of the three estates and one further above them, the king.[1] In 1483,
Bishop Russell, drafting his address to Richard III's only Parliament,
spoke of 'three estates as principal members under one head' (*not* 'knit
together', as Henry VIII had it), and when he actually delivered himself
he was more precise still in describing 'this high and great court' as
composed of the three estates of lords spiritual and temporal and the
commons.[2] The same definition appeared in the same year in the
statute affirming Richard III's title to the Crown, which declared him
to be king 'at the request, and by assent of the three estates of this
realm, that is to say the Lords Spiritual and Temporal, and Commons
of this land, assembled in this present Parliament'.[3] Russell at one
point came closer to the other doctrine, in a draft of a sermon for
Edward V's Parliament (which never met): there he spoke of the
prince, the nobles, and the people all assembled on this occasion, but
even then he did not call these three parts of the 'public body' a
Parliament, as Henry VIII did.[4]

For the definition offered in 1543 clearly thought of the institutional
body of Parliament as comprising the king, the (House of) Lords, and
the House of Commons. The pre-Tudor Parliament was rather a body
of Lords and Commons only. The difference is large, and fundamental.
To Fortescue's concept we may compare that of Sir Thomas Smith,
the more so because Smith is usually regarded as simply continuing
Fortescue's tradition concerning the constitutional government of
England.[5] Not only does his careful discussion, in a book similarly
concerned to describe the English constitution, contrast strongly with
Fortescue's remarkable neglect of Parliament, but what he thought of
the institution was very different from Bishop Russell's view and
entirely in accord with Henry VIII's: Parliament consisted of king,
Lords, and Commons, and its acts were 'the prince's and whole realm's
deeds'.[6] This is the familiar doctrine of the king-in-Parliament, a
sovereign body in the real sense, because it has absolute discretion in
the making and unmaking of law. But while that doctrine has been
commonplace ever since, it should be recognized that when Smith

---

[1] Cited in Chrimes, *Constitutional Ideas*, 121.   [2] Ibid. 123.
[3] Ibid. 125.   [4] Ibid. 123.
[5] George L. Mosse, 'Change and Continuity in the Tudor Constitution', *Speculum*, 22 (1947), 18–28.
[6] *De Republica Anglorum*, ed. L. Alston (Cambridge, 1906), 48.

wrote, in 1565, it was of recent enough origin. Nevertheless, to him it was obviously already self-evident.

As late as 1483, the only concept we can find thought of 'king and Parliament', two bodies that must co-operate – the one acting, the other advising and assenting – if certain things were to be done. Thereafter, there was a long gap without any remark on Parliament. Remarkably enough, Edmund Dudley's *Tree of Commonwealth* (written 1510, published Manchester, 1859), written to praise limited government, did not even mention Parliament, in striking contrast to the manner in which the constitutional platitudes of a parliamentary system were to become commonplace from the 1530s onwards, in the writings of St German, Starkey, Aylmer, Smith, and so on. By 1534 the new concept was in being: we have seen that Cromwell's Dispensations Act was unambiguous on the point that king, Lords and Commons together formed the Parliament. However, Cromwell probably adopted rather than invented what was then a new notion, thereby making it dominant; at least, it is possible that Christopher St German revealed in the versions of his *Doctor and Student* how very recent the precise definition of the concept was. In its original form, the dialogue referred to statutes made 'by our soueraygne lorde the kyng and his progenytours, & by the lordes spyrytuell and temporal and the commons of the hole realme in dyuers Parlyamentes'.[1] This certainly recognized the joint legislative authority asserted since the middle of the previous century, but still treated king and Parliament as two different bodies acting in concert. This statement was written about 1523. In 1531, when St German brought the book out with an additional section, he allowed himself to speak quite plainly of 'the kynge the whiche in the sayd Parlyament was the hed and moste chyef and pryncypall parte of the Parlyament, as he is in euery Parlyament'.[2] But the following year, firmly asserting parliamentary authority over the Church, he reverted to the older commonplace by speaking of 'the King's Grace and his Parliament'.[3] A similar uncertainty of interpretation still appeared in John Aylmer's *Harborowe* of 1559. Calling the Parliament the image, and even 'the thinge indede', of the mixed English constitution, he spoke of the three estates (king, Lords, and Commons) in Parliament,

[1] *The fyrste dyaloge in Englysshe, with new addycyons* (1531), fo. 25v.
[2] Ibid. Sig. O.4.
[3] *Treatise concerning the division of the spiritualtie and the temporaltie* (1532), 21. Interestingly enough, J. W. Allen, *A History of Political Thought in the Sixteenth Century* (1928), 167, when discussing St German and citing this very phrase, consistently speaks of 'the king in Parliament', thus underlining the failure of historians to see the important difference.

yet also said that the laws were made by the monarch and Parliament together.[1] It was only with Smith, six years later, that the ghost of Fortescue and the middle ages was laid at last.

Thus, in the course of the sixteenth century, the medieval 'king and Parliament' jointly capable of doing certain things, the former acting, and the latter controlling, were transformed into the modern 'king-in-Parliament', a single (mixed) sovereign body. There is every reason to think that the full grasp of the doctrine upon which English government has ever since rested was delayed until the 1530s. Interestingly enough, at that point it was best enunciated not by writers or theorists (who were to take a little longer to become clear on the point) but by the makers of policy themselves; we should think of Henry VIII's reform administration as already working on the assumption that the existence of this new kind of Parliament liberated sovereign action in the body politic. That the practical difficulties of operating a mixed sovereign, together with the incompetent authoritarianism of Stuart governments, revived in the seventeenth century a 'medieval' situation in which king and Parliament stood opposed to each other should not conceal the fact that the principle of a single mixed sovereign body never disappeared,[2] and that both in theory and in practice the king-in-Parliament doctrine returned in 1660 and especially in 1688. Whether the Parliament that entered the seventeenth century was by experience and organization qualified to share in the exercise of rule is something to be discussed later. Nevertheless it should be remembered that in the prevalent doctrine of the constitution it was conceived of as doing precisely such sharing – in the creation of law, though not in the administration of the realm. This was not true of the medieval Parliament, as late as the accession of Henry VII and even later. The practical difference was not, perhaps, very substantial – though lawmaking (as we shall see) took on a strikingly new force after 1530 – but it lay at the very heart of the country's thinking about its polity. Once again, the significant fact may be noted that hardly anyone concerned with political thought before 1530 had anything, or anything much, to say about Parliament, whereas thereafter it became the automatic point of reference for those who wished to treat England's government as mixed, limited, and constitutional. To the examples already cited one may add William Marshall's uncalled-for introduction of Parliament

---

[1] *An Harborowe for faithfull and trewe subiectes* (Strasbourg, 1559), Sig. H.3.
[2] It was fully stated, on the eve of the civil war, by Charles I himself. Corrinne C. Weston, 'The Theory of Mixed Monarchy under Charles I and After,' *EHR* 75 (1960), 426–43.

into his translation of Marsiglio of Padua's *The Defense of Peace* (London, 1535), or Thomas Starkey's casual references, in about 1533, to Parliament as the obvious constitutionalist element in the English state.[1]

Naturally, the developed doctrine of the king-in-Parliament derived from the earlier concept of the king and his high court of Parliament. The doctrine inherited useful convictions as well as practices; in particular, it inherited the usual philosophical justification for the claims made on Parliament's behalf, namely that it was representative. As Smith was to put it in the reign of Elizabeth:

Every Englishman is intended to be there present, either in person or by procuration [proxy] and attornies, of what preeminence, state, dignity or quality soever he be, from the Prince (be he King or Queen) to the lowest person in England. And the consent of the Parliament is taken to be every man's consent.[2]

With the exception that Smith, faithful to the new doctrine, listed the prince as simply another part of the realm present in Parliament, he was stating sufficiently ancient views. That 'Parliament represents the body of all the realm' was asserted by Thorpe, C.J., as early as 1366 to circumvent a plea of ignorance of a statute.[3] And though a view of Parliament as a court (the king's court) for a time rather dominated over the representational concept,[4] the latter was commonplace enough by 1525 to be enunciated by so lowly a person as a member of the common council of London who quoted the act forbidding benevolences (1484) against Cardinal Wolsey's attempts to levy one.[5] When Wolsey protested that the acts of so evil a man as Richard III could not be good or honourable, he received the reply: 'Although he did evil, yet in his time were many good acts made not by him only but by the consent of the body of the whole realm, which is the Parliament.'[6] It will be seen that this London councillor still thought in 'medieval' terms, for he did not include the king in the Parliament; yet the idea of representation was evident enough to him.

Not even this had been accepted without question for very long, despite the fact that the whole binding force of parliamentary legislation and assent to taxation depended on the supposition that the

---

[1] See below, pp. 229–30, Starkey, *A Dialogue between Reginald Pole and Thomas Lupset*, ed. K. Burton (1948), 100, 155, 165–6. [2] *De Rep. Anglorum*, 49.
[3] Cited in Chrimes, *Constitutional Ideas*, 76. [4] Cf. ibid. 76–81.
[5] Hall, *Chronicle*, 698. [6] Ibid.

agreement of Lords and Commons equalled the agreement of, and therefore called for obedience by, every individual within the realm. In 1441, counsel in a case that turned upon a grant confirmed in Parliament tried to argue that a grant so made need not bind everyone, while in 1480 it was maintained that an act of Parliament 'binds everybody to whom it extends, forasmuch as every man is party and privy to the Parliament'.[1] One may perhaps suppose with Plucknett that this marks the stride forward in political thinking which he discerned in the fifteenth century, though this view of 1480 did not differ from Thorpe's in 1366. Perhaps it would be sounder to think of these notions as still being debatable, not yet commonplace. It seems that the idea of Parliament as a representative body, containing all members of the realm either in person or by delegation, was currently developed, until it emerged plainly in such statements as those of Henry VIII or Thomas Smith. It was not until the sixteenth century that it became the ordinary and universal justification for the claims to obedience made by Parliament and its edicts.

The importance of the doctrine lies far more in its practical consequences than in its theoretical subtleties (which are not very great). Unless the actions of a Parliament bound everyone in the realm, it was hardly worth the trouble of calling one. This had been recognized from the first. In particular, the practice of granting taxation in Parliament depended on the willingness of those paying the taxes to accept an obligation agreed by their representatives; from the reign of Edward I onwards, knights and burgesses came equipped with *plena potestas*, with full power to commit the members of the communities that had elected them.[2] But it is, of course, notorious that the medieval electorate was in no sense democratic. Just how representative were these Parliaments, and to what extent did they reflect the realities of power within the body politic?

REPRESENTATION AND POLITICAL POWER

Despite the frequent talk of 'three estates' in Parliament, especially from the fifteenth century onwards,[3] the English Parliament, unlike similar institutions elsewhere, never in any real sense consisted of

---

[1] Plucknett, 'The Lancastrian Constitution,' in *Tudor Studies*, 166, 173.

[2] J. G. Edwards, 'The Plena Potestas of English Parliamentary Representatives,' in *Oxford Essays in Medieval History* (Oxford, 1934), 141–54.

[3] Chrimes, *Constitutional Ideas*, 115–26.

representatives of the bodies to whom conventional medieval thought attached that title. Superficially, it was true, there was some point in that talk. The three orders of society – *Lehrstand, Wehrstand, Nährstand*, those who pray, fight, and labour – could be supposed present in the lords spiritual, the lords temporal, and the commons. In actuality, none of these sections of the Parliament corresponded with the estates. These groups did not sit or act separately, which would have marked an estate-based structure. No one ever regarded the spiritual estate as confined to those higher clergy who received a summons to Parliament, and yet the lower clergy had no share there at all, not even voting for members of the Commons. The noble estate should have included the knights, but even the distinction between a higher and a lower nobility did not correspond with the line drawn between the Lords of Parliament and the knights of the shire. Men who received an individual summons to one Parliament on occasion sat for a shire in the next. As late as the reign of Henry VIII, the *Lords' Journals* preserved an ancient social fact by describing barons in Parliament as 'X. Y., chevalier', indistinguishable so far as nomenclature went from knights who sat as elected members of the Commons. If the Parliament was in any way representative, this was not because the three conventional social orders were present there.

The Lords, in fact, cannot be thought of as having been representative at all. Both spiritual and lay peers owed their presence to the royal summons, not to any form of election from among their kind. The Church, in particular, was not present at all. Those clergy who sat in Parliament were there on account of a writ of summons which by the end of the fifteenth century had become a matter of entitlement. The Crown regularly called the archbishops, bishops, and a large part of the abbots, but these men were called as tenants-in-chief or as royal officials, or as both, not as an estate of the realm. The lay lords, too, came because they were called. They were called because their position as the king's great feudatories and natural counsellors entitled them to a summons. By the reign of Edward IV, though possibly not much before then, the right to a writ had become well established in what may already be called a parliamentary peerage, and the Crown had little flexibility left.[1] Nevertheless, the whole character of the Lords

---

[1] The summons had become so much a matter of right and not of grace and so much attached to identifiable persons (peers) that it could not really be withheld. Therefore, when the government of Henry VIII thought it advisable to secure the absence of some well-known opponent from Parliament, it had to resort to accompanying the summons with an intimation that disobedience would be well received (*Tudor Constitution*, 241).

was not that of representatives but of king's councillors – the enlarged Great Council of the realm – a fact underlined by the continued practice, down to 1529, of calling occasional meetings of the Lords without the Commons.[1] These 'assemblies of notables' could deliberate and advise but do nothing else; here, the conciliar function of the Lords in Parliament stood out very clearly.

In these respects, the English Parliament was like some other assemblies and unlike others. In the French provincial estates, for instance, the principle prevailed that the great men both lay and clerical had a title to summons.[2] In the Estates General, the Crown retained the power to call whom it would and used it with much flexibility until 1483, after which date both clergy and nobility turned 'democratic' and began to elect representatives for their estates in the individual *bailliages*, as the third estate had always done.[3] In the Spanish kingdoms, clergy and nobility similarly came in response to a summons to which they never established a right, but which treated them as members of their order, not as tenants-in-chief. The same principle prevailed in those Italian assemblies (Sicily and Sardinia) where Spanish influence was strong, whereas in other parts of the peninsula the higher clergy were treated like the English bishops, and the nobility obeyed an individual summons (a matter of entitlement) which was sometimes confined to the top rank and sometimes extended to all who claimed to be noble.[4] Thus it is clear that the Lords of the English Parliament were not anything very exceptional in composition or function. What was exceptional was the degree of precision, the thoroughness of systematic organization, which the control of the Crown had created in this body of 'natural advisers and counsellors'.

Moreover, this greater precision lay behind the fact that what had been fairly commonplace in late-medieval assemblies became, in the sixteenth century, something almost peculiarly English. As has been said, the French estates of Church and nobility consisted from 1484 onwards of elected representatives – in no sense royal councillors –

---

[1] Robin L. Storey, *The Reign of Henry VII* (1968), 217–18. These 'Great Councils' were not, of course, any longer called Parliaments.

[2] *Representative Government in Western Europe in the Sixteenth Century*, ed. G. Griffiths (Oxford, 1968), 124.

[3] J. Russell Major, 'The Loss of Royal Initiative and the Decay of the Estates General in France, 1421–1615,' *Album, Helen Maud Cam*, ii. 254–9.

[4] Roger B. Merriman, 'The Cortes of the Spanish Kingdoms in the Later Middle Ages,' *American Historical Review*, 16 (1910–11), 476–95; A. Marongiu, *Medieval Parliaments: A Comparative Study*, trans. S. J. Woolf (1968), 226–7.

while in Castile both these orders, having obtained the privilege of tax exemption, withdrew from the Cortes after 1538, a move which reduced that body to unicameral ineptitude. And while the form of summons endured in such diverse places as Sicily and the Low Countries, both the prelates and the nobles in those assemblies came to act as separate chambers and agents of self-conscious sectional interest. The Tudor House of Lords, on the other hand, retained enough of the character of a king's Council in Parliament to remain useful to the Crown, while at the same time it became a member of the parliamentary trinity, a House of the Parliament and therefore a working part of a legislative assembly. If the Lords had ever been representative of an order – that is, acted in the interests of an identifiable sector of the nation – this had been in the days of magnate struggles with the Crown, between 1376 and 1470; there is certainly no evidence of it in the sixteenth century when this, like other marks of medievalism, had disappeared. The point comes out most clearly in the pre-eminent area of self-interest, in matters of taxation. In 1593, for instance, the Lords tried to interfere with the by then reasonably established principle that money grants were the province of the Commons.[1] But they did so in order to vote larger supplies – acting, that is, in the interests of the Crown (and the nation), not of themselves. They were still, in many ways, a Council of the realm, though also a House of Parliament. But in what sense they represented anyone, even themselves, is less apparent.

The English Commons, on the other hand, were not only somewhat peculiar by comparison with other 'third estates' but also more evidently representative. In all medieval assemblies, the unit represented in the third estate was not the individual but a 'community', a territorial segment of the realm. In nearly all assemblies the communities in question were towns. This was to be expected in those well-urbanized regions, Italy and the Netherlands, but it was true also of Spain, even though the enfranchised towns of Castile included some of the open country.[2] It was not true of France, the largest territorial area that attempted to create (with moderate success only) a representative assembly. Here the third estate consisted of representatives of the administrative divisions only (*bailliages* and *sénéchausées*),

[1] J. E. Neale, *Elizabeth I and Her Parliaments* (1953, 1957), ii. 301–12.
[2] Merriman, *Am. Hist. Rev.* 16, 479–86. Oddly enough, in Germany, where a number of towns achieved territorial power and independence, there was no third estate at all in the earlier medieval Diets (Marongiu, *Medieval Parliaments*, 106 ff.). Some towns, however, sent representatives to *colloquia* in the twelfth and thirteenth centuries, and by the sixteenth century the 'imperial cities' formed one of the chambers of the Diet.

the towns being absorbed into the territorial electoral system. In England, on the other hand, the king's administrative organization of his realm took very little account of the towns (mostly self-governing by the time that the calling of assemblies became frequent) but rested on the ancient and eminently durable structure of the shires. Yet from the first, mainly because consent to taxes was required, the Crown summoned both knights for the shires and burgesses and citizens for the towns; that is to say, the concept of communities of the realm was extended beyond the administrative divisions to the embedded lesser units. Both shires and towns were, in fact, real communities in the sense that they had self-consciousness, self-government, and self-purpose; and the composition of the House of Commons in the later middle ages quite exceptionally reflected the reality. The knights and burgesses could speak for the realm because the areas which they represented covered both territory and opinion to a remarkable degree. Only perhaps in the estates of the various territories which made up the sixteenth-century Netherlands was opinion so fully reflected as in the English Parliament. In the Netherlands the States General, which might have acted as unifiers, failed for a long time to do so because they were composed of delegates from the particular estates who could rarely act without reference back to their parent bodies.

The House of Commons was representative in theory because every community of the realm (in theory!) had sent its delegates; the notion meant something in practice because the shire organization was general and uniform, and because so many towns were summoned. The House was extraordinarily large. In the reign of Henry VIII, thirty-seven counties and 112 boroughs sent two representatives each, a total membership of 298.[1] This may be compared with the size of the third estate in Castile – eighteen two-member constituencies from the 1480s onwards.[2] Yet at the time, Castile had something like twice the population of England. In the large and teeming realm of France (four times as populous as England), none of the estates had anything like a fixed membership, partly because not all parts of the kingdom were summoned every time even after they had been reunited under the Crown, and partly because returns varied. Even so at no time did the third estate approximate to the size of the English House of Commons. A large French gathering, like that of 1576, produced only 150 members.[3]

[1] Tanner, *Tudor Constitutional Documents*, 514.
[2] See Merriman, *Am. Hist. Rev.* 16, 480.
[3] R. Doucet, *Les Institutions de la France au XVIe siècle* (Paris, 1948), i. 314–21.

And the English Commons furthermore grew enormously throughout the sixteenth century as statutes added members for Wales, Chester, and Durham, while Crown enfranchisement produced another 141 borough members. The House of Commons known to the Virginia colonists was 462 strong, far and away the largest representative body in existence not only proportionately to population but absolutely.[1] These numbers become even more impressive when one remembers that the Lords' size varied between sixty and ninety, especially after the Reformation removed the abbots. The French Estates of 1576, on the other hand, balanced the 150 members of the third estate with 176 men from the other estates.

Moreover, members of the House of Commons were, by medieval and early-modern standards, properly elected to a degree unknown elsewhere. The representatives of Castilian and Aragonese cities were chosen by lot. Attempts in France to standardize returns from the *bailliages* failed; in the sixteenth century, the various constituencies elected what numbers they pleased, a practice which in the assembly led to a voting by *bailliages* (or even by the twelve *gouvernements*) only, to equalize things. As a result the real discussions took place in preliminary private meetings of deputies from a given region, and the voting reflected a prearranged collection of compromises.[2] In England, county knights were chosen by the freeholders of the shire, a body large enough to call for the introduction of a property qualification for the franchise in 1429 (possession of freehold worth 40s. a year qualified). In the boroughs various rules prevailed, but the commonest practice awarded the right to vote to all burgage tenants or to all who paid certain local taxes. This electorate was often small and sometimes rendered smaller by oligarchic usurpations on the part of borough dignitaries. The Tudor age certainly knew pocket boroughs; still, the total of people entitled to vote in a general election was large by the standards of the time, and both the subterfuges of returning officers and the evidence of contested elections show that these events were real enough.[3]

Thus the commonplace that Parliament represented the body of the realm – the king and Lords being present in person, and the rest (as communities) by proxy – was better justified in an institution in which

---

[1] *Tudor Constitution*, 243.
[2] Major, *Album, Helen Maud Cam*, ii, 560. After 1560, when the three estates sat separately and each held discussions within the structure of *gouvernements*, there were then, as Major says, thirty-six separate deliberative assemblies.
[3] For all this, cf. J. E. Neale, *The Elizabethan House of Commons*.

reality of election and numbers of representatives involved a much higher proportion of the nation in the meetings of these assemblies than was the practice in any other territorial state of the time. Nevertheless, one must ask just what this representation meant in practice. The communities were there, by proxy. How far were ascertainable interests, let alone the individuals bound by the decisions of the assembly, there at all? And are we to take at face value the evidence of numerical superiority in the House of Commons as against the small number and the unrepresentative character of the Lords in Parliament?

There has been a good deal of controversy about the place of the Commons in late-medieval Parliaments, from the confident assertions of Stubbs – who treated the Commons in Lancastrian Parliaments as politically dominant in the manner of the seventeenth-century House – through the confident assertions of earlier Tudor scholars who were sure that the Commons were merely the instrument and mouthpiece of the Lords, to more recent (but still quite confident) descriptions of them as men politically mature and highly influential.[1] The true position is complex and so far still not clear. It is also certain that the situation varied a lot from one age to another, sometimes from one Parliament to another. It would be a great gain if historians could free themselves from the conviction that all these constitutional developments always moved in one line, up or down, forward or back.

A great deal must depend on the sort of people who sat in the Commons. In theory, only men of knightly status resident in the county were able to represent the shire, while borough members were supposed to be resident burgesses of their towns. Thus the locality was to appear in Parliament in the person of a characteristic and respectable representative, well able to speak for the interests of those who had sent him there. However, the fact that several statutes of the mid-fifteenth century attempted to enforce observance of these rules sufficiently indicates that they were not being obeyed.[2] Indeed, it is by now a well-established fact that, from Henry VI's reign at the latest, boroughs increasingly returned members whose connection with the

[1] See the short account of fifteenth-century Parliaments in Wilkinson, *Const. Hist.* . . *Fifteenth Century*, 278–320, and especially the bibliography on pp. 277–8. Wilkinson is a neo-Stubbsian. The most authoritative recent statements restoring the Commons to an influence once denied them are K. B. McFarlane, 'Parliament and Bastard Feudalism,' *TRHS* (1944), 53–79, and J. S. Roskell, *The Commons in the Parliament of 1422* (Manchester, 1954).

[2] Cf. Ludwig Riess, *The History of the English Electoral Law in the Middle Ages*, trans. K. L. Wood-Legh (Cambridge, 1940), 78–83.

constituency could be very tenuous and who in social status were hard to distinguish from shire knights. In the age of Edward III, the Commons seem genuinely to have consisted of local men with local concerns; in the Parliament of 1422, though three-quarters of the burgesses were still nominally resident, men of gentry status already outnumbered genuine burghers by four to three; in 1478, some half the borough members were gentlemen; and by the end of the sixteenth century, four gentlemen sat in the House of Commons for every townsman, thus neatly reversing the proportions that would have obtained if the old qualification laws had been observed.[1]

This 'invasion of the gentry', as it has been called, had consequences, though these may have become overemphasized in recent accounts. For one thing, the fact that English towns were mostly small and lived very much inside their surrounding countryside somewhat reduced the difference of interests between burghers and gentry (London never returned anyone but its own people). Many gentlemen sat for boroughs in which they had a perfectly genuine interest and represented the locality quite as competently as a butcher or shoemaker would have done. It therefore matters less what the social status of the elected member was, and more whether he was truly a local man (in or near the borough). Local ties snapped when strangers began to use boroughs simply as a means for getting into Parliament and as the basis of a career. In this respect it would appear that only in the sixteenth century did residence become nominal in any large number of cases. It has also been inferred from the growing number of gentry that a House which once consisted of humble men, easily overawed by the great and especially by the king, came to include men of standing, experience, and independence, till it was able to assert itself against the other parts of Parliament; this development has been assigned to the latter half of the sixteenth century. There is some measure of truth in this. Shire knights, for instance, seem to have taken the lead in medieval Parliaments; they certainly supplied every known Speaker before the session of 1533. By the reign of Elizabeth, a member's constituency was no longer any sort of guide to his standing in the House, whereas a report on the Parliament of 1485 certainly made the burgesses look quite small and deferential.[2] Yet, as has been proved often enough and

---

[1] Roskell, *Commons of 1422*, 131; May McKisack, *The Parliamentary Representation of the English Boroughs during the Middle Ages* (Oxford, 1932), 109–10; Neale, *House of Commons*, 146–8.

[2] *The Red Paper Book of Colchester*, ed. W. G. Benham (Colchester, 1902), 60 ff.

effectively, the burgesses of Edward III's and Henry IV's Parliaments showed little subservience and much independence in fighting for their concerns. It seems to me that the 'invasion of the gentry' had a different, and more far-reaching, effect upon the House of Commons than that of introducing a lot of vigorous men capable of conducting an opposition to the Crown.

The crucial questions touch the political structure of the gentry and the political activity of the House of Commons. In the very active Parliaments of the fourteenth century there were no genuine signs that the Commons, as such, wished to assert an authority over the king's government. The Commons worried about matters economic, especially the use of their taxes, and complained of bad government, but did not attempt to tell the king who his councillors should be. Even the engineered attack on the king's ministers in 1376, when the Commons were put forward to complain on behalf of the realm, and the appointment in Parliament of a Council to rule the realm during Richard II's minority form no exception to this statement, for on both occasions the magnates were in the lead. That these striking events did not mark the assertion of novel 'constitutional' claims but only attempts to provide for government when the medieval system found itself in the usual dither produced by the absence of an active king is proved by the very evident dominance of royal or aristocratic interest in the Parliaments of Richard's majority, from 1386 onwards. Then, in the reign of Henry IV, the Commons suddenly, and repeatedly, tried to force a king who was of age and capable of government to attend to their wishes in the appointment and control of his councillors. Constitutionalism seems to have arrived. Or so one would think until one looks at the Parliament of 1422. On that occasion it became necessary once again to provide for a royal minority, and a regency (protector and Council) was appointed in Parliament. But in these doings the Commons played no part at all; on this most favourable occasion they made no attempt to assert the principle of conciliar responsibility to Parliament, quite explicitly claimed in 1406. Both in doctrine and in fact, the government of the realm in such an emergency was recognized to be a matter for the lords, the magnates, in or out of Parliament.[1]

Small wonder that this event has troubled those who see in the Lancastrian Commons a politically self-conscious body, and that they resort to various exculpatory conjectures to explain it. But worse was

[1] Roskell, *Commons of 1422*, 107–9.

to follow: through all the long years of Henry VI's minority, when misgovernment at home combined too often with military failure abroad, the regency government was frequently in trouble with its own members but never subjected to the sort of attack from the Commons which had troubled Henry IV in 1404, 1406, and 1411. Yet the problem looks less difficult if one abandons the curious and ingrained practice which treats the Commons in Parliament as a monolithic and self-contained body. They were a large collection of individuals whose interests, concerns, and ties differed widely. From the early fifteenth century onwards, the intrusion of so many gentlemen of the shire produced in the House a political structure which in most essentials was to remain unaltered until the social transformations of the early nineteenth century. This is the fact called variously affinity, clientage, and connection – the fact that the politics of both shire and nation were dominated by groupings of interest gathered round the territorial, economic, and political ascendancy of certain great men to whom lesser men attached themselves. This concise description overlooks the flexibility of the system and the many exceptions that can readily be produced, but it states the lasting and underlying reality of the social and political structure of the governing classes. How strong the affinities – the interest groups of the magnates – were in 1422, Professor Roskell has himself shown. In the appointment of a magnate Council in that year, the followers as well as the leaders of the groups achieved their ends – the take-over of the king's government in respect to both the making of policy and the control of the royal patronage. This has been the ambition of various sets of lords ever since the Barons' War of 1258, with variations on the theme. Parliament had provided the scene for these efforts from Edward II's reign onwards. In 1422, the purpose was achieved, a purpose no less agreeable to the powerful gentry in the Commons anxious to enlarge the influence of the great men to whom they attached themselves, than to the magnates who in turn depended on a following among the lesser landowners for their local power and national position.[1]

This complex story can here be but sketched, but the implications are manifest. In the first place, of course, it should be recognized that in respect to issues of higher politics the fifteenth-century Commons were instruments of aristocratic policy; they were so because it suited the book of the leading men in the Commons themselves. But, in the

[1] For details of the way in which affinities and connections worked in the fifteenth century, see Robin L. Storey, *The End of the House of Lancaster* (1966).

second place, it puts the question of the Parliament's representative character in a new light. The lords were not the only men with political power, but the hierarchic structure of society, the interdependence of greater and lesser landowners, and the importance of a man's ascendancy in his locality still gave them the political leadership and the ultimate political opportunities in both country and Parliament. Just because their interests coincided with those of the classes which prevailed in the House of Commons, they could and did use Parliament to fight the battle for political control – through the Commons in the reign of Henry IV – but without this weapon and in Council only once the king had been (temporarily) eliminated, Edward IV, himself a faction leader, demonstrated his understanding of the situation when he built up a Crown interest in the Commons, a policy continued by the Tudors. The Commons did not originate political conflict by their demands; they simply provided both the instrument of attack and the scene of battle, so long as the king's control of his Council deprived the magnates of the chance to transfer the conflict there.

Thus, in real terms, the fifteenth-century Parliaments were representative because there, in the interaction of Lords and Commons, the political nation was fully present – not the 'people', a concept of neither ideological nor practical significance, but those interests powerful and concerned enough to engage in the activities which constituted the politics of the day. On the eve of the Tudor era, the English Parliament already stood for the political embodiment of the nation; that was the reality behind the commonplaces about a body of the realm present in person and by proxy. In this setup, however, it was the magnates who predominated. The lords remained foremost, as Lords of the Parliament, and the distribution of power within the political nation entirely favoured them, a fact reflected in the relative standing of the parts of Parliament.

This position of the Parliament as the political nation in being injected vitality into the institution; too many varied concerns found it useful, even indispensable, for it to be anything but thoroughly alive. As the Yorkists recognized (though, as we have seen, comprehension and theory were slow to catch up with the fact), these concerns included the king himself. He might indeed be at war, literally or metaphorically, with other powerful elements in the state, but the Parliament could be his political instrument as easily as it was that of his opponents – indeed, more easily because it was after all still his institution, his high court, to be called and dismissed only by him. He needed political skill and enterprise to handle and manage it, but he could also enjoy the advantages which consent in Parliament gave to his actions. The vitality of the English Parliament is not to be measured by its willingness to oppose or its success in defeating the ambitions of kings, but by the degree to which it gathered all the interests – all the political nation – together to allow the conflict of interests to be resolved into positive action. This, its original purpose, may have been overshadowed for both contemporaries and historians by the drama of scenes of conflict and by false analogies drawn from the seventeenth century, but it was recognised well enough by the magnates of 1422 and by the stronger kings who recovered the government from 1461 onwards.

The purpose, moreover, was greatly assisted by another aspect of parliamentary history to which the books have paid too little attention. The Parliament we have been discussing was a working institution; by comparison with similar assemblies elsewhere, its organization and practice were much more workmanlike. Kings could employ it because it was geared to the production of results. True, such an assembly as the Cortes of Aragon had a highly developed organization, with powers over the Crown superior to anything that the English Parliament achieved in the middle ages.[1] But it was an organization deliberately designed to shackle kings, and when in the sixteenth century the poverty of the region made it pointless for monarchs to seek financial support there, they could afford to ignore the Cortes, letting them still go through their meaningless motions in a political vacuum. By contrast, the Parliament of England operated to achieve positive action on behalf of whoever could run it, and except in times of deep monarchical trouble kings could always do so. The representatives' *plena potestas* had for two centuries ensured that agreement in Parliament meant agreement in the nation. In contrast, the Burgundian estates could do nothing of significance without constant reference back to their constituents. As late as the reign of Charles V, the Crown of Castile was trying to obtain this elementary necessity by dictating clumsy letters of attorney to be made out by the constituencies to their delegates.[2] In the early fourteenth century, English burgesses had often arrived in Parliament with similar formal letters of authority, but the practice had long been abandoned as superfluous, a fact which underlines how much more routine and businesslike the English assemblies were. The French Estates General did take decisions

---

[1] Merriman, *Am. Hist. Rev.* 16, 486–90.
[2] Griffiths, *Representative Government*, 2–3, 30 ff.

without reference back, but there was no guarantee that their constituents would think themselves bound.[1] What point was there in holding long, tedious, and contentious meetings if even final agreement did not necessarily mean that action would result?

The English Parliament was also a much better defined body than most of the parallel institutions elsewhere. Its bicameral organization was unique; elsewhere, assemblies met either in plenary session, or by estates, or in *ad hoc* and variable arrangements. The two bodies of Lords and Commons could and did give substance to such concepts as that the king and his Council hears and remedies the grievances of the realm, brought to their notice by the communities of the realm. From this resulted the vital fact of legislative monopoly. The presentation of grievances – *cahiers, capitulos* – was common practice; the production of law by the co-operation of various parties on the occasions of Parliament was not. If we want to understand why an assembly like the English Parliament – in which the convenient principle of redress of grievances before granting of supply was never pressed for long, though it prevailed extensively in Mediterranean assemblies – should have succeeded in subjecting the royal lawmaking power to the control of consent, we need only look at a lawsuit of 1455. The court, confronted with the question whether a private act of Parliament pleaded by the defendant was properly made, called in two expert witnesses, a Chancery clerk and the clerk of the Parliament. Their description of how an act was passed stands suitably at the head of a long line of technical notes on the procedure of Parliament which culminates in Erskine May's handbook.[2] They spoke calmly and professionally of what happened to bills first introduced in the Commons or the Lords, of the proper way with amendments, of the technicalities of endorsements. Though the judges rightly deplored the failure of the organization to register the date on which a bill was introduced, their criticism only highlights the thoroughly sophisticated administrative procedure which lay behind the political conflicts beloved by chroniclers and historians and behind the bald record of legislative achievement presented in the rolls of Parliament.

One can cite other details to prove the point. The Lords' Journal for

[1] On the whole problem see H. G. Koenigsberger, 'The Powers of Deputies in Sixteenth-Century Assemblies,' in *Album, Helen Maud Cam*, ii. 211–43.

[2] Chrimes, *Constitutional Ideas*, pp. 231–3; Wilkinson, *Const. Hist. . . . Fifteenth Century*, 312. The whole case is reprinted in the original French (in which the wording even more obviously expresses routine and professionalism) in Dunham, *Fane Fragment*, 99–102.

eight sittings in 1461, which has accidentally survived in a copy, gives elaborate proof of the working system of a working institution: regular record of attendances, regular practices as to the introduction and treatment of bills, appointments of committees, all are illustrated here.[1] And other things: the office of Speaker, continuous from the reign of Richard II;[2] the rules of debate and parliamentary order to which Thomas Smith testified in 1565 but which were clearly much more ancient; the developed distinction between public and private acts; the standard formulae of the royal assent – in all these the hidden efficiency of parliamentary meetings appears to the eye. Compare the English royal veto, *le roi s'avisera*, with the response in 1506 to a Castilian petition complaining of clerical absenteeism: 'That his highness is pleased to refuse his consent, and he will try to find a remedy for this with our most Holy Father, and will not permit any action to the contrary.'[3] Indeed, compare the petitioning procedure of the sixteenth-century assemblies anywhere outside England with the regular production of statutes in England out of bills introduced *in forma statuti* described as early as 1455. Even the writ of summons, brief and standardized in England from the early fourteenth century onwards, had no real equal elsewhere. Behind all this stood the ancient business organization of the king's Chancery and the relative effectiveness of the Crown's action in medieval England. The outcome was a Parliament ready made for business.

By the beginning of the sixteenth century, therefore, Parliament was a regular institution, with recognized powers and functions. It was superior to similar institutions elsewhere because it had no rivals in regional assemblies, because it genuinely provided an opportunity for all political interests to argue and resolve their conflicts, because it was quite exceptionally organized for business, and because (all these facts combining) it not only participated in government but was positively useful to the monarchy. Such a description might suggest that those who regard the late medieval Parliament as 'complete' and can see no

---

[1] Dunham, *Fane Fragment*. The editing and discussion of this document leave a good deal to be desired, cf. K. B. McFarlane in *EHR* 53 (1938), 506–8, and are affected by reliance on Howard L. Gray's misleading *The Influence of the Commons on Early Legislation* (Cambridge, Mass., 1932). Cf. Chrimes, *Constitutional Ideas*, 236–49. However, the text, reproduced in facsimile, tells the necessary story.

[2] See generally J. S. Roskell, *The Commons and Their Speakers in English Parliaments, 1376–1523* (Manchester, 1965).

[3] Griffiths, *Representative Government*, 16. This is quite apart from the fact that when a similar request came up at Westminster in a bill of 1529, the royal response was *le roi le veult*!

important developments in the sixteenth century have the right of it. But this is not so. Institutions as vigorous were to die or at least languish elsewhere, and the English Parliament's survival – indeed, its marked increase in importance – was no foregone conclusion. By 1500, it was already something markedly different from the Cortes or Etats Généraux, but it was by no means yet the assembly which King James I was to encounter.

PARLIAMENT IN THE SIXTEENTH CENTURY

At a casual glance, the busy parliamentary scene of the sixteenth century did, indeed, provide little more than continuations of the sort of things already described. The House of Commons, large before, increased further by nearly 60 per cent. These additions, on the one hand, completed the principle of territorial representation, in that Wales, Chester, Durham, and (for a while) Calais now also sent members. At last, all the king's dominions were truly present.[1] On the other, the increase gave a larger number of the governing sort, themselves increasing in an age of population expansion, the chance to be present, so that the second principle – that political weight should be represented – was also given fuller play. The two Houses stood ever more equal to each other, and organization developed further, but these matters had been tolerably evident from at least the 1480s. Both Houses began to keep Journals, a new form of record; yet, though the Commons never had one before 1547, the Lords' Journal, now extant from 1510, probably had a fifteenth-century predecessor. In the Commons, in particular, internal procedure acquired many new details; the history of the House in this century may be summed up by saying that it finally achieved its ambition to be a court, a self-governing institution. It is in this period that the main precedents were set for the various privileges – freedom from arrest at a private suit, the right to determine disputed elections, the power to control members and deal with outsiders – upon which the House rested its self-sufficiency and with which it protected its influence. The business practices of Parliament were further refined; by the end of the century, three readings for every bill were customary in each House, and the use of committees both standing and specific had become common. And much of the time, despite the ascendancy of strong monarchs and the continuous government provided by a powerful Council, the political history of

---

[1] Ireland had a Parliament of its own.

the age must concentrate on the debates and doings in Parliament where the great issues of the day were handled and frequently decided, as in a less marked way they had been in previous centuries.[1] None of this sounds particularly new. Starting from the existence of an effective Parliament, and resting upon the twin pillars of an exclusive competence in the making of law and granting of supply, the Tudor age actively enlarged the competence and efficiency of the institution. If the old view once current that the century was marked by a lapse of parliamentary activity can no longer be held, neither, it would seem, can the more recent view that, on the contrary, Parliament really began its proper political career only at this time.

Yet a closer look quickly dispels the appearance of mere continuity, however accentuated. It is always worth remembering that many important features of Parliament have been seemingly continuous from the fourteenth to the twentieth century; however, behind the show of sameness, things have really changed drastically at times. Despite the obvious life found in the late-medieval Parliament, the institution was by no means sure to survive in an age of increasing monarchical strength. Those Continental assemblies which concentrated on opposition and the protection of sectional privilege were increasingly abandoned by monarchs who found them only troublesome; the Parliaments of 1515 and 1523 impressed both Cardinal Wolsey and King Henry VIII in much the same way. What made certain of the continued life of Parliament was neither custom nor mystique, but the problem of Henry's divorce and the break with Rome which grew from that. Once it had been shown that the autonomy of England could express itself in every way through the legislative sovereignty of the king-in-Parliament and in no other manner if a constitutional revolution was to be carried through with strict attention to the facts of common law and statute, the Crown ceased to be able to dispense with Parliament unless in turn it wished to start another revolution. By being tied to statutory penalties which only Parliament could decree or remove, the upheavals of the Reformation compelled meetings to continue; between 1529 and 1559 there were only six years without a session of Parliament. In those same thirty years, the Cortes of Castile met (futilely) nine times and the French Estates General not at all; and though those of Sicily, for instance, or the Netherlands were almost as frequent as those of England, they were politically quite unimportant by comparison. In the reign of Elizabeth, meetings were

---

[1] Cf. the section on Parliament in *Tudor Constitution*, 228–317.

relatively few – thirteen sessions in forty-five years – but they came at regular intervals, lasted longer, and made a lot more noise. In the history of Parliament, as in so much else, the 1530s reset the stage upon which the fortunes of England were playing themselves out.

We remember the evidence, already cited, that from the 1530s onwards Parliament occupied a very different position in thought about politics than it had done in the past. We have noted that the vital concept of the king-in-Parliament – the principle of legislative sovereignty vested in a mixed assembly of king, Lords, and Commons – cannot be discovered before the days of the Reformation Parliament but was commonplace some thirty years later, and that from that time those who wished to call England a limited monarchy talked in terms of Parliament rather than about moral principles or the king being under the law. It is therefore important to realize that in organization and practices, too, the 1530s marked the final establishment of a situation in which the three partners to the lawmaking process became equal. Despite the earlier acceptance of the Commons into the legislative authority of Parliaments, and the Lords' effective reduction to one of the two Houses, older attitudes had endured until that time.

The evidence for this assertion is found in the procedural details recorded on the original acts, the documents which passed through Lords and Commons and received the royal assent.[1] It is clear from the account given in 1455 that at that time bills originating in different Houses were treated differently, so as to stress the superiority of the Lords.[2] Bills that started in the Lords were sent to the Commons without annotation but required the Lower House's assent to be inscribed; those coming from the Commons carried a note recording their despatch to the other place, but the Lords did not trouble to write their assent on them. This was still the practice in 1497, the first year for which original acts survive. The clerk of the Parliament put *Missa a dominis* on the bill, but not *soit bailli as Communes*, nor did he add the Lords' assent to a bill sent up on which only the words *soit bailli as seiniors* appear. In this Parliament, too, and contrary to conventional notions, public bills started in the Lords, a practice which embodied the old principle that while the Commons presented grievances it was

---

[1] Preserved at the Record Office of the House of Lords. The collection is not complete; the original acts are missing for the two important sessions of 1523 and 1529.

[2] See p. 49 above.

for the king with the advice of the Lords to devise remedies.[1] This last point still held true in 1504, in two measures originating in a Commons' petition; so far was this still from being merely a procedural device that in such cases the bill was first handled in the Lords and then sent to the other House which noted its consent to a measure it had in fact promoted![2] By 1512, this archaic survival had gone, and bills in the form of a Commons' petition were treated like all bills originating in the Commons.

A major change in practice, in fact, came about in 1504, the first Parliament since 1497 and the last of Henry VII's reign. It may be connected with the appointment of a new clerk, Richard Hatton, who made a practice of signing his name on bills.[3] Though he still entered the *Missa* clause which marked the Lords' superiority, he also added a *soit bailli* clause, as well as the Lords' assent on bills received from the Commons. Even so, complete equality of treatment for the three partners had not yet arrived; in particular, the king still signed all the bills to which he agreed, and his sign manual was all that appeared on provisos attached to the bill which bear no evidence that they were ever passed by either House. These practices continued under Hatton's successor, John Taylor, clerk of the Parliaments till 1523, though the last evidence for his doings belongs to the previous Parliament of 1515. In these twenty years, it had also become clear that public bills could originate indifferently in either House. Procedurally speaking, the Parliament of 1497 was the last medieval Parliament.

These changes, which reflected so much political reality, were brought to completion in the Reformation Parliament by Taylor's successor, Sir Brian Tuke, incidentally the first lay clerk of the Parliaments. Now there was perfect routine, total equality, the full transformation of a Parliament held by the king with his Lords, with the Commons looking up to them, into a Parliament consisting of king,

[1] The only exception is 12 Henry VII, c. 6 (1497), which started as a petition of the Merchant Adventurers to the Commons, went from there to the Lords, and received the private-act response. Two private bills (cc. 9, 10 for the queen and for the earl of Surrey) oddly enough started in the Commons and are endorsed *le roi le veult*.

[2] Original acts of 19 Henry VII, cc. 7, 8 (1504). The exception is one Commons' petition which received the Lords' assent but was vetoed by the king; it seems that the Commons could push their demands in this way if the normal procedure was denied them by Crown opposition.

[3] Richard Hatton, Ll.D., a career cleric, Chancery clerk, and member of the king's Council, ended his days as provost of King's College, Cambridge. He died in May 1509, soon after Henry VIII's accession. *CPR Henry VII*, ii. 389; *Calendar of Close Rolls, Henry VII*, ii. 14; *LP* i. 54 (84).

Lords, and Commons working in equality. The king no longer signed bills to signify his acceptance, so that the last truly petitionary aspect of legislation was gone.[1] Nor did the clerk splash his signature over the documents. Two standardized lines recorded the resolution to despatch to the other House and that House's consent; and the royal assent, instead of being endorsed, was written across the top. The formulas of consent noted whether provisos were included; the attached slips bearing provisos carried the same phrases as the bill itself (making it possible to know where such amendments originated). The notion that a Commons' petition formed the basis of statute had disappeared to the extent that a bill, public in purpose but cast in the petitionary form, received the assent proper to private acts (*soit fait comme il est desire*), even though as recently as 1515 such bills had turned into public acts. These procedural details, it may be said, walked in the footsteps of constitutional fact, but they matter nonetheless. They demonstrate conclusively that the changes which transformed the medieval into the modern Parliament were not complete or fully grasped until the Reformation Parliament.

This is not an original or surprising conclusion, though in the face of some recent misunderstandings it must be reasserted. The conclusion is supported by the events of the day. After all, this was the Parliament which so remarkably extended the powers and competence of the institution because of the developments in Church and state. The religious legislation which accrued between 1529 and 1559 by degrees subjected every aspect of life in the realm to the authority of statute; for the first time, it could be truly said that acts of Parliament were omnicompetent in England.[2] If one compares the lawmaking activity of Tudor Parliaments – at its height in the 1530s but massive enough for the rest of the period – with the attempts of Spanish assemblies to press demands, constantly ignored, upon their lawmaking kings,[3] or

[1] An exception must be made for bills touching the person or family of the monarch. On these, the royal signature signified not approval of a petition but permission to proceed and was presumably required (as well as probably added) before the bill reached whichever House saw it first. [This is a rash statement: the problems both of the royal sign manual and other endorsements continued in some confusion after 1536. But in essence Tuke's practice became standard.]

[2] There has been much argument about the earlier competence of Parliament, but it is certain that no pre-Tudor statute involved the sort of authority as that which stood behind the 1539 Act of Six Articles or the various Acts of Uniformity (1549, 1552, 1559). Cf. Penry Williams and G. L. Hariss, 'A Revolution in Tudor History,' in *Past and Present*, 25 (1963), 3–58, and my reply, ibid. 29 (1964), 26–49.

[3] Cf. the documents printed by Griffiths, *Representative Government*, especially 44 ff., 68 ff.

with Bodin's opinion, already quoted, concerning the location of legislative authority in France, one can readily see how much more formidable the English institution was and how much more definitely an essential part of the government of the realm. If one compares this legislation with medieval practices, the increase in size and range is sufficiently striking.[1] While earlier Parliaments had stood high in this function, post-Reformation Parliaments stood sovereign; no matter was outside their cognizance. The change is fundamental, not superficial.

With it went a quite major change in the acts themselves. Anyone who is convinced that nothing much happened to Parliament in the sixteenth century might like to compare the shape of legislation in the reigns of Henry VII and Elizabeth. Statutes grew longer and acquired much longer preambles; they *looked* quite different. This, again, mainly happened in the 1530s, and the use of preambles to make major points was probably initiated by Thomas Cromwell. In the acts of the Reformation Parliament, too, the enacting clause achieved its regular standard form. There is a good example of this in the acts touching the person of the king himself. An act of 1504 (19 Henry VII, c. 26) dealt with the king's family, a personal enough matter. Procedure was still flexible enough to take account of this fact. The king signed the bill, and his assent was endorsed, but the two Houses simply accepted it, so that the bill bore the record of each House's agreement and no note about despatch, unlike a bill handled in the ordinary way. The enacting clause omitted the king – since he had asked the Parliament to help him – and spoke only of the advice of the Lords and Commons and the authority of Parliament (presumably here seen in its 'medieval' form as not including the king). By contrast, the Succession Acts of Henry VIII's reign, settling the dynastic circumstances of the royal family, though the first two for political reasons pretended to be derived from a joint petition of both Houses, were otherwise treated like any ordinary statute.[2] The king also abandoned a well-entrenched practice of attaching provisos to acts already passed by both Houses, a practice which had underlined where legislative authority was really conceived of as residing. Edward IV blandly qualified his assent to

[1] In the printed *Statutes of the Realm*, all extant legislation from Magna Carta to 1509 fills 1,092 pages, the thirty-five years of Henry VIII fill 1,032, and the years 1547–1603 another 1,014. This very rough indicator is, moreover, biased inasmuch as the first includes a mass of material duplicated by being given in both French and English, while no private acts at all are printed in the last.

[2] 25 Henry VIII, c. 22 (1534); 28 Henry VIII, c. 7 (1537); 35 Henry VIII, c. 1 (1544).

legislation on some occasions by last-minute reservations and amendments not agreed to in Parliament.[1] Henry VII did even more surprising things; thus, for instance, in December 1499 he sent the clerk
of the Parliament a signet letter which, two years after the Parliament
had gone home, ordered the clerk to add a saving clause to a statute
already on the roll; the roll was being specially released to him by the
Chancery for the purpose.[2] A slightly less dubious form of interference
is exemplified in a letter of 1504 to the Speaker (Edmund Dudley) and
the chancellor of the Duchy (Sir John Mordaunt), ordering them to
erase a name in a comprehensive bill of attainder then before the
House.[3] By 1534, the omission of Sir Thomas More's name from the
attainder of the Nun of Kent was handled by the councillors in the
House of Lords, after Henry VIII had been privately persuaded and
without any direct instructions from him. By then the king was no
longer in the position of a man who owned a court and could use it as
he willed, but in that of a member of the assembly who had to manage
things 'politically'. Nor was the monarch alone in conceding the
sovereignty of statute and his inability to change it once it was made;
the judges, too, came to treat acts of Parliament as quite different in
kind from the judgments of the ordinary courts – as legislative edicts
capable of being interpreted according to certain rigorous rules, not as
decisions to be used at discretion.[4] By the later sixteenth century it was
axiomatic that only another Parliament could alter what an earlier one
had done; the only creatures not bound by Parliament were its
successors.

From the 1530s on, discussions of the English constitution, themselves more frequent, stressed the place of Parliament in ways which
were quite unprecedented and especially missing from Fortescue.
Details of internal procedure and attitudes to statute law reflected this
novel position of Parliament and its legislative work. Institutional
development, however precedented, made different things out of
Commons and Lords. And the Parliament attracted ever more attention
as the centre of politics. Indeed, ever since Sir John Neale showed how
lively, active and difficult the Parliaments of Elizabeth commonly

---

[1] *England under the Yorkists, 1460–1485*, ed. Isobel D. Thornley (1921), 142–3.
[2] Letter in box of original acts for 12 Henry VII (1497), House of Lords Record Office;
cf. Pollard, *Reign of Henry VII*, 16–17, for examples found on the roll.
[3] House of Lords Record Office, box of original acts, 19 Henry VII (1504).
[4] *Tudor Constitution*, 232–4, partly summarizing the important discussion in Samuel E.
Thorne's introduction to his edition of *A Discourse upon the Exposicion & Understanding
of Statutes* (San Marino, Calif., 1942).

were, it has taken a degree of bigotry to ignore the transformation of the institution – its elevation to sovereignty in law and power in affairs – after the 1530s. But the essence of that transformation lies not in the outward and visible signs of opposition and resistance to the policy of the Crown, but in the inward and partly spiritual grace bestowed by the extension of competence to the Church, to every corner of the realm, and to all the affairs of men. It was as an indispensable arm of government, not as a restraint on power and policy, that the Tudor Parliaments achieved their eminence; in them stood embodied the effective and effectively growing power of the state because in them all the realm, king and lords and commonalty, were present.

The change in the relative position of Lords and Commons went, in fact, beyond the establishment of equality. While the Commons grew so hugely in numbers, the Lords lost membership. Thirty-one abbots went in 1536–40, leaving the spiritual peers in a permanent minority, and the temporal lords, thanks to the Tudor policy of making few peers, never exceeded about sixty. The Commons were not only 462 strong by 1601, but about four out of every five members can only be called gentry – representative of the substantial middling landowners. This social cohesiveness gave the House a great deal of purposeful strength. On the face of it, the Commons were markedly less representative than they had been. Many members had virtually no ties with the constituencies for which they sat – many parliamentary boroughs had become no more than a gateway into politics – and the Elizabethan House of Commons cannot be said to have expressed territorial representation in the manner of its fourteenth-century predecessor. And despite the presence of some merchants and many lawyers, often themselves country gentry in origin and habits, the varied interests of the realm were also less obviously present than they had once been. What the House did represent very effectively, however, was the political nation of England, that part of the people that concerned itself with affairs, was indispensable to the effective administration of the realm, and wished to participate in the deliberations and decisions of government. The role filled quite properly by the magnates (with their followers) in Lancastrian and even Yorkist Parliaments was now in the hands of a much larger and more diffuse group of landowners; and this was true even though the local ascendancy of individual lords and the hierarchic ties of patron and client were manifest throughout Elizabethan society. There were more men than ever of independent means and independent minds in the Commons, at the very time that the Crown had gained a degree of control over the Lords which it had never enjoyed before the days of Henry VIII. Behind this change stood the facts of a numerical increase in the population, which may just about have doubled between 1470 and 1600, and the opportunity created by the secularization of Church lands for cadet branches of gentry families to establish new landed dynasties. On any democratic principle the Elizabethan House of Commons obviously represented a highly partial and sectional interest only, but in terms of political reality it effectively embodied the only politically significant sector; and it did so now much better than the Lords whose social and political ascendancy had still been properly depicted in the Yorkist Parliaments. In this there lay great strength and the possibility of a novel role.

That the novel role was played, Neale's books have fully demonstrated. The story of political conflict, of determined and sophisticated opposition meeting determined and sophisticated government leadership, is by now so familiar that it requires no detailed examination here. Yet this picture of puritan agitation, frequent clashes between queen and Commons, and the sheer difficulties of every session puts an essential point in danger of being overlooked. Of course, the Parliaments of the sixteenth century were, as they had always been, arenas for debate, argument, opposition, resistance to royal claims, the working out of compromises. Though the Commons of Elizabeth proved much more active in this respect than those of Henry VIII, they only accentuated an ever present fact of life. The bringing together of divergent interests and views was one of the major purposes of every parliamentary session. But a Parliament which did nothing else was a Parliament of the 'continental' type – a counterweight to the power and rule of the monarchy. The English Parliament (as we have seen) had in large measure been something more: a partner in government affairs, a business organization for attending to some of the foremost tasks of government. As we have also seen, this vital function was enormously enlarged, to the point of transforming the place of Parliament in the constitution, in the consequences of a Reformation carried through from above and by the use of common law and statute. The parliamentary troubles of Elizabeth's reign should not hide the continued governmental function of the assembly. A meeting of Parliament continued to be an occasion for doing work, for achieving ends, not simply one for parading protests or making claims. The whole important story of the struggle over free speech in Parliament should be seen as an endeavour to increase the efficiency of the institution as a positive, not a negatively restricting, element in the system.[1] It is a cardinal error, unconsciously perhaps encouraged by knowledge of what happened under the Stuarts, to concentrate on conflict. Assemblies that had nothing but criticism and resistance to offer died because they were useless to governments and failed to impress the powerful interests with their pointless vapourings. When, under Charles I, the English Parliament at last seemed to be going the same way, there were many influential voices that doubted the value of these empty meetings. The criticism and argument produced in the Elizabethan Parliament led generally to agreed results – to action, to laws, to remedies, to political adjustment. The emergence of the Commons as the leading House not only did not reduce the distinctive function of the English Parliament, it enormously increased it. To all men who cared about government, wished to share in it, had causes to promote or interests to serve, Parliament became in the sixteenth century the continuous forum of political life, a role which it had never filled in the middle ages but which it has never since ceased to play.

This essential fact had practical consequences for statesmanship which under the Tudors were fully recognized. To be able to carry on the king's government, a Tudor politician needed, certainly, the confidence of the monarch, personal ascendancy in Council, good ties with the local interests upon which individual political power ultimately rested. But he also needed to be able to manage and steer Parliament, especially the House of Commons. After Thomas Cromwell had first demonstrated the importance of these skills, the ministers of the Crown developed and maintained them, changing details as circumstances changed, but ever mindful of the existence of the House of Commons and thoroughly familiar with its peculiar ways. It is hard to avoid a kind of sentimentality in discussing this point, but the fact remains that there has been, from the Reformation Parliament onwards, a recognizable entity, with its own self-conscious ethos and practices and reactions, to be called the House of Commons, despite the fact that the entity consisted of hundreds of diverse and constantly changing individuals. There is an unmistakable mixture of vigour and arrogance, volatility and touchiness, frivolity and seriousness, a ready response to the right kind of touch, which every competent student of Parliament soon comes to take for granted. These almost mystical

[1] For free speech, see *Tudor Constitution*, 254–7, and the works there cited.

things do exist, over and above the divisions of faction or party, amazingly persistent through the changes brought by time. By the same token, there has ever since the 1530s been a breed of men whose political instincts were in tune with the House – men who understood the House – and they have not necessarily included the noticeably great. But Cromwell and Cecil, who were great men, have had their successors down the ages. The whole character and effective working of English government have since the days of Thomas Cromwell depended on the coexistence of a Parliament, in which the Commons provided the real scene of political activity, with ministers of the Crown who could manage Parliament into the achievement of positive results: into exercising its true function as the ultimate embodiment of the nation in political action.

None of this the Stuarts and too many of the men they chose for their servants understood at all well, or sometimes at all. When the representatives of the young colony of Virginia met in assembly in 1619, the latest news they had of the English Parliament was shocking indeed – of a session which had achieved nothing, which had run away in conflict, which had ceased to be an organization for business. They inherited ancient traditions of representation and participation in government, but they started their own enterprise at a bad moment in time if what they wished to achieve was co-operation with constituted authority, orderly and agreed government, and continuous non-violent change through the passage of the centuries.

23

PARLIAMENTARY DRAFTS 1529-1540*

The period which opened with the meeting of the Reformation Parliament on 3 November 1529 and closed with the fall of Thomas Cromwell on 10 June 1540 was one of revolution. A great many things were done that overthrew accepted notions, and a great many more were planned. A new 'polity' was being shaped, though the revolutionaries were conservative to a degree in the manner of their work. The characteristic note of those years is one of calm assurance that things ought by rights always to have been even as they are now being fashioned; there is really no innovation – only a clearing away of the false and usurped encrustations of the ages. The preamble of the Statute of Appeals with its invocation of 'histories and chronicles' sets the tone. In keeping with their backward-looking words, the revolutionaries also employed the strictest legality in putting through their measures. There was no attempt to do away with the supremacy of the law; on the contrary, nothing was done without giving the courts a hand in applying it. The place of Parliament in the establishment of the royal supremacy and in dealing with the vast social and political consequences of that establishment has been consistently misunderstood. Henry VIII and Cromwell did not appeal to Parliament for moral authority, nor did they use it (having perhaps packed it) to pretend a unity in the nation for propaganda purposes. They had no choice in the matter if they were to make their measures enforceable at law – if they hoped, as everything shows they hoped, to carry their revolution through on conservative and legal lines. The reformation statutes do not make the king supreme head – they accept that fact as their starting point; what they do is to work out the administrative details and impose the penalties which alone could secure the revolution against opposition. Only Parliament – only the lawmaking body – could do this; there was nothing new in this use of Parliament, though a great deal that was new in the scope and magnitude of the work.[1]

* [*BIHR* 25 (1952), 117–32; and 27 (1954), 198–200. Some of the points made here are corrected or developed in *Reform and Renewal*.]

[1] It is, of couse, true that one result of the 1530s – part of their revolution – was Parliament's greatly enhanced standing as a maker of law.

The importance of legislation in Parliament has not been overlooked, and ever since the existence of drafts for Acts of Parliament was revealed by the publication of the *Letters and Papers . . . of Henry VIII*, historians have remarked on their significance. Stubbs and Maitland, great guides indeed, were the first to point it out.[1] Some have since investigated the genesis of enacted legislation from the sequence of extant drafts, false starts and dead ends; the treason law, the Statute of Uses, the Act of Appeals and the Supplication against the Ordinaries have all received this treatment.[2] Others have discovered some of the very interesting plans cast in the form of parliamentary bills which never came to fruition, and have sought to divine the government's intentions from them.[3] But here the difficulty begins. It has been too easily assumed that every draft act of Parliament preserved among the state papers necessarily represents government planning. This was an age of turmoil, not only among the makers of policy but also among men of ideas unconnected with the government. The 'commonwealth's men' of the 1540s[4] had their predecessors in the 1530s. Though more obscure, the Clement Armstrongs and Rastells were no less active in thought than the Haleses and the Levers, and Latimer, so prominent in the later group, provides a link with the earlier. Such treatises as those on the staple and the provision of labour for industry and agriculture which are ascribed to Armstrong[5] display a lively interest in reform and incidentally an equal predilection for the term 'commonwealth' or 'common weal'. It is at least not inconceivable that some of the more extravagant ideas may have sprung from brains less committed to responsibility than those of Thomas Cromwell and his staff. Rastell's plans for the reform of Church and state included suggestions for five statutes ('bills to be drawn against the next Parliament') – to permit priests to marry, to prohibit offerings to images, for reforms in the common law and the court of Chancery,

[1] W. Stubbs, *Seventeen Lectures* (Oxford, 1886), 321; F. W. Maitland, *English Law and the Renaissance* (Cambridge, 1901), n. 11.
[2] I. D. Thornley, 'The Treason Legislation of Henry VIII,' *TRHS* (1917), 87 ff.; W. S. Holdsworth, *Hist. of Eng. Law*, iv. 449 ff. (on the Statute of Uses) [better now: E. W. Ives, 'The Genesis of the Statute of Uses,' *EHR* 82 (1967), 673 ff.]; below, nos. 24 and 25.
[3] T. F. T. Plucknett, 'Some Proposed Legislation of Henry VIII,' *TRHS* (1936), 119 ff.; L. Stone, 'The Political Programme of Thomas Cromwell,' *BIHR* 24 (1951), 1 ff.
[4] S. T. Bindoff, *Tudor England* (Harmondsworth, 1950), 129 f. I owe much in this paragraph to points made by Professor Bindoff in conversation, but he is not, of course, in any way responsible for the conclusions at which I have arrived.
[5] Tawney and Power, *Tudor Economic Documents*, iii. 90 ff., 115 ff.

to prevent the taking of excessive fees in the various courts.[1] There was but a small step from suggesting reforms and asking that bills be prepared for them, to the drawing up of such ideas in usable form and sending them to the man who could use them.[2] They would then survive as parliamentary drafts among Cromwell's papers. It should be possible to discover some means of determining whether a draft emanated from the government or not, and all that will be attempted here is to provide such a classification and discuss the 'private' drafts. The sixty-odd extant drafts of those eleven years have therefore been studied and compared. It was supposed from the start that a government machine as highly developed as that of the early Tudors, working moreover through most of this time under the direction of one chief minister, would show a marked uniformity in its products, and this supposition has been borne out.[3]

Taking those drafts that resulted in legislation – drafts, that is, whose government provenance can nearly always be taken for granted – the following characteristics emerge. They are written on one side only of large sheets of paper (about 18 in. by 12 in.); spaces one to one and a half inches wide are left between the lines for corrections; they are almost invariably in a typical clerical script otherwise found in the offices of the privy seal and especially the signet;[4] corrections on them, when not by the drafting clerk, are nearly always in an identifiable government hand, either Cromwell's or Lord Chancellor Audley's. In other words, they are obvious drafts, written out so as to make correction easy, and in fact are as a rule corrected. The form does not appear to have been original, for there are among Cromwell's papers drafts of indentures and patents which would seem to be its prototype. They are, then, lawyers' drafts. Some evidence, mostly of the negative kind, suggests that the application of this form (and indeed the practice of prolonged drafting and redrafting) to parliamentary business may

---

[1] *LP* vii. 1043. That this paper was composed by Rastell was proved by A. W. Reed, *Early Tudor Drama* (1926), 24.

[2] Armstrong sent his treatises to Cromwell (S. T. Bindoff, 'Clement Armstrong and his Treatises of the Commonweal,' *Econ. Hist. Rev.* 14 [1944], 68). Cf. also his scarcely veiled appeal to Cromwell: Tawney and Power, iii. 112.

[3] All the drafts have been studied in the original MS, but for simplicity's sake they will, wherever possible, be cited by reference to the calendar (*LP*).

[4] Handwriting in the offices of the lesser seals was not so definitely departmental as were Exchequer and Chancery hands. At this period, however, it can be identified within limits: it is a large, round and well-formed mixture of late Bastard and early Secretary which is met with occasionally in other clerical scripts but predominantly among government clerks; it can never be mistaken for anything but a professional hand and is easily distinguished from more individual writing.

have been due to Cromwell, but this point does not matter in the present context and cannot be pursued any further. The point to note is that the typical genuine government draft of an act of Parliament cannot be mistaken.

It would be too much to expect no exception to this simple rule, and a number of drafts which do not obey it while yet being part of enacted legislation must be mentioned. It will be seen that they do not really affect the rule because there is something out of the ordinary about all of them. They will be taken in order as they are listed in the calendar.

(*a*) A draft of the Supplication against the Ordinaries:[1] on smaller sheets and written on both sides; but in the clerkly script and corrected by Cromwell. This is a draft of the year 1529 and part of Cromwell's work before he became a member of the government; though connected with Cromwell, it had nothing to do with the government.[2]

(*b*) Two drafts for the Act of Appeals (24 Henry VIII, c. 12) are a little out of the ordinary.[3] They are the first in the series, a draft which is 'proper' in every respect except that it was written on sheets smaller than the usual size, and the draft made when it became apparent that a fresh start on the problem was required. This second draft was again 'proper' but for the handwriting; not a clerk but men a little higher in the official world wrote it (Sir Richard Riche? and others) because it required renewed thought and fresh phrasing. There is nothing in these drafts to make nonsense of the definition given. They were different in minor details and for special reasons.

(*c*) A draft for the attainder of the Fitzgeralds (26 Henry VIII, c. 25).[4] Closely written on both sides of smaller sheets, in an uncharacteristic clerical hand; uncorrected and cast in the form of a Commons' prayer. It is likely to be the first draft and the work of the Irish opponents of the defeated Fitzgeralds who may have been asked to submit a suitable bill as they were the party most interested and most knowledgeable.

(*d*) A draft for the bill to exonerate the universities from the payment

---

[1] *LP* iv. 6043 (7).

[2] Cf. below, pp. 108ff. The other drafts of the Supplication may be included here; only a brief notice is required as they are discussed in full in no. 25 below. The first of them (*LP* v. 1611 [3]) is a Commons' draft; of the remaining three, one (ibid. [4]) is also Cromwellian and non-government; while the others (ibid. [1, 2]) come from Cromwell and the government. Only no. 2 is an altogether 'proper' draft.

[3] The drafts are E and F in my numbering (below, p. 82, n. 4). For F, cf. also below, p. 90.   [4] *LP* vii. 1382 (1).

of first fruits and tenths (27 Henry VIII, c. 42).[1] Correct in every way, except for narrow spaces between lines. This together with a decorated first line suggests a final draft ready for submission to Parliament.

(*e*) A draft of the act extinguishing the authority of the bishop of Rome (28 Henry VIII, c. 10).[2] Like (*d*); endorsed by Cromwell's clerk 'An Acte towch . . .' and by Cromwell (?) 'the busshop of Rome'. Also likely to have been the final draft.

(*f*) Two papers concerning theological matters.[3] Though endorsed 'An Acte of parliament concerninge the true vnderstandinge of holy scripture', these papers are not draft bills; the endorsement may have been a note as to steps to be taken. The form of the papers – smaller sheets written on both sides in a clerical script with narrow spacings – is quite typical of the many treatises, opinions and memoranda on such matters.

(*g*) Three drafts identical in form; one for the Act of Six Articles (31 Henry VIII, c. 14),[4] and two for the Statute of Marriages (32 Henry VIII, c. 38).[5] They are on both sides of smaller sheets (15 in. by 11 in., to 12 in. by 9 in.), in one of the known clerical scripts, with well-spaced lines, and corrected by the king. It seems certain that this special form was adopted only for drafts which Henry VIII himself wished to see and revise. Only these matters of theological interest attracted him, and his hand does not appear on any other draft except on one of the many for the Act of Appeals which is also a little unusual in form, having originally been a roll.[6] Specially handy drafts were apparently made for the king.

(*h*) A draft preamble to an act for a subsidy.[7] Though written on both sides of smaller sheets, this is otherwise a 'proper' draft; it is endorsed by Cromwell ('ffor a subsidie'). Whether it was ever used is not certain, and in any case it was a draft of only part of a bill and therefore does not have to conform to the pattern.

(*i*) A draft for an act concerning maltsters.[8] A 'proper' draft except that the spacing is very narrow, and that it is in the hand of John Uvedale, clerk of the council in the north. Endorsed by Cromwell's clerk: 'Againste Maltes – merchauntes of yorke.' It adopts the form of a petition. In fact, it was drafted not by the government in London

---

[1] *LP* x. 246 (11).
[2] Ibid. 1090.   [3] *LP* xii. II. 1313 (1, 2).
[4] *LP* xiv. I. 868 (9).   [5] *LP* xv. 499 (1, 2).
[6] This is draft H in my numbering (below, p. 82, n. 4), now cut up and bound in separate sheets in BM, Cleo. E. vi, fos. 179–202.
[7] *LP* xv. 502 (1).   [8] *LP Add.* 1453.

but by the government in the north, in deference to local interests, and was never enacted.

These are all the drafts which we can be sure had some connection with the government and which do not fit the normal pattern. It will be seen that they do not affect the argument; there are reasons why they should be a little different, and in any case it would be surprising if the form had been always followed without fail. The great number of 'proper' drafts still makes it possible to say that government draft bills were written on large paper, one side only was used, the lines were widely spaced, and the writer was as a rule a government clerk (usually a signet clerk?) with a distinctive clerical hand. Corrections and endorsements in the hand of ministers or their known servants confirm the identification. From this it follows that a considerable number of drafts which never resulted in legislation, but which answer to the description of 'proper' government drafts, may be taken to have emanated from the government. With them we are on safe ground; plans outlined there may be used to illustrate the lines on which the government was thinking and working.

However, there is nothing very striking among these abortive government drafts. Sometimes the ideas are interesting enough, but as a rule they are dull – simply details of administration. The vast plans embodied in the drafts printed, for instance, by Professor Plucknett and Mr Stone are not among them. But ought we really to be surprised at this? It is, on the face of it, much easier to believe that the government was worried about the rebuilding of Dover harbour or the fate of the weaving trade, than that it wished to set up revolutionary courts to supersede the common law or build a standing army. That is merely on the face of it: intrinsic improbability does not disprove a case otherwise sound. We must see how sound the case is for ascribing a number of interesting drafts to the government, and it must in the first place be remembered that none of the documents now to be discussed answers to the description of true government drafts which has already been given. 'Diplomatically' they are not government drafts. Indeed, it is really incumbent upon those who would have them be such to prove their case, for they can only have been government drafts if they broke all the ordinary rules. Once again we shall do best by taking the drafts in turn as they are listed in the calendar and discuss them individually. There are only nine of them. The points to consider, apart from their diplomatic appearance, are such details as corrections and endorsements, and their contents; the language employed can be a useful guide to the source whence the idea came.

(1) Draft bill to restrain the bishops from citing or arresting any of the king's subjects for heresy.[1] The draft is written on one side of large sheets of paper, but there are no spaces left for correction, and it is in an individual hand, so far unidentified. Its contents suggest the amateur at work. Citations for heresy were not to be allowed unless the bishop or his commissary was free from any private grudge against the accused, and there were to be at least two credible witnesses. The accused was to know the charge and the names of his accusers. The draft embodied, in effect, standing grievances against ecclesiastical courts, especially in their attitude to heresy trials, grievances which also found expression in the Supplication against the Ordinaries. Since these grievances were entertained by the Commons themselves (the Supplication originated in that House),[2] it seems likely that this draft represents work on the part of the Commons, or of some one individual interested in these matters and connected with the Commons. It should probably be ascribed to the first (1529) session of the Reformation Parliament. Nothing seems ever to have followed from it.[3]

(2) Draft bill to prohibit the sale of goods except at fairs and markets.[4] Almost a 'proper' draft, but in an individual and unknown hand. Endorsed: 'Mr Gybson – A bill concernyng Cyttes borowhs towns and portes.' The suggestion in the calendar that this referred to Richard Gibson, member for Romney,[5] is quite unsupported; we suggest instead that the endorsement referred not to the man entrusted with the bill or responsible for sponsoring it in the House, but to the author who had sent the document to Cromwell (the endorsement is by a Cromwellian clerk). The significance of this will appear below.[6] The contents of the bill bear strong marks of a special kind of source: they speak of the engrossing of merchandise by rich men and their unethical dealings in the privacy of their own houses, of the decline of market towns and the impoverishment of artisans compelled to seek a living in the countryside or go begging. The bill provides for public and controlled trading and compels all artificers, except blacksmiths and farriers, to reside within some town or borough. Not

---

[1] *LP* vi. 120 (2).   [2] Cf. below, pp. 110–11.

[3] There is only the vaguest echo in the act restraining bishops from citing suspects out of their dioceses, passed in 1532 (23 Henry VIII, c. 9), but this too arose out of a clause in the Supplication.   [4] *LP* vii. 67.

[5] Ibid. footnote.   [6] Pp. 72–3.

even pedlars are to sell any goods except at markets and fairs. The draft evinces a concern for decaying towns of which there is much in the programme of the economic reformers of the 1540s, but nothing in government action until 1554;[1] it attacks merchants much as Armstrong did;[2] and the absurdity of its desire to restrain craftsmen within the limits of towns sufficiently indicates that we have here no responsible government plan. It reads like the suggestions of an ardent reformer with ideas of his own on the troubles of the realm. Needless to say, there is no trace of such a plan in any other document of the period.

(3) Draft bill for the setting up of a court of six Justices or Conservators of the Common Weal.[3] This is the draft printed and brilliantly commented upon by Professor Plucknett.[4] To him it was a sign both of high juristic reasoning and administrative skill. It planned the erection of a court, assisted by a police force (serjeants of the common weal), to enforce 'statutes penal or popular', statutes creating offences breach of which was brought to trial by private persons (informers) bringing a civil action and taking part of the statutory fine. The scheme outlined would have given England an early system of public enforcement of the law in criminal cases by means of a true criminal procedure, and would have saved such matters both from the malice of individuals and the confusion introduced by the principle of civil action. Whether it could have been established in a society whose local government was so markedly unbureaucratic is another matter. There is no other trace of so far-reaching a revolution in the administration of the law; the common practice then and for many years before and after was to commit the enforcement of penal statutes to conciliar committees, especially the 'king's council learned'.[5] The draft would therefore show the government considering the adoption of entirely new methods. But whether one can, in fact, see the hand of the government in this draft, is the question. It is written on both sides of small sheets with a little space between lines for corrections; the scribe, though a clerk of some sort, did not write any known government draft. All the few corrections are by him. There is thus no trace of government provenance in the appearance of the draft.

Many points about the document suggest an origin outside govern-

---

[1] 1 & 2 Philip and Mary, c. 4.   [2] Tawney and Power, iii. 122 f.
[3] *LP* vii. 1611 (4).   [4] *TRHS* (1936), 125 ff.
[5] Cf. R. Somerville, 'Henry VII's "Counsel Learned in the Law",' *EHR* 54 (1939), 427 ff., and such statutes as the 'Star Chamber Act', 3 Henry VII, c. 1.

ment circles. The reiteration of 'common weal' – the catchword of the later economic pamphleteers – not only in the title of the officers to be appointed but also in the sweeping adjurations of the last clause, is in itself significant. There is the fact, remarked by Mr Plucknett, that the one citation of a previous statute is a serious misquotation.[1] The extreme provisions of clause 20, extending the competence of the court to offences not yet created and left to its discretion, are very different from the almost painful legalism commonly observed in the statutes of the 1530s. There are some very odd and oddly phrased sentences which it would be difficult to parallel in known government work: acts are not observed 'and bettir it were they neuer had bene made onlesse they shuld bee put in due and perfite execucion',[2] 'there is neuer at any tyme any sutis . . . entreated of but oonly such as concerne meum and tuum',[3] 'the prisone of the flete shalbe the place to commytte all such offendours vnto' – a curious inversion suggesting the sermon rather than the statute.[4] There are others. The enacting clause is highly peculiar, especially in that it refers in general to the ordinances following instead of to the first section, an invariable practice in genuine acts. Equally unusual is the use of 'Item' instead of 'Also' to introduce each section. Finally, there is the business of the seal of the court. Several new courts with seals of their own were erected in this period, but this is the only one to be described. And in so strangely romantic a way – a ship and the king's arms on one side, a plough with two handcarts, a hammer, and a spade on the other – to signify the place occupied by husbandry, crafts, and fishing in sustaining 'the greate bourdene of the Common weale of the Realme'.[5] One might be reading a political pamphlet; indeed, the seal suggested to Mr Plucknett the hand of Thomas More and echoes of *Utopia*,[6] though – as he himself says – the draft cannot be earlier than 1534 by which time More, two years out of politics, was awaiting his fate in the Tower. The last folio seems to clinch the matter: it suggests the words to be engraved on the seal 'if it bee the kingis pleasure', surely no way to express things in a statute prepared by the king's ministers.[7]

To sum up: this is almost certainly not the work of the government, but was produced by one of those men interested in economic and

---

[1] Plucknett, *TRHS* (1936), 128, 137.   [2] Ibid. 135.
[3] Ibid. 136. These two sentences provoked Mr Plucknett's special admiration, and rightly so: but are they in any way comparable to the usual tone of statutes at the time?
[4] Ibid. 140.   [5] Ibid. 138.
[6] Ibid. 132 f.
[7] Ibid. 144. The words underline the ideas represented on the seal.

social reforms of whom there is growing evidence in the 1530s. If we could point to a man closely associated with Latimer, Armstrong and Hales, whose chief interest lay in the law, we might be able to identify the author. The plan was in any case too vast and difficult to find favour with the government to whom it was sent.

(4) A bill described as 'The copye of an Acte of Parlyament agaynste Pilgrimages and supersticious worshippinge of Reliques &c.'[1] It is drawn up in a very 'improper' manner: on both sides of smaller sheets, with hardly any spaces between lines but very wide margins, and in an unfamiliar clerical hand. Its phrasing gives it away. The preamble is full of moral reflections, which is not unusual, but also adopts some very fanciful words; thus it inveighs against the man who 'addict hym self to any priuate or common place where yn ease and ydlenes he may lede his lyfe and like a drone bee eate and suke vpp suyche allmys and sustentation as shulde be geven to poore impotent and miserable persons'. The bill uses sermonizing terms like 'spices of ypocrisy' and is vague when it comes to legal points. Throughout the enactment phrases of moral censure and justification recur, whereas they ought to have been concentrated in the preamble. Altogether, taking into account appearance, purpose and phrasing, this paper was most likely drafted by an advanced religious reformer, perhaps at the instigation of interests either in Parliament or government, and must not be taken as evidence of the government's considered intentions. The fact that it was described as a 'copye' does not mean it was taken from a real draft of an enacted statute; 'copye' here signifies much the same as draft.

(5) Draft bill (the preamble only is now extant) concerning the payment of tithes in London.[2] Nearly a 'proper' draft, but the clerk's hand is unfamiliar and the spacing is unusually narrow. The paper seems originally to have formed a roll. The point at issue, affecting only the interests of the citizens and parsons of London, and the fact that the bill was intended to clarify doubts arising out of an arbitration made between them, make it plain enough that this bill was drawn up by the city authorities; that it was submitted by them to Cromwell is suggested by the endorsement, in the hand of one of his clerks, of the description 'Bytwene the Cytizens and Curattes of London'.

(6) Draft bill for 'A Reformacion for the pow[re] benefices thorough the Realme'.[3] 'Proper' except for spacings and handwriting which is very individual, though so far unidentified. The bill grants powers

---

[1] *LP* x. 246 (16).   [2] *LP* xi. 204.   [3] *LP* xiv. I. 868 (15).

to abolish poor benefices and transfer their emoluments to others; it envisages a necessary and not very difficult reform. The fact that the vicegerent in spirituals is specifically given authority by it also suggests that it may have come from Cromwell and the government. Against this is its form, not a very weighty objection since it is nearly enough correct and may be a first and rough draft to be worked up later; more important, a correction (not by the draftsman) has changed the perfectly accurate reference to the authority of 'the kinges highnes . . . and of his lordes spirituall and temporall and comens in this present parlament assemblyd' to 'the three estattes assemblyd in this present parlament', a meaningless and unparalleled form of the enacting clause. For the rest, the phrasing is not inconsistent with official origin. Possibly this draft was in some way commissioned by the government but never got near enough acceptance to be put in the hands of official draftsmen. As it is, its provenance must remain suspect.

(7) Draft bill concerning the use of confiscated monastic lands, the creation of a standing army and the erection of a court of centeners to administer it.[1] This draft recently acquired special importance when it was used to clinch a general argument alleging vast plans to build a 'Renaissance despotism' in England.[2] Mr Stone used his view of this document to support his general thesis, and his general thesis to prove that this document was drafted by the government; his circular argument makes it necessary to tackle both these points.

The document is quite 'improper': written on both sides of small sheets with hardly any spacing between lines, it does not look like a government draft. The handwriting is individual and not clerkly; I have kept an eye open for its recurrence in four years' reading in the records of this time without ever coming across it again, in itself not a bad argument for suspecting that it did not belong to anyone connected with the government. Most significant is an endorsement on it of the name 'Thomas gybson'. This is not only contemporary (and not, as Mr Stone supposes, possibly Elizabethan),[3] but moreover in the familiar hand of a Cromwellian clerk much employed in endorsing the names of senders on Cromwell's incoming correspondence. It is at least likely that a Thomas Gibson sent the paper to Cromwell, and – despite Mr Stone's failure to make anything of the name – there is a Thomas Gibson, obscure enough but interesting, in this context. He was a protégé of Latimer's, an executor of Clement Armstrong's will, a grocer turned printer and a man who communicated some rather

---

[1] *LP* xiv. I. 871.   [2] Stone, *BIHR* 24 (1951), 1 ff.   [3] Ibid. 11.

absurd ideas to Cromwell.[1] In other words, he admirably fits the part for which the endorsement seems to cast him, and it is quite probable that the endorsement on document (2) refers to the same man. 'Diplomatically', the paper suggests private provenance.

Its phrasing and contents support this conclusion. Mr Stone's view that only a statesman could frame a draft satisfying to so many interests[2] is in conflict with the evidence of private excellence provided, for instance, by document (3) above; moreover, the desire to see the monasteries north of the Trent saved and to keep the dispossessed monks from contact with the world by reconstituting a propertyless monasticism went clean contrary to express government policy. On the other hand, that the dissolution had bad social consequences became one of the commonplaces of the Latimer group of reformers.[3] Especially noticeable is the reference to monks 'accomptyd ded persons in the law',[4] correct enough but never allowed to interfere with the dissolution and in fact irrelevant to it; it recalls the juristic philosophizing of draft (3). To Mr Stone, the petitionary phrase with which the document opens is categorical proof that it was 'either drawn up by the same hand as' the second act of succession, 'or was based upon it'. 'As such,' he goes on, 'it must be the work of a lawyer, and one in the employ of the government.'[5] The deduction hardly follows; moreover, it is wise to avoid all dogmatism where the petitionary or enacting clause is concerned. There was little regularity or definition about the practice in such matters, except that there had to be a mention of king, lords,

---

[1] His figure emerges from the following few notices: Thomas Gibson, grocer of London, signed Clement Armstrong's will (Bindoff, *Econ. Hist. Rev.* 14 [1944], 72; Armstrong himself was a grocer before he turned pamphleteer – ibid. 69); he may still have been a grocer in 1538 (*LP* xiii. II. 1192); before that, however, he had taken up printing in the reforming interest, and Latimer recommended him to Cromwell for the 'Bishops' Book' of 1537 (*LP* xii. II. 295). The Thomas Gibson who some time in 1537–8 wrote to Cromwell, offering to prove the king's coming victory over the pope from many curious prophecies which he had collected (*LP* xii. II. 1242), may well have been the same man; such mild forms of religious mania went commonly well enough with reforming ideas in Church and commonwealth.

[2] Stone, *BIHR* 24 (1951), 4. His reference to 'a crank reformer' shows his misapprehension of the true position: the more far-reaching and complicated a suggested piece of legislation was, the less likely it is to have originated with the government. Those who had to carry the laws into effect knew well the possible limits of the bureaucracy at their disposal.

[3] Chambers, *More*, 261.   [4] Stone, *BIHR* 24 (1951), 14.

[5] Ibid. 4. The form of a petition by both Houses also occurs in the attainder of Elizabeth Barton, the act confiscating the property of the knights of St John, and the Cleves divorce (23 Henry VIII, c. 12; 32 Henry VIII, cc. 24, 25; the last two are referred to by Mr Stone). It proves nothing.

and commons. Remarks in the preamble about the hurt to the realm which the suppression of the monasteries had caused would read most surprisingly if they had been drafted by the government. The concern with husbandry, hospitality, unemployment and old age was at least as marked among the social theorists of the time as in Henry VIII's government; most people would say the former cared more. The sum of £1,000 allocated to the upkeep of fortifications is absurdly small when compared with the actual expenditure on such items in these years.[1] The choice of Coventry as the seat of the court – because it is 'not farre from the mydell of the realme' – provides the sort of fanciful touch one would expect in a private plan. All government was being more and more concentrated at Westminster, and no responsible states-man would have dreamt of sending so important a department as a virtual war office half way across the country. The further argument that the decay of Coventry might thereby be arrested recalls the re-formers' concern with towns.[2] It is impossible to recite all the detail here: if the draft stood by itself, it could not seriously be thought to have been a plan devised by the government.

But Mr Stone has argued that it was meant to provide the coping stone in a system of despotism, and if his view that Cromwell was planning a despotism were tenable the draft would indeed fill that place well. This is not the place to enter into a consideration of Crom-well's real plans, though one may remark in passing that it was a strange despotism that relied so largely on the legislative supremacy of parliament. But Mr Stone's own arguments in favour of his thesis must be rapidly reviewed.[3] Maitland's suggestion that in the 1530s the common law was nearly displaced by the civil law, and liberty there-fore by despotism,[4] was long ago severely modified by Holdsworth:[5] the supremacy of the common law itself was never threatened by the conciliar courts, though these looked likely to become permanent rivals to the common law *courts*. The court of commonweal was not a government project, and if it had been it would not have threatened the common (and statute) law whose enforcement it was meant to secure; no basis for a 'Renaissance despotism' there.[6] Treason by words

---

[1] E.g. between Sept. 1532 and June 1533 the treasurer of Berwick alone received £23,368 (*LP* vi. 664); in 1538, financial assistance to be given to 'certain garrisons' if some plans were followed was put at 20,000 marks (*LP* xiii. II. 1).
[2] In draft (2) above; and there too the name Gibson appears.
[3] Stone, *BIHR* 24 (1951), 2.   [4] Maitland, *English Law and the Renaissance*.
[5] Holdsworth, *Hist. of Eng. Law*, iv. 252 ff., esp. 283–5.
[6] Cf. Plucknett, *TRHS* (1936), 130.

was recognized by the common law in the fifteenth century and only reduced to statute in 1534, not invented then.[1] The supposed nation-wide network of informers is a myth; men who wrote delating offenders were either magistrates whose ordinary duty it was to do so, or – very occasionally – men with a grudge; there is no trace of evidence for a government-organized system.[2] Cromwell's attempts to influence elections to Parliament are not to be properly described as packing, being but mild precursors of the ordinary policy of the next 300 years and certainly not 'dictatorial' except perhaps in the one known case of Canterbury in 1536 – and even there we are not familiar with the circumstances.[3] Whatever the purpose of the lost original draft of the Act of Proclamations may have been, no argument can rest on it *in absentia*; it is certain that the act as it stands only provides machinery for the enforcement of proclamations and it is at least likely that its first form was designed to do the same thing, though probably by less palatable methods.[4] In fact, there is not one piece of genuine evidence to suggest that Cromwell planned a despotism, 'Renaissance' or otherwise; the casual remarks of opponents like Chapuys or the virulence of personal enemies like Cardinal Pole are hardly worth calling evidence. No one can doubt that his government was vigorous, direct and often ruthless, employing the legitimate and constitutional means to hand; but that is a very different thing.

Mr Stone sees the 'key to the whole of this elaborate programme' in the need for financial and military power, to be supplied from the wealth of the Church and its suitable employment. Since there was no such elaborate programme it is the less necessary to look for a key. Nor were such far-reaching ambitions required to make Henry and Crom-

---

[1] I. D. Thornley, 'Treason by Words in the Fifteenth Century,' *EHR* 32 (1917), 556 ff.

[2] The argument (which is not peculiar to Mr Stone) for this network relies on Merriman, esp. i. 116 ff. That book is marked by an unfounded overemphasis on the supposed sinister and terrorizing activities of Cromwell. From it an idea seems to have arisen of Cromwell as a sort of premature Metternich organizing a police state. [See *Policy and Police*, ch. 8.]

[3] Cf. my remarks on the question of Cromwell and elections, above, vol. i, pp. 200 ff.

[4] Cf. Stone, *BIHR* 24 (1951), 2, n. 11. E. R. Adair's discussion of this act (*EHR* 32 (1917), 24 ff.) must stand. Cromwell's letter of 1535 (*LP* viii. 1042; Merriman, i. 409 f.) only proves that the judges held sound views on proclamations; he himself was so far from wishing to replace statute by proclamation that he doubted whether proclamations not grounded upon a specific statute were legal. Marillac (*LP* xiv. I. 1207) shows that, as so often, he had only heard an inaccurate rumour. Much of the 'despotic' flavour given to this period comes from excessive reliance on the hostile and ill-informed reports of ambassadors. The argument cannot be saved by what King James said seventy years after. [Cf. further no. 19 above, and on the fact that Cromwell's letter belongs to 1531, above, vol. i, p. 274, n. 2.]

well look to the Church for the filling of coffers left empty by Wolsey. Mr Stone argues that the employment of clerical wealth for the creation of an army was much mooted; if he were right, one would indeed have to think differently of the draft under discussion. He prints a document which, he says, contains 'the basis of the government's policy' for a decade from 1533 onwards.[1] Perhaps so – but about as many of its suggestions as were adopted were never put through, and there is in it no trace of a plan for an army.[2] Where indeed is the 'considerable other evidence that the need for a standing army was preoccupying the government through those years'?[3] Chapuys said in 1535 that the king had enough money to equip a force of 1,000 men 'as they have sometimes said';[4] does this prove any intention to create a large army, or is it not rather in line with the setting up of the bodyguard of 200 (ultimately 50) gentlemen-pensioners, much discussed before it was established in 1539,[5] an altogether tamer affair? As for the projected garrisons in the north, the document quoted by Mr Stone shows that Cromwell did not plan them so much as express doubts whether they would not lead to more trouble than they would cure,[6] while the plan of 1538 referred to a slight reinforcement for existing garrisons (probably those of Berwick and Carlisle).[7] Mr Stone himself admits that attacks on episcopal wealth did not necessarily come from the government; his example – John Parkyns's scheme – is, within its narrower field, as detailed as the plans for the court of centeners.[8] Not all devices to increase government revenue at the expense of the Church arose in government circles; one of the most extraordinary, advocating the confiscation of all Church property down to parish glebes, was certainly a private extravaganza.[9] Mere elaboration of impracticable ideas does not mark them as coming from the government. Mr Stone does not improve one's trust in his conclusions when – to

---

[1] Stone, *BIHR* 24 (1951), 3, 9 ff. This paper was probably, though not certainly, produced by the government.

[2] The confiscation of episcopal lands and the payment of salaries to bishops did occupy the government's attention; Mr Stone could have found better proof in a document written by Thomas Wriothesley and therefore certainly coming from the government (*LP* vii. 1356).

[3] Stone, *BIHR* 24 (1951), 5. His arguments are taken in turn.

[4] *LP* viii. 121.

[5] *LP* xii. I. 237; xiii. I. 503, 510; II. 1, 111; xiv. I. 29, 719, 745–6.

[6] *LP* xi. 1410: 'If the King will have garrisons planted they should be thought of in time and so ordered as not to offend the people . . . '

[7] *LP* xiii. II. 1. The sum to be allotted was the same as that to be reserved for the upkeep of 200 gentlemen-at-arms.

[8] *LP* xii. I. 261.

[9] BM, Lansd. MS 1, fos. 215–16.

prove that the government contemplated the seizure of Church orna-
ments and chantries – he quotes a list of Cromwell's notes in which
nothing of the sort occurs and a vague view of the government's
possible intentions expressed by the imperial ambassador.[1] There is
practically no sign that Cromwell's government ever seriously intended to proceed further with the confiscation of Church revenues than
the dissolution of the monasteries and Order of St John. What matters
more here, there is no sign at all that a standing army was ever contemplated. In 1539, when the government was faced with the danger
of invasion, it worked hard to bring the militia up to strength, as plentiful muster rolls evidence,[2] but no army of mercenaries was hired or
even considered. What Sir Edward Coke said in the reign of James I
is hardly evidence; he may well have seen some such paper as that
under discussion here and also have thought it a government project.
His summary reads as though something like this document, or perhaps the Lansdowne MS quoted above, had been the basis of it, and
even Coke could err.[3]

The conclusion must therefore be that Mr Stone has failed to prove
any 'despotic' intentions on the part of Cromwell's administration.[4]
We repeat that we cannot here join issue on the larger aspects of his
paper, we cannot enter our plea for a true view of the 1530s; what
matters is that the draft for the court of centeners – which in itself is
about as sure not to have originated with the government as any draft
of this period – cannot be made part of a 'political programme of
Thomas Cromwell' which never existed. It follows that nothing
stands in the way to seeing in this document a private plan, communicated and perhaps thought up by Thomas Gibson.

(8) A draft bill for abolishing some liberties enjoyed by the Church.[5]
On both sides of small sheets, in an individual hand and with no

---

[1] *LP* viii. 475; x. 282. Stone, *BIHR* 24 (1951), 5, n. 5.

[2] *LP* xiv. I. 652.

[3] Mr Stone says (p. 17) that Coke must either have seen such a plan or simply invented
it. Of course he did not invent it; the point is rather whether the plan he saw really
emanated from the government. That he said it did proves nothing at all.

[4] For a warning against Mr Stone's too definite assertions cf. his statement that Chapuys
reported Cromwell to be in favour of slowing down the dissolution, but was opposed
by the king (p. 8). The letter he cites (*LP* x. 601) only shows that Chapuys was relating
the merest rumour (even he said he had only been told); yet this unreliable rumour becomes the basis for a confident assertion on Cromwell's attitude to the dissolution, to
be followed by a quite unsupported and equally confident allegation about his attitude
to bishops.

[5] *LP* xv. 501. *LP* refer to 32 Henry VIII, c. 12 (concerning sanctuaries) but I can see little
connection between the two.

spacings; therefore probably a private draft. As it is endorsed by a Cromwellian clerk with a rather lengthy title ('of grauntes by the noble prynces of this Realme for good intent yoven to spirituall men, nowe abused'), it may again have been sent to Cromwell for consideration. The fact that the bill would have subjected the inhabitants of these liberties to municipal and not to royal jurisdiction supports the view that the draft did not emanate from the government.

(9) A very long draft bill for a poor law.[1] A 'proper' draft, except that it was written on both sides of small sheets; it seems to be in the hand of a government clerk. Its provisions were to come into operation on 1 March 1536–7, so that it may have been planned to take the place of the act of 27 Henry VIII, c. 25 (passed in the spring of 1536). Its vast scope, general scale, and great administrative difficulties – it is a real though short-term poor law code, envisaging a system of public works paid for out of a general graduated income tax and complete with a health service for the labourers – would have caused it to be dropped in favour of a stop-gap measure when the government found itself confronted with the work caused by the dissolution of the monasteries. The draft deserves a detailed study which the present writer hopes to devote to it some time;[2] in the meantime he can only give it as his opinion, for what it is worth, that it represents a plan drawn up not by the government but on its initiative. Possibly several ideas for a poor law were commissioned and collected, and the simplest put through.

That concludes the discussion of parliamentary drafts in the 1530s. Some represent the early stages of enacted legislation, some are government plans which came to nothing, some – and they include the most interesting – are the fruit of private labour, the work of men interested in social, economic and religious reforms who sent their ideas to Cromwell as their best hope, and at times prepared them in the form of parliamentary bills so that the minister might the more readily adopt them. About a few of the documents we cannot be sure. A list of the extant drafts classified accordingly is appended.

APPENDIX

This list does not claim to be beyond cavil, but it is hoped that at least it may be exhaustive. A number of documents described as drafts in the calendar are not

[1] BM, Royal MS 18. C. vi. (not calendared in *LP*).
[2] [See no. 26.]

included because they are in fact not drafts but later copies, or not parliamentary material at all. Two drafts listed in *LP* v. 50 and vii. 1380 (2) cannot now be traced at the Public Record Office and have been omitted. All references but the last in the list are to volumes of the *Letters and Papers*.

Drafts for acts passed, originating with the government.
iv. 6043 (6); v. 52 (1, 2), 721 (1, 4, 8, 9, 11), 1016 (1, 2); vi. 120 (3–8); vii. 57 (2), 62, 1381 (1–5); x. 246 (1, 2, 4–6, 8, 11, 14), 1090; xiv. I. 868 (9, 12); xv. 499 (1–3).

Drafts for acts passed, originating outside the government.
iv. 6043 (7); v. 1016 (3, 4); vii. 1382 (1).

Abortive government drafts.
v. 721 (10, 12); vii. 66 (2), 1611 (1, 2); x. 246 (18); xiv. I. 872, 876; xv. 502 (1); *Add.*, 663, 824, 899, 1453, 1480.

Abortive drafts from outside the government.
vi. 120 (2); vii. 67, 1611 (4); x. 246 (16); xi. 204; xiv. I. 871; xv. 501.

Abortive drafts possibly commissioned by the government but drafted outside it.
xiv. I. 868 (15); BM, Royal MS, 18 C. vi.

A FURTHER NOTE

In a previous discussion of the surviving 'Parliamentary Drafts 1529–40', I stated that the two drafts listed in *Letters and Papers of Henry VIII*, v. 50 and vii. 1380 (2) could not now be traced at the Public Record Office and had therefore been omitted. That statement was made in good faith after several attempts to discover the missing documents. Nevertheless it was mistaken, largely because I had not turned for help to the right quarter. Thanks to the knowledge and kindness of Mr N. Blakiston, the drafts have been found and the 'Key' to *Letters and Papers* has been amended to show their proper place. Since it seems desirable to complete that earlier analysis, a few words on these papers may not come amiss here.

LP vii. 1380 (2)[1] is a straightforward draft for the statute transferring the first fruits and tenths to the Crown.[2] It is a 'proper' draft, in the hand of a government clerk and plentifully corrected by Cromwell, Audley, and very likely another unknown reviser. Thus it falls ob-

[1] PRO, E 175, file 9.   [2] 26 Henry VIII, c. 3.

viously within the category of 'Drafts for acts passed, originating with
the government'. The other draft presents a more difficult problem.[1]
As at present preserved it consists of several separate pieces of writing
assembled to make one document twenty-two pages (i.e. eleven folios)
long; there are many gaps, a few mutilations, and one page is totally
blank. The paper used appears to have been of a size smaller than that
employed in government drafts, though the present state of the document makes it hard to be sure. The writing is tidy but unfamiliar, spaces
between lines being narrow; in a few places, another unfamiliar hand
has added corrections. In appearance it is thus clearly a private draft,
and its contents support this conclusion. It asserts that the people want
an English Bible and that therefore Parliament has set up a body called
'the great standyng counsayll' with powers to search out heresy but
not to prosecute or punish. There follows a general hotch-potch of
matters – the outlines of a general, if highly eccentric, programme of
reform in matters spiritual which it would be pointless to enter into
here. It is so much of an outline that five points are simply listed as due
to be remembered for fuller development. Its tone is orthodox but
suspicious of priests. Beyond question it should be put in the category
of 'Abortive drafts from outside the government'.

Two things about this draft are of special interest in connection with
the general classification attempted. One is that we have here yet another of these large schemes of reform which rely on the establishment
of a new government organ called a 'council'. The same idea dis-
tinguishes the three outstanding non-government drafts of the period,
those proposing a reform of criminal procedure, the setting-up of a
standing army, and an ambitious poor law.[2] The suggestion of a
common origin is strong: may one not see here the work of one group
of reformers, presumably of that group which in the next decade
acquired the name of commonwealth-men? Calling these drafts 'non-
government' does not involve denying their authors' acquaintance
with and access to government circles; indeed, the survival of the
drafts proves the contrary. On the point that the distinction between
genuine government plans and outside plans submitted to the government is a valid and important one, I remain as convinced as ever. The
other point worth noting is that in this present draft the pretence of a
parliamentary statute wears very thin. There is no real preamble, and
the body of the paper is simply an assembly of barely related matters –

---

[1] PRO, SP 6/7, art. 14. [Discussed at length in *Reform and Renewal*, 71–7.]
[2] Drafts 3, 7 and 9.

a rag-bag of mixed ideas linked only by a general concern with ecclesiastical and spiritual matters. This underlines a point I made in my article.[1] A parliamentary statute was the end aimed at, and so the idea was written down to look not unlike a bill in Parliament, though very unlike the shape which such a bill would ultimately have to assume. The suggestion has been made that the casting of an idea in this form is presumptive proof of government origin, and it is therefore significant that a document so very far from being a genuine bill for submission to Parliament yet pretends to the same form.

In view of the fact that I have made reference to both these drafts, as it were *in absentia*, I may conclude this note by saying how far their discovery has affected earlier conjectures. The poor law clauses of *LP* v. 50, bear, indeed, a marked resemblance to some of the provisions of the draft I have discussed at length elsewhere,[2] mentioning as they do public works and the collection of a poor rate. A full comparison, not possible here, would be interesting. It looks as though this rag-bag draft may have been used by the author of the developed poor-law draft; perhaps it was always intended to work up the separate parts of a mixed programme into separate acts, a conjecture supported by headings in *LP* v. 50 which refer to various separate 'articles'. At any rate, while some of the ideas of the full poor law may be traced in this draft, they are here only unintegrated suggestions. As for *LP* vii. 1380 (2), I have said elsewhere that 'one might conceivably discover a good deal' about Cromwell's influence on the statute from corrections on this draft.[3] Certainly he had much to do with the final form of the act, and it is noteworthy that the clause which made possible the appointment of a special treasurer for first fruits and tenths in place of the treasurer of the chamber was a later insertion in the draft. Unfortunately for the perfection of proof, it does however look as though the insertion was made by Audley, a point of spelling ('Succesorz'– Cromwell never, to my knowledge, used the plural ending in z) deciding the issue. That does not mean that Cromwell could not have been responsible for the idea, even if the actual words were written in, in revision, by his close associate, the lord chancellor.

---

[1] Above, p. 63. [2] Below, p. 138, n. 3. [3] *Tudor Revolution*, 191, n. 1.

24

THE EVOLUTION OF A
REFORMATION STATUTE*

The Act in Restraint of Appeals to Rome[1] was the first step taken in Parliament towards the extinction of the papal jurisdiction and power in England. Considerable importance therefore attaches to anything that it might be possible to discover about the origin and development of this measure. Among the state papers at the Public Record Office and the British Museum there survive no fewer than eight drafts and four fragments of drafts of the act, all on paper and most of them bearing corrections which are usually in the hand of Thomas Cromwell. The drafts are listed in *The Letters and Papers of the Reign of Henry VIII*,[2] though one fragment is there wrongly attributed to a different act.[3] In order to make reference easier, we shall assign the letters A to H to the drafts in the order in which they are now bound, and the abbreviations frg. 1 to frg. 4 to the fragments.[4]

The correct sequence of these drafts can be established from the corrections made in them. A reasoned exposition of the whole evidence would fill many pages and is therefore impossible. The alternative is a practically dogmatic statement, but it is hoped that the relations between at least some of the drafts will become clearer in the course of this paper. Normally, corrections made in one draft are found embodied in the text of another. In a few cases, minor discrepancies, such as the retention of an uncorrected version in a copy obviously made from a corrected draft, can only be explained as being due to clerical errors.

---

* [*EHR* 64 (1949), 174–97.] I owe thanks to Professor J. E. Neale and Mr S. T. Bindoff, who read this paper in manuscript, for their most valuable help and criticism.

[1] 24 Henry VIII, c. 12 (*Stat. of the Realm*, iii. 427 ff.).

[2] *LP* vi. 120 (6–9).   [3] *LP* vii. 1611 (2).

[4] A: PRO, SP 2/N, fos. 32–44; B: ibid. fos. 45–54; C: ibid. fos. 55–65; D: ibid. fos. 66–74; E: ibid. fos. 91–102; G: ibid. fos. 103–8; H: BM, Cleo. E. vi, fos. 179–202; frg. 1: PRO, SP 2/N, fos. 109–11; frg. 2: ibid. fos. 112–13: frg. 3: ibid. vol. Q, fo. 137; frg. 4: ibid. vol. N, fos. 75–6. This last fragment has been wrongly attached to D. It is in a different hand from D and does not follow on where any of D's folios end. The second of its two folio sheets has been pieced together from three strips which do not make one composite whole. The first continues fo. 75, but the third is a surviving part of the final clauses of D, and the middle probably does not belong to the act at all. Its wording (which might be from any act) does not recur in the drafts, and it will here be ignored.

It must also be remembered that not every stage of the development through which the wording passed has survived. With these general reservations in mind, we can reduce the drafts to order. E was the earliest draft. It was followed by G, together with frg. 3 which stands at the same stage as G. Next F, a very rough draft, was made, and before it was corrected it was copied fair into C. A few of F's corrections were afterwards transferred to C on which other original corrections were also made. After F had been corrected another copy – H – was made and corrected, and both C and H with their corrections were used in producing the next draft. Of this, two identical copies were made, A and D, of which only D was used in the further development of the bill. A is therefore uncorrected; the corrections in D, except for the last part, are in B, which is thus a fair copy of D corrected. This last part (the new course of appeals to be established by the act) caused some difficulties. One clause survives in two identical drafts (frg. 1 and frg. 2) of which only the latter is corrected: the last part of B is a fair copy of frg. 2 with its corrections, as far as it goes. Frg. 4 also contains a clause of the last part, but not in a form that can be linked to any other draft. All that can be said is that its import places it between D and B. B is the last link in the chain of drafts, but it differs in a number of points from the act as finally passed. Perhaps it will be best if we describe this development in a diagram:

$$E \dashrightarrow \begin{Bmatrix} G+ \\ frg.\ 3 \end{Bmatrix} \rightarrow F \overset{F\ corrected \rightarrow H}{\underset{\longrightarrow C}{\nearrow}} \Bigg\} \rightarrow \begin{Bmatrix} A \\ D \end{Bmatrix} \longrightarrow B \dashrightarrow Act\ as\ passed$$

with frg. 1, frg. 2, and frg. 4 branching below

Because intervening stages were sometimes never written or have been lost we cannot always go straight from the corrections in one draft to the body of the next. A broken line therefore indicates where such a word-for-word demonstration of descent is not possible, but where the sequence is established beyond doubt by a comparison of individual passages and the general tenor.

Were any of these drafts ever before the House of Commons?[1] Except E and F, they are all in the form proper for introduction into Parliament: fairly written on one side of large sheets of paper, with wide spacings between lines for corrections. None of them, however,

---

[1] The original act, extant at the Parliament Office, House of Lords, proves that it was introduced in the Commons. It is marked 'Soit baille aux Seniours' and 'A cest bille les s's sont assentus'.

bear endorsements (such as notes of readings) which would assure us of their origin and fate. The fact that they were all, presumably, among Cromwell's papers is some evidence against their having been parliamentary material.[1] It may further be considered as normal that no drafts before the House, or a committee of the House, could have gone outside for alterations. This would exclude all drafts up to and including H on which the king himself wrote some corrections. It may be objected that parliamentary procedure was still undeveloped in the Reformation Parliament, and that no rules or customs applicable to later times should be taken to apply to the reign of Henry VIII. It is certainly conceivable that Henry and Cromwell might be capable of removing a bill out of Parliament for further revision by king and Council, but there is no evidence of such things. One rather gathers from Henry's general attitude that he would not do anything to hurt Parliament's feelings unnecessarily, and here he had no need to do so. Cromwell sat in the House, and if the government wanted any further changes made he could see to their inclusion in the ordinary way. The existence of two identical fair copies in A and D does suggest that it was intended to introduce the bill at this stage. It seems credible that one copy was intended to go to Parliament, while the other would be retained by Cromwell for his private purposes.[2] However, the further stages in our chain prove plainly that this intention had to be abandoned because the bill was still not considered ready. We have frg. 2, corrected in a hand which had already occurred in F, a draft definitely made before the bill reached Parliament,[3] and we have in

---

[1] The present arrangement of the state papers of Henry VIII at the PRO was made in the nineteenth century when the calendaring of these papers was undertaken. It is thus impossible to be certain of the provenance of our drafts. However, the MSS volumes for 1530–40 are largely composed of Cromwell's papers, and the drafts – so plentifully corrected by Cromwell – were most likely found among them.

[2] This conclusion is supported by the fact that A alone of the drafts (except E) was endorsed with a title. It would be put away among Cromwell's files, and a ready means of identifying it would therefore become necessary. Cromwell's correspondence was always endorsed before being filed.

[3] Its very roughness proves this. The hand which wrote the first part of F, and corrected frg. 2 and parts of F, may well have been that of Richard Riche. There are many striking similarities, yet I cannot feel absolutely sure of the identity. If Riche did write these parts the evidently higher standing of this particular 'clerk' would be explained, but the main argument would remain unaffected. Riche was at the time attorney-general for Wales, i.e. a law officer of the Crown (cf. *DNB*), and might well be used to draft legislation. He was also member of Parliament for Colchester, but if he took part in drafting the act he did so as one of the king's legal counsel and not as a burgess. F was drawn up outside Parliament: it is thus more than probable that the other trace of Riche also originated outside Parliament.

frg. 4 a separate piece of drafting which seems to show some outside influence at work. Perhaps the strongest point of all is the existence of another uncorrected fair draft, B. We suggest that B corresponds to A – that it was a second copy of the bill as it was finally introduced in the Commons. The actual bill which went before the House is lost, and all we have is Cromwell's office copy.

It follows that all the drafts and fragments which survive constitute the genesis of the act in the hands of the government, while the differences between B and the act as passed will tell us what changes were made in Parliament.

We turn to E, a first draft not ready for Parliament and submitted for the consideration of the government. The title endorsed on it ('concernyng the Kinges matter & other that none shall sue appeales hereafter to rome but only within this realme') strongly suggests that the bill was proposing to deal with two things – the king's divorce in particular and all cases in general. That this was not the original intention is proved by a draft which purposed to deal with 'the king's matter' only, a draft in the hand of Thomas Audley, since 16 May 1532 lord keeper of the great seal.[1] It was thus the draft of a government bill which never came to anything.

This abortive predecessor of the Act against Appeals began with a preamble which declared the opinions collected in the king's favour, the injustice of the pope in withholding a decision, and the ability of the clergy of England to resolve the matter. It went on to enact, first, that the decision should be entrusted to the archbishops whose sentence was to be final; secondly, that papal censures were not to be obeyed, so that attempts to deprive the nation of the sacraments and services of religion were not to be successful; thirdly, that persons suing out at Rome an appeal or other process against the archbishops' decision were to come under the penalties of the Statute of Provisors (16 Richard II, c. 5). Pressure was to be put on Queen Catherine: she was to keep her possessions if she accepted whatever judgment was given, failing which she was to lose all she had. There are here quite a few points familiar to anyone who has studied the drafts of the Act against Appeals. The remarks on the pope's insolence find an echo in E; the statute of 16 Richard II is mentioned, as it is in nearly all the drafts; the phrases concerning the continued practice of religion are

---

[1] The draft is in PRO, SP 2/N, fos. 155–62 (*LP* vi. 311 [4]). The editors claimed that both the drafts listed under *LP* vi. 311 (4 and 5) were in Cromwell's hand; they were, however, certainly written by Audley whose writing is somewhat similar.

similar to the corresponding clause in the earlier drafts of our act. The enacting clause employs the disguise of a parliamentary petition, a device also found in E but in none of the later drafts. Everything points to this abortive bill having been drawn up before the first draft of the Act against Appeals. It would therefore seem that it was originally planned to introduce a bill simply to enable the king's divorce to be settled in England and to prevent papal intervention in this one matter, an intention also suspected by Catherine's partisans.[1]

However, here was an opportunity for something better. A fatal blow could be struck at papal authority in England, and the theory of sovereignty for which both Henry and Cromwell stood could be placed on the statute book. Parliamentary authority was not really needed for submitting the divorce to the judgment of the English Church, represented by its metropolitans. The important point was to prevent an appeal to outside authority. A powerful and striking preamble was required,[2] to be followed by a careful stopping of all loopholes. The result of this was E.

The preamble opened with a roll of drums, with a phrase which it was to retain through all the changes made: 'Where by dyuers sundry old autentike stores and cronicles it is manifestlie declared and expressed that this realme of England is an Impier and so hath byn accepted in the world gouerned by one supreme hedde having the dignitie and roiall estate of the Imperiall crowne of the same vnder whom a body politik compact of all sortes and degrees of people deuided in termes of spiritualtie and Temporaltie bere and owen to bere next to god a naturall and humble obediens . . .'[3] These words at once provide the dominant note of the whole statute. More than two years before the Act of Supremacy and the extension of the royal title, Henry was declared to be the 'supreme head' of England by virtue of his 'imperial' power, the word 'empire' being defined by the description of England as a body politic composed of laity and Church over both of which the king's rule was qualified only by their obedience to God. Medieval Europe knew only one possible rival to the pope – the emperor, and no mere king could have claimed equality with either. But if England was an empire, Henry could establish his supremacy in state and Church with some show of principle.

---

[1] *LP* vi. 89, 142.

[2] Preambles were probably a pet subject of Cromwell's. It is very noticeable, as one goes through the *Statutes of the Realm*, that preambles seem suddenly to become *de rigueur* in 1529, and that they achieve their full form of expounding policy only when we know that Cromwell was in charge of affairs, i.e. about 1532.   [3] E, fo. 78.

The preamble continued as it still stood in the act as passed, with an exposition of the king's power over all legislation and jurisdiction in England and a reference to the old statutes of provisors; then, however, it branched out into a whole-hearted attack on the papacy which included the point under consideration – papal jurisdiction by means of appeals and citations to Rome – as well as a number of standing grievances: provision to bishoprics and exaction of first-fruits from them, the bishops' oath to the pope, visitations of regular and secular clergy for the benefit of the papal coffers, pluralism for a similar purpose, and usurped jurisdiction over the legality of marriages which it was alleged gave the pope great powers in settling the succession to the royal crowns of Europe.[1] The enacting clause, pretending a petition from Parliament,[2] pressed home this last point by suggesting that the nobles and commons besought the king because of their anxiety that a disputed succession might lead to renewed dynastic troubles.[3] Of the things objected against the pope this was most likely to find strong support in the Commons. The preamble was also careful to remind the Commons of the drain of money to Rome and of the insult offered to the king by the pope's claim to sovereignty, two points which had always roused national feeling since the fourteenth century. Another significant point was the complaint that the pope had habitually taken from the bishops on their institution 'a corporall othe of obedience and subieccion to the see Appostolik contrary to their naturall dutie of obedience and alegiaunce that they shold and own to the Kinges of this realme'. At the end of the previous session, on 11 May 1532, Henry had summoned the Speaker and twelve members of the House of Commons in order to show them this very oath, claiming that it proved the bishops to be 'but half our subiectes, yea, and scarce our subiectes', and had asked them 'to inuent some ordre' to deal with this state of affairs.[4] We may suspect Henry's sudden realization of the bishops' duplicity; it is certain, at any rate, that contemporary opinion ascribed the discovery to Cromwell and thought that he had gained the king's

---

[1] E. fos. 81–5.

[2] 'The nobles and commens of this realme assembled in this present parliament . . . do therefore most humbly beseche the Kinges highnes that it myght pleas his grace to ordeyn and enact by the assent of the lordes spirituall & temporall & the commens in this present parliament assembled and by auctorite of the same . . .' (E, fo. 86).

[3] 'Calling to their remembraunce the great diuision which hath byn hertofore in this realme for dyuersity of titles to the crowne of this realme' (E, fo. 86).

[4] Hall, *Chronicle* (ed. 1809), p. 788.

favour by pointing it out.[1] Thus, by May 1532, Henry and Cromwell were planning to use the bishops' oath for the purpose of breaking the papal power in England. Hall goes so far as to say that 'the openyng of these othes, was one of the occasions, why the Pope within two yere folowyng, lost all his iurisdiccion in Englande',[2] a view which, coming from a member of Parliament, shows what effect the disclosure had on opinion in the Commons. The oath was not mentioned in any statute, and the only mention it gets in the measures abolishing papal jurisdiction is in the first draft of the Act against Appeals. The presumption is that it was included there because the government knew well how strongly members had been affected by Henry's dramatic announcement. The first draft of the preamble was designed to plead and persuade.

The main body of the bill proposed to enact a prohibition on all 'sumons citacions inhibicions suspencions excomunicacions' and other processes touching any acts done in the king's dominions, all such acts to be finally determined within the dominion of the Crown 'in such courtes spirituall or temporall as the causes shall requier' without any interference from 'the see apostolik or any other foreyn princes or potentates of the world'.[3] This was the core of the act, and in its essentials it remained unchanged to the end. The draft appointed the penalties for transgressors to be those of high treason, covering both the offender's life and his property, and there was to be a final clause concerning the possessions of such a traitor to save the rights of the lords of any fees he might have.[4]

So much for E. It differs considerably from the shape the act was to assume. Its preamble was well over half its entire length and contained all sorts of complaints against the pope which had little to do with the matter in hand. The penalty it established was as for high treason and not as for *praemunire*, the chief difference being that the former involved loss of life as well as property.[5] It did not provide for a course of appeals

---

[1] Thus Pole (*Apologia*, 121) and Foxe (*Acts and Monuments*, v. 367). Their stories are quite unreliable as evidence for the manner of Cromwell's rise to power, but they show what ideas he was generally believed to have put into Henry's head.

[2] Hall, *Chronicle*, 789. [3] E, fos. 87–8.

[4] E, fo. 90. He was to forfeit entailed property for life only, but if he held in fee simple the forfeiture was to be complete, 'Saving alwayes to the lordes of the fees thereof their rentes & seruices due and accustumed'.

[5] As we shall see, the penalties finally enacted were those of the statute of 16 Richard II, c. 5, usually called 'the *praemunire*'. These were: forfeiture of all possessions and imprisonment for the purpose of examination by king and Council (*Stat. of the Realm*, ii. 85–6). They did not include the death penalty. When the act was passed, Chapuys

to take the place of appeals to Rome. The bill was now submitted to Cromwell for consideration, for the next draft, G, was written by a government clerk and corrected by Cromwell.

This draft is without a preamble, starting with the words 'Do therfore by thassent of the Kynges Royall Maiestie and of the lordes spirituall and temporall and the co[mmons in] this presente parliamente assembled and by Auctorite of the same Inacte'.[1] This enacting clause now assumed the form usual in all the Reformation statutes: the pretence of a petition was dropped, and no room was left for doubt that the initiative lay with the king. Traces of a preamble surviving in frg. 3 also show new features. This preserves part of the passage, found in later drafts, in which the act asserted the true Catholic faith of its promoters. The prohibition of appeals to Rome assumed the form in which it continued, with minor adjustments, till the end of the whole process. The draft enacted the penalties of *praemunire* against all transgressors, 'their ffautours eydours Counfortours Abbettours procurers executors and Counsaillours', and added a new clause establishing a course of appeals in England. As this part of the act caused the greatest difficulty we reserve it for comprehensive discussion in all its stages later. At the end of G, Cromwell wrote 'And it ys fferther Inactyd': F shows that the additional clause was to declare that all Statutes of Provisors and *Praemunire*, and all acts concerning the maintenance of papal jurisdiction in England were to stand in full strength and to be obeyed and executed 'as though they were rehersed in this present acte particularly worde for worde'.[2] The clause was dropped again during the revisions of F, probably being absent already from H (the end of which is missing), and certainly from A and D. It would have added nothing of importance as the new statute went so much further than any of the old. The rest of Cromwell's corrections were concerned with giving precision to the act. One change, however, deserves notice. The draftsman had still referred to Rome as 'the See Apostolic', but Cromwell now changed this to 'the See of Rome'.[3] The change indicated the hardening temper of the government. To Cromwell,

---

reported that offenders were to be considered as traitors 'and without any further process be sent to an ignominious death' (*LP* vi. 324). He was undoubtedly mistaken; high treason was mentioned in E and never again. But the difference between treason and *praemunire* was not always clear even to contemporary Englishmen.

[1] G, fo. 103. This passage was cancelled by Cromwell who substituted for it 'and ffurther do Inacte by the Auctoryte aforsayd'; as, however, the enactment which followed was in fact the first, the original reading was restored in the later drafts.

[2] F, fo. 102.

[3] He overlooked the phrase once or twice in the *draft* (e.g. G, fo. 105).

the act was from the first the gage of battle thrown down to the pope who would from now on be but bishop of Rome and without authority in England.

However, G was discarded, and there followed a most complicated process of drafting and re-drafting, embodied in F, C, and H, the details of which would only be tedious. Suffice it to say that F was very rough, in three different hands and consisting of different parts which did not always fill whole pages but made one composite whole. Naturally enough it was copied fair before correction (C), and as a consequence some of the corrections later made in F were transferred as corrections into C. H was a fair copy of F corrected, prepared specially for the eye of the king. It is the only draft which has corrections in his hand. At this stage, corrections were freely transferred from one draft into another, and a general confusion ensued which made a new fair copy necessary after the drafts had gone through the hands of Cromwell and Henry. It will be best to follow their minds by taking the parts of the act separately.

The preamble as given in C retained the invocation of history with which E had started, but it now confined itself to asserting the imperial right of the English Crown to govern fully both its lay and clerical subjects. Attention was concentrated on the jurisdictional aspect of the act, and the grievances against the papacy disappeared. The preamble is now an unequivocal statement of undoubted rights, with no apologies or explanations for the action proposed. This action, it claims, rests on the statutes of the fourteenth century, now rendered insufficient by recent encroachments on the rights of the Crown and the jurisdictions, spiritual and temporal, of England, which those statutes had tried to preserve 'frome the Annoyance aswell of the see of Rome as frome the vsurped auctoritie of other foreyne Potentates attempting the dymynysion or violacion thereof'.[1] What is new is a long clause, of which we saw a trace in frg. 3, anticipating that 'evyll Interpretours . . . of the laws insuyng' would accuse their makers of heresy. King and nation therefore asserted their true catholic faith and explained that they had to pass these laws because their duty to their native country compelled them to withstand 'the Ambition and vsurpacion of all foreign powers'.[2] The passage was crossed out in correcting F, but was not cancelled in C and reappeared in A and D. It seems, then, that either Henry or Cromwell wished it to stand. Of the two, Henry was certainly more likely to be concerned about an asser-

[1] C, fo. 57. [2] C, fos. 57–8.

tion of his true catholic faith, and it is probable that he insisted on the passage being restored after reading H which was without it. Cromwell, who was presumably behind its deletion from F, wished to remove the one passage from the preamble which still retained an element of apology, but was for the time being defeated by the king's desire to appear a true son of the Church. He did, however, insert a more detailed statement of reasons why it was thought necessary to prevent appeals to Rome.[1] 'Dyuers and sondry inconuynences and dangiers . . . hathe risen and sprongen by reason of appeales to the see of Rome,' which had led to great trouble and costs to the whole realm, and to much delay in the administration of justice because Rome was far and the papal courts could not therefore properly examine witnesses and evidence which were left behind in England. Cromwell thought it wiser not only to introduce some concrete points into the preamble, but also to bring home to the Commons how they suffered materially from the appeals to Rome. Perhaps the abstract assertion of the king's imperial power seemed to him insufficient ground on which to meet parliamentary opposition.

Henry's influence on the act as shown by his corrections was small, but in two points he showed how strongly he felt on the question of the royal prerogative. F said that both the temporal and spiritual jurisdictions in England proceeded 'of & from the seid imperiall Crowne and none other wyse' (fo. 92), but the words were cancelled in correction. Henry, however, working perhaps with F at his elbow as he read the roll prepared for his study, reinserted them in H (fo. 185), and they reappear in A (fo. 34). On the other hand, Cromwell had added to the phrase defining the basis of ecclesiastical jurisdiction in certain matters (given originally as 'the goodenes and long sofferance of princes of this realme and by the lawez and customes of the Same') the words 'the grauntes of the Kynges most noble progenytors' (F, fo. 94). This phrase, which would have convicted the royal prerogative of enhancing the power of the Church, Henry crossed out in H (fos. 189–90).

In the main body of the act, the changes made at this stage were of no great importance. Lengthy passages were crossed out, largely for the sake of greater brevity. There was a new clause, enacting ('to thintente that all the suiectes of this realme may haue the more tender Respecte to the preseruacion of the liberties and prerogatyves of the

---

[1] This was embodied, badly drafted, in H (fos. 186–8), but the fuller and better version which went into the next draft was interlineated in C (fo. 58) by Cromwell himself.

Crowne of this realme') that persons suing, under the act of 16 Richard II, against transgressors under the present act should recover treble damages in addition to costs from the defendant's lands, goods, and chattels, 'the forfaiture thereof to the Kynges Highnes notwithstonding'.[1] But this passage was no sooner put in than it was crossed out again, perhaps because it deprived the Crown of some of the forfeited property. The last part of the act, the new course of appeals which underwent considerable alterations and was largely responsible for the multiplication of drafts, we again leave for later discussion.

As we have seen, it was now apparently thought that a bill could be produced for submission to Parliament. The act now had a preamble which asserted the fundamental idea behind this aspect of Reformation legislation, that is to say, the absolute sovereignty of the Crown over all its subjects, and which claimed that the proposed law was merely an enlargement of existing legislation. In the body of the bill, the essential points – prohibition of appeals, prevention of the consequences of papal counteraction, penalties for offenders – had been fully set down. Finally, a new course of appeals was to make sure that justice should continue to be served.

With this bill the government intended to go to Parliament, but it proved to be not final yet. Essential changes had once more to be made, and as most of these occur in the last part, it is there that the reason for the renewed delay will be found. But the other parts, too, were altered. In the preamble a passage was cut which had been there since the first draft. It asserted that the kings of England, having been named vicars of God in papal epistles, used to make laws for spiritual matters as well as for temporal, 'so that no wordelie [sic] Lawes ordenaunces iurisdiccions, or auctoritie of any persone . . . was practised experimented or put in execucion within this realme but only suche as was ordeyned made, dyryued and depended of thimperiall crowne of the same'.[2] This was certainly a rash claim, for the spiritual courts had for a long time been in the habit of administering the canon law derived from Rome.[3] Another phrase cancelled was one which Henry had reinserted in H, and this time the whole passage disappeared. It had stated that both the temporal and spiritual authority and jurisdiction 'ar deryved and dependeth frome and of the same Imperiall crowne of this

---

[1] C, fos. 62–3.   [2] D, fos. 66–7.

[3] F. W. Maitland, *Roman Canon Law in the Church of England* (1898), esp. 17–18, 78–81. Cf. also his *Coll. Papers*, iii. 137–56. The history of the Act against Appeals indicates that Cromwell and his legal advisers agreed with Maitland's views.

Realme . . . and in this manner of wise procedeth the Iurisdiccion spirituall and temporall of this realme of and from the said Imperiall Crowne and none otherwise'.[1] Apparently someone disapproved of these assertions of the Crown as the fountain-head of the law administered by the Church in England – assertions which it would have been impossible to substantiate.

A victory for Cromwell was the final deletion of the long defence against a possible accusation of heresy which had been crossed out once before (in F), and had been brought back, as we have seen probably at the king's command. With it went the last trace of uncertainty in the government's attitude to its own policy: Henry and his advisers were to declare their intention of breaking the pope's authority in England without hesitation, taking their stand on the existing laws and the somewhat mystical sovereignty of the Crown supposedly proved by 'dyuers sundrie olde autentike histories and Cronicles'. As the various corrections show, it was Cromwell who had deleted all passages detracting from this unequivocal assertion, and who had even overcome Henry's reluctance to incur the charge of heresy which, of all accusations, he liked least.

Certain changes were made in the list of causes dealt with by ecclesiastical courts which were to come under the terms of the act. The list read in A and D: 'causes testamentarie causes of matrymonie rightes of tithes oblacions obuencions and coreccions of synnes'.[2] Of these, the last was now cancelled,[3] and Cromwell inserted 'deuorse' after 'matrymonie'. This insertion was not embodied in the next draft, B, but does appear in the act as passed; its omission from B was perhaps due only to a scribe's mistake, and in any case, Cromwell had his way in the end. The word added merely precision to the enumeration, for divorce would naturally be included among matrimonial causes, but it added precision in the interests of that case which had started the whole ball rolling, and anything that might smooth Henry's way in his 'great matter' was well worth putting beyond doubt.[4] The exclusion of corrections of sin from the terms of the act meant that purely

---

[1] D, fo. 67.

[2] D, fo. 70.

[3] There had been an attempt to delete it in F, but no attention was apparently paid to the cancellation there.

[4] It is commonly asserted nowadays that Henry's separation from Catherine was not a divorce but a declaration of nullity. That is true enough by the standards of modern usage, but in the sixteenth century nullity was called divorce. Thus Stokesley, bishop of London, describing events in Convocation in 1533, spoke of Cranmer pronouncing sentence of divorce (*LP* vii. 15).

spiritual jurisdiction, in particular jurisdiction over heresy, was not to be touched. The act was to confine itself to matters affecting the king's subjects in their temporal affairs. Here again we have an abatement of over-large claims. The other material corrections occur in the last part of the act, and to that we must now turn. Except for this, D with its corrections was copied into B, which means that we have now reached, for both preamble and main enactment, the form that was put before the Commons.[1]

The first attempt at establishing an order of appeals to replace those to Rome was made in G. A subsidiary preamble stated the need for some provision to ensure the execution of God's law and to prevent 'the greate lycens to lyve [in] libydine and Syn whiche at this houre & tyme is vncorrected within this Realme by reason of Appeles dayly Sued to the sayd See of Rome',[2] and the following course of appeals was then briefly appointed: from the archdeacon where the cause is begun to the bishop of the see, from the bishop to the archbishop ('of Caunterbury'), and from him to the king who was to appoint a commission of 'Indifferente Iudges for the clere and fynall Determynacion of any suche causes of Appeale'. However, this version was patently unsatisfactory, and F, even in its original form, extended the clause to include every archbishop as the proper judge of appeal within his own province. It was, however, when Cromwell set to work on this part of the act that real changes were made.[3] The moral platitudes of the preamble disappeared, and in their place Cromwell wrote at the bottom of the page: 'and in escuyng of the sayd gret inormytees Inquyetacyons delayes charges and expenses daylye Sustaynyd in pursuyng of such appellys and fforeyn proces ffor and Consernyng the Causes afforsayd'.[4] Again he gave definite and material reasons for his legislation. The course of appeals still ran from archdeacon to bishop and from bishop to metropolitan, but the whole passage concerning

---

[1] With one exception. In B, there appeared a clause enacting one year's imprisonment and fine at the king's pleasure for any 'spirituell personn' obeying the 'fulmynacions' of Rome and refusing to administer the services of religion. This closed a loophole in the act, for up to that stage it had apparently been thought that all priests would cheerfully administer the sacraments despite a papal interdict, feeling reassured by the authority of Parliament. The penalty now enacted was more realistic and strongly suggests Cromwell's hand; but as the clause first appeared in a fair copy we cannot name its author, and, as we shall see, not all corrections after D were made on Cromwell's initiative. [2] F, fo. 107.

[3] All the corrections in this part of F are in Cromwell's hand, and so are the corrections in the corresponding part of H. In C, the whole last part was struck through by him, and the form embodied in A was taken from H. [4] F, fo. 99.

appeals from the archbishops was cancelled. On a separate sheet,[1] Cromwell wrote out a clause which introduced a new principle: causes affecting the king or his realm were to go from the archbishops to Convocation of the province concerned. In this form, H was drawn up, but here Cromwell made further changes.[2] In particular, he remedied an omission caused by the crossings-out in F, by interlineating a provision that causes concerning only subjects were to go from the archbishop to 'the Kynges highnes . . . and suche spyrytuall lernyd persons[3] beyng Indeferent as his highnes . . . shall name and appoynt by his Commyscyon from tyme to tyme', and he substituted 'the Spyrytuall prelates and other discret Abbottes & pryours of the vpper howse of the conuocacion' for the whole of Convocation as the court of last instance in the king's causes.[4] In F, too, he altered the penalties for transgressing this part of the act (again those of *praemunire*) by removing the provision for treble damages mentioned in G.[5] One other change was made in A and D of which there is no previous sign in the drafts: the appeal to Convocation was to be made within fifteen days after the archbishop's court had given its decision.

When, therefore, Cromwell thought that he had prepared the act for submission to Parliament, he had worked out the new course of appeals as follows: a short preamble gave practical reasons for it, and it was to run, for all cases, from archdeacon to bishop and from bishop to metropolitan. Here, however, it was to divide, ordinary cases being heard by a commission of ecclesiastical lawyers appointed under the great seal, and the king's causes going to the upper house of Convocation. The division was essential, for matters of state could hardly be treated on the same footing as ordinary cases. Whereas the latter could be fairly and expeditiously dealt with by *ad hoc* commissions, it was obviously impossible to claim justice for a procedure which would have allowed the king to appoint judges in his own causes. These were, therefore, passed to the highest and most authoritative assembly in spiritual affairs. The changes so far made did thus serve the

---

[1] F, fo. 100A.

[2] Opposite the beginning of this part of the act he wrote a marginal note: 'this must com in the latter ende', presumably intending to put the whole clause after the passage about the validity of existing laws. But as this passage disappeared from A and D, the marginal note lost its point.

[3] I.e. ecclesiastical lawyers – canon and later civil lawyers.   [4] H, fos. 201–2.

[5] G, fo. 107: 'euery person and persones greved contrarie to this Acte shall have their Accion and sutes vpon this estatute in any the Kinges Courtes . . . and shall Recouer treble Damages'. Deleted in F (fo. 102) as had been the provision of similar damages for transgressing the whole act on fo. 99 (above, p. 89).

interests of justice. But Cromwell can hardly have forgotten that the lower house of Convocation was notoriously more likely to oppose the king,[1] and that the appointment of bishops and abbots could be controlled so effectively that it was quite safe to entrust them with deciding the king's causes.

However, A and D were not to go to Parliament yet. Cromwell made some changes in those parts of D itself which survive. He tried to limit the number of appeals from the archbishop's court by reserving to the king the right to decide whether an appeal was justified,[2] and to circumscribe the king's freedom of action by stipulating for a commission of five[3] spiritually learned men 'wherof on at the lest to be a bushop'. But this was not enough, and a number of further drafts were made. One (frg. 4) attempted to re-draft the passage concerning the king's cases by appointing for them a full course of appeals from archdeacon through bishop and archbishop to the upper house of Convocation. It did not, therefore, make any changes in the proposed law, and it had no influence on further developments. More important is frg. 2 which admitted that cases might be started elsewhere than in the archdeacon's court. The fragment begins in a manner which makes it clear that another provision was meant to go before;[4] this was undoubtedly the point about cases started in the archdeacon's court already included in the full draft, for what we have in frg. 2 are cases commenced before the bishop or his commissary, or before the archbishop's archdeacon or his commissary (with appeal, in both cases, to the archbishop and no further), or before the archbishop (with appeal to 'the hole house of conuocacion'). In the subsequent correction the Court of the Arches was interpolated between the archbishop's archdeacon and the archbishop, and the appeal to Convocation was dropped. As a consequence of these alterations, which were embodied in B, the archbishop's court became the final court of appeal in all cases which did not touch the king.

When the bill was submitted to Parliament the last part stood as follows. Cases begun in a bishop's diocese were to go from the arch-

---

[1] Cf. J. A. Froude, *History of England*, i. 439.

[2] 'And in case the Archbusshop will not doo Iustyce yf the partye grevyd do Complayn to the Kyng So that it may appere to the Kynges Highnes that the partyre grevyd hathe cause to complayn of Iniurye don to hym by thesayd archebusshop.' Passage interlined by Cromwell on fo. 74.

[3] Ibid. This word has been inserted, corrected, and crossed out again, and the reading is somewhat doubtful. But between one word reading something like 'ffyndee' and another like 'ffyne' corrected to 'ffyve', I suggest that 'five' was meant. That would also make sense of the passage.   [4] 'Likewise yf it be commenced . . .'

deacon or his official to the diocesan bishop and from him to the archbishop, as were also cases begun before the bishop or his commissary.
Cases begun in the diocese of Canterbury or York, before the archdeacon of an archbishop, were to go to the Court of the Arches and
from there to the archbishop. In all these cases the archbishop was to
have the last word. If a case commenced before the archbishops it
was there to be decided without appeal.[1] All appeals from a lower to a
higher court were to be made within fifteen days after the judgment
in the lower court. A saving clause reserved to the archbishop and
church of Canterbury their prerogative right of appeals 'likewise as
they haue been accustumed and vsed to haue heretofore'.[2] If a matter
touching the king was brought into any of the courts mentioned,
'the partie greved . . . may appeale from any of the said Courtes

[1] This whole course of appeals raises a difficult question: what did the act mean by cases
going to the archbishop? What court was it thinking of? In pre-Reformation times, the
normal court of appeal for a province was the 'court of Canterbury' (or York) which
was early confused with the court of the archbishop's peculiars in London, and acquired
its name of Court of the Arches (I. J. Churchill, *Canterbury Administration* (1933),
424 ff.). Here the dean of the Arches (or rather the archbishop's official, by this time usually
the same person) presided by virtue of the archbishop's commission. Did the act mean
that cases from diocesan courts were to go to this court? At all events, that is what
happened and the Court of the Arches continued to exercise the archbishop's appellate
jurisdiction for his province. But what, in that case, was the point of the course of appeals
as established for the diocese of Canterbury or York? Here the normal diocesan court,
the court of the archbishop's commissary general, does not appear to be mentioned
at all. On the other hand, we find that the court which exercises final appellate jurisdiction in the province occupies a secondary position in the diocese; unless, indeed, we
should wish to argue that the Court of Arches mentioned in the act was the original
court of the London peculiars. This, however, is impossible, as that court never exercised any jurisdiction outside the thirteen peculiar churches. No, the act directed appeals
within the archbishop's diocese from the archdeacon to the provincial court of appeal,
with a final appeal to the archbishop himself. Our questions cannot really be answered
until detailed investigation has revealed the way in which the system worked in the sixteenth century and after. The solution will perhaps be found along the line suggested
by Stubbs (*Report of the Eccl. Comm. 1883*, Hist. App. i. 39) who thought that the
mention of clerical dignitaries rather than courts was possibly intended to secure the
personal hearing of appeals by the appellate judge. In that case, what happened was
that the archbishop continued to delegate his appellate jurisdiction in the province
to the Court of Arches, possibly contrary to the (ill-expressed) intention of the statute,
while in his diocese appeals would go to the Arches anyway. In neither case would his
competence himself to hear appeals be exhausted by the delegation. In pre-Reformation
times the archbishop would hear appeals from the provincial court of appeals (Churchill,
497), and he seems to have preserved at least a theoretical right to do so after the Reformation. The wording of the Act against Appeals suggests that it tried to turn this right
into a practice.
[2] The reference is to the claim of the metropolitan court known as the Prerogative Court
of Canterbury to hear all cases of probate affecting property in more than one diocese
(Churchill, *Canterbury Administration*, 380).

gradatim to the spirituell prelates and other abbotes and pryours of the vpper house . . . in the convocacion', their decision to be final. Here, too, the fifteen days' clause applied. Finally, the penalties of 16 Richard II, c. 5 were appointed for anyone offending against this part of the act. The main change from A, apart from a more detailed exposition of the scheme, was therefore that in cases touching not the king but his subjects the archbishop, and not a royal commission, took the place of Rome as the final court of appeal. It would almost seem that Cromwell met clerical opposition which he first tried to appease by narrowing the commission to five men of whom one at least was to have been a bishop, but that this was not enough and he had to give way completely on this point.

Thus the changes made in D, the changes which caused the introduction of the bill to be delayed, were mainly of two kinds. A number of excessive claims for the royal origin of the law administered in the spiritual courts were deleted, and the king lost the last word in the course of appeals. Both these alterations went against the high pretensions of the 'imperial crown', and therefore neither would have been made by Cromwell without influence and pressure from outside. The people most likely to have known how false were statements about the king as the fountain head of the law of the Church were the canon and civil lawyers, and the people interested in retaining the final decision in all cases before the courts Christian and in saving the prerogative of Canterbury were the leaders of the Church. It is therefore of great interest to find that in the period during which the Act against Appeals was under consideration, there was also drawn up a list of names containing representatives of these two classes.

This list was written by one of Cromwell's clerks on part of a sheet already used by Cromwell himself for some of his 'remembrances'.[1] Both list and memoranda were drawn up at about the same time, for the clerk who wrote the list endorsed the paper 'Rememb' and the names of certen byshopes and abbottes'. The date of the paper can be established with some accuracy, for action is known to have been taken on some of the notes. The earliest result was a warrant dated 6 February 1533 by which Cromwell was to receive £2,000 from Thomas Alvarde and to pay half to Cranmer and half into the king's privy coffers.[2] The list was therefore drawn up not later than 5–6

[1] PRO, SP 1/74, fo. 170 (*LP* vi. 150).
[2] *LP* vi. 131. The relevant 'remembrance' reads: 'my warraunt for Thomas alverd for the last ij° thowsand powndes the on payd to my lord of Canterburye & the other to the kinges Cofers'. *LP* vi. 150 misreads 'to the king's uses'.

February 1533. Its earliest date is supplied by the mention of 'My lorde of Cantorburye' in it; Warham died on 22 August 1532, and the first mention of Cranmer as archbishop-elect[1] is on the occasion of Audley's promotion to the chancellorship on 26 January 1533.[2] It is not likely that he was elected much before that date. He returned to England in January and was appointed within about a week, in readiness, Chapuys asserts, for the meeting of Parliament where he was to authorize the king's second marriage.[3] Parliament was to meet on 4 February, and as late as 31 January Bonner wrote to Benet at Rome to tell him that Cranmer was sending his bulls:[4] as Henry was certainly in a hurry with his appointment, Cranmer cannot have been elected much before the end of January. The list was therefore drawn up some time between 25 January and 5 February. On 9 February, Chapuys reported that Queen Catherine had heard that four days earlier one of the king's chief councillors 'had assembled several doctors, both clerical and lay', in order to discuss with them the possibility of the king's marriage being dissolved.[5] There was, then, a meeting concerning 'the king's matter' on 5 February, and we suggest that our list was drawn up for that purpose.

Who was present? Let us copy the list.[6]

★ My lorde of Cantorburye	★ Doctor Lee
My lorde of Yorke	★ Doctor Gwent
My lorde of London	Doctor Alryge
★ My lorde of Wynchester	Doctor Goodrige
★ My lorde of Lyncolne	Doctor Trylbe
★ My lorde of Saynt Asse	Doctor Curwyn
★ Thabbat of Hyde	★ The fryer Carmelytane
★ Thabbat of Burtton	ffryer Nicolas
The Deane of the chappell	Doctor Tresham
★ The Almosnyer	Maister Bedyll
★ Doctor Olyuer	Maister Leighton
★ Doctor Tregonwell	

Taking only those pricked, that is, those actually called:[7] the arch-bishop-elect, Gardiner of Winchester, and Longland of Lincoln were

---

[1] He was not consecrated until 30 March, but that would not prevent Cromwell from calling him by his new title once the election formalities were over.
[2] *LP* vi. 73.   [3] Ibid. 89, Chapuys to Charles V on 27 Jan. 1533.
[4] Ibid. 101.   [5] Ibid. 142.
[6] The names marked with an ★ are pricked in the original. Presumably the full list was drawn up for Cromwell to choose his conference from, which he did by pricking the names.
[7] Authority for most of the points mentioned here can be found in *DNB*, and they could be further amply illustrated from *LP*.

probably the leading churchmen in politics. Standish of St Asaph was the senior bishop and had presided in the Convocation of the southern province after Warham's death. Of the two abbots, Salcot of Hyde was to be bishop of Bangor within a few months of the meeting; he was reputed a 'great clerk', and was one of the three men to whom, two years earlier, Henry had asked the pope to commit the decision of his case.[1] Boston of Burton resigned in April 1533,[2] and nothing further can be discovered about him. Edward Foxe, the king's almoner, D.D. and provost of King's College, Cambridge, was a brilliant scholar, diplomatist and reformer, and later to be a bishop. He presided in Convocation in April 1533 when the legality of the king's marriage was discussed. Oliver and Tregonwell were probably the leading civilians of the day; both were also doctors of canon law, officers of the chancery, agents of Cromwell's, and active about the divorce.[3] Rowland Lee, the future bishop of Coventry and Lichfield and president of the Council in the Marches of Wales, was not only one of Cromwell's most trusted agents, but also probably the man who, as king's chaplain, married Henry to Anne on 25 January 1533.[4] Gwent was dean of the Arches, that is to say, vitally concerned in matters affecting church courts. The 'fryer Carmelytane' was probably the provincial of the White Friars. Thus Cromwell assembled some of the leading divines and doctors *utriusque iuris*.[5]

Chapuys says that the conference considered the problem of the king's divorce, and that the assembled doctors were induced to pronounce Cranmer capable of settling it.[6] That may be so, but we have reason to think his information either misleading or incomplete. Henry and Cromwell were preparing to submit the question to the archbishop of Canterbury; Cranmer's hurried appointment proves that, and so does (what concerns us more) the projected legislation

---

[1] *LP* v. 327. [2] *LP* vi. 417 (20).

[3] Tregonwell was principal judge of the Admiralty court (the acme of a civilian's career) by 1535. He was later active about the dissolution of the monasteries in the taking of surrenders. Oliver, 'an active official of the new way of thinking' (*DNB*), had been consulted by Henry about the consecration of Cranmer and was later one of the court which pronounced Catherine contumacious.

[4] Cf. *DNB* (under Rowland Lee) for the likelihood of the story.

[5] Of those not called, Lee of York was always busy in the north and therefore not in London; Stokesley of London presided in Convocation on 5 February (*Eccl. Comm. 1883*, Hist. App. I. 94), so that his being unmarked in the list strengthens our collation of it with the meeting reported for that day; and a number of leading clerics, future bishops (Thirlby was to occupy three sees), and government propagandists like Curwen and Nicholas del Burgo, were considered but apparently thought superfluous. [6] *LP* vi. 142.

against appeals to Rome. It was rather late in the day, after the secret second marriage, to be seeking the approbation of these churchmen and doctors. Is it not more likely that they were called together, at the beginning of the parliamentary session, in order to be acquainted with the government's plans? Even allowing Chapuys to have been correctly informed, he might well report a discussion concerning the prevention of appeals to Rome, particularly in the matter of the king's marriage, as turning on the point whether Canterbury was competent to pronounce sentence, for the question of that competence arose only with the prevention of appeals to Rome and the fate of the queen was all that mattered to Chapuys. That does not mean that the government were not more concerned with the fate of their revolutionary measure. We remember that we can point to a stage in the history of the Act against Appeals when it was obviously ready for Parliament, and that it afterwards underwent changes best explained as the result of representations from the higher clergy and the doctors of both laws. We remember further that a meeting of such persons assembled on the second day of the session which was to pass this act. Can we doubt that this meeting considered this very draft of the act? The government had got the act ready in time for the session. They then informed a selected number of churchmen, calling in legal experts for assistance, and the delay in the introduction of the bill was due to certain of its points rousing opposition which had to be appeased before a smooth passage in the Lords and no trouble from Convocation could be relied on.

At last, on 14 March 1533, the bill was read in the Commons.[1] Chapuys reported that it came as a surprise:[2] probably, people had not expected such sweeping legislation, thinking that Henry would content himself with having his own case settled alone, as indeed had been the government's original intention. For a fortnight, opposition continued strong and the Commons would not pass the act. According to Chapuys, resistance was based mainly on the argument that the pope would be able to ruin England, by inducing other countries to treat her as schismatic and refuse to trade with her.[3] To this the government replied that the chances were rather that England's example would encourage her neighbours to follow suit. One of the members for the city of London, out of partisanship for Catherine, apparently suggested

---

[1] *LP* vi. 235, Chapuys to Charles V on 15 March: 'Yesterday and to-day it was proposed in Parliament to make a statute declaring the Pope had no authority in this kingdom.'
[2] *LP* vi. 235, 'which many people found very strange'.
[3] Ibid. 296, Chapuys to Charles V on 29 March.

a grant of £200,000 to the king in return for his agreeing to submit the divorce to a General Council of the Church.[1] The sum would have been fantastically large (about twice the annual revenue of the Crown at the time),[2] and if the proposal was actually moved it showed little sense of the real situation. No money grant would have moved the government, not then in financial straits, to abandon the one important project of the session, and no one, least of all the pope, wanted a General Council. In the first week of April, the opposition collapsed and the act was passed.[3] The length of time taken in the Commons makes it likely that the bill was committed; if so, we may be sure that Cromwell, who had so far watched every step of its progress, sat on the committee. In the absence of any journals that is all that can be said or conjectured about the passage of the bill through Parliament.

In its passage, the act underwent some alterations which were all made before it was engrossed, for the parchment bill at the Parliament Office shows no traces of any corrections or additions. The Lords did not touch it. A comparison of the finished product with B shows that most of the alterations (and there are not many) touched points of detail and phrasing. To enumerate the more important differences: in the act as passed, the word 'dyvorces' was inserted after 'causes of matrimony' in the recital of judicial business affected by it. But we have seen that such an insertion was made by Cromwell in D. It may have been in the bill as introduced, having been left out accidentally in Cromwell's private copy (B); at any rate, it embodied Cromwell's wishes. From the list of foreign processes not to be allowed in English courts the words 'prouocacions, prouysions' were removed. The 'spirituall prelates' were added to the 'pastours, Mynysters, and curates' who were to ignore Rome's strictures in continuing to administer the services of religion. In the last part of the act it was now declared that appeals from the archbishop's archdeacon should lie to 'the Courts of the Arches or Audyence of the same Archebisshopp or Archebusshoppes'. These two courts were parallel courts from both of which similar appeals went later to the High Court of Delegates.[4] More must be said of another change: by the act as passed, appeals

[1] Ibid. 324, Chapuys to Charles V on 10 April.

[2] Cf. F. C. Dietz, *English Government Finance 1485–1558* (Urbana, Ill., 1920), 140, and his table of subsidies actually granted (p. 225).

[3] The session ended on 7 April, and if there were any doubt whether the act got through both Houses in time, Chapuys' report of 10 April (*LP* vi. 324) would remove it.

[4] Cf. *Parl. Papers, Accts. and Papers 1867–8*, vol. lvii, p. xxv. The Canterbury court of audience, a court of appeal held by the archbishop himself, was early superseded in

in cases touching the king were to go to the upper house of Convocation direct from any lower court where they had begun. They were thus to miss the ladder of appeals applicable in ordinary cases. A certain degree of hesitancy had been evinced before about this matter. Draft A had stated that in cases of appeals 'concerning the King or his realme the partie greved obseruyng the order afore lymyted shall and may appele' to the upper house of Convocation.[1] An attempt to clarify the phrase 'obseruyng the order afore lymyted' was made in frg. 4 where this order was set out in detail, but it was deliberately disregarded, for B had the even more ambiguous phrase 'the party greved ... may appeale from any of the said Courtes gradatim'. Gradatim, by degrees, certainly implied 'going through the whole course, from court to court', and was therefore equivalent to the meaning of A, but the phrase was very vague. Taken together with the refusal to use a draft clause of perfect clarity (frg. 4), this fact suggests strongly that Cromwell meant all along to prevent the king's causes from being dragged through the whole course of appeals. But he was probably unable to persuade the conference of 5 February to agree to a change in the act which would have taken much business away from the higher Church courts. The phrase was apparently challenged and redrafted in Parliament, a step so much in accordance with Cromwell's desires as shown in the previous history of the passage that it is possible that he foresaw or even intended it. Cromwell's victory in this matter – his in spirit and probably in fact – did two things. Any appeal in a cause affecting the king's interests would now go only and directly to a tribunal whose constitution was, in the last resort, in the king's hands. On the other hand, it was likely that few men would trouble to appeal if such action meant waiting for the next meeting of Convocation and an expensive contest before that august body.[2] There would be fewer appeals in our day if the House of Lords were the only court of appeal in the land.

importance by the court of the official principal, or court of the Arches (Churchill, *Canterbury Administration*, 470 ff.; Holdsworth, *Hist. of Law*, i. 601; Phillimore, *Eccl. Law*, 922–3). Coke (*Fourth Inst.* 337) thought that the phrase 'court of the arches or audience' meant the Arches court only. He wrongly ascribed the phrase to the act of 25 Henry VIII, c. 19 where it does not occur, though the appeal to Chancery, also mentioned by Coke, is in that act.

[1] A, fo. 43. The scribe wrote 'lynyted' by mistake.
[2] The right of appeal to Convocation was further limited by the provision that such appeals had to be made within fifteen days of the decision of the inferior court. If Convocation was not sitting by then the appeal would presumably lapse. The king could always summon Convocation if he desired to have a case reviewed. As a matter of fact, no use was apparently ever made of Convocation as a court of appeal (Stubbs in *Eccl. Comm. 1883*, Hist. App. I, 39).

This was the one essential change which the act underwent in its passage through Parliament, and it was a change which favoured the king and was therefore most probably sponsored by the government. The Act in Restraint of Appeals to Rome was a government measure, affected slightly by opposition from the Church and not at all by Parliament. A proposal to authorize the archbishops by act of Parliament to dissolve the king's marriage was soon replaced by a comprehensive attack on papal jurisdiction in England. In Cromwell's hands, the preamble turned into an unhesitating statement of the theory which underlay the whole practice of Henry VIII and his government: the theory of the imperial crown of England sovereign within its own realm over both laity and Church. In contrast to the wide sweep of the preamble, the severely practical enactment dealt only with certain definite business transacted in the ecclesiastical courts. Even some of this, the spiritual jurisdiction proper, was dropped from the act. There remained all the work done in those courts which affected the laity materially, either in their private lives (testamentary and matrimonial causes, causes of divorce) or in their relations with the profits of Church benefices (rights of tithes, oblations, and obventions). Outside the preamble there was no pretence that the act was directed against anyone but Rome. In only one point the government suffered defeat, being compelled to allow the archiepiscopal courts final jurisdiction in all matters not affecting the king. This defeat was not final. A clause (sec. 4) in the Act for the Submission of the Clergy (25 Henry VIII, c. 19), passed in the next session of Parliament, declared that appeals were to run as established by 24 Henry VIII, c. 12, but that an appeal was to lie from the archbishops to the king in Chancery upon which a commission was to issue under the great seal for the final determination of the case. Thus the protest of the conference of 5 February 1533 was at length overruled.[1]

The act claimed to be a development of the Statutes of Provisors of the fourteenth century. Even the most important of these (16 Richard

---

[1] Hall (*Chronicle*, 795) says of the act against appeals that appeals were to go from 'Commissarie to the Bishoppe, and from Bishop to the Archebishop, and from Archebishop to the kyng, and all causes of the kyng to be tried in the vpper house of the Conuocacion'. This was the law as it stood before 5 February 1533, and again after the session of 1534. It seems to me unlikely that Hall was remembering an earlier draft of the 1533 act (had he been, it would be of some importance that he should have known of it); he was confusing the two acts. In the next sentence, he states that the same session (1533) passed the act declaring Catherine to be but princess dowager. But this act (25 Henry VIII, c. 28) also belonged to 1534; it is clear that Hall, writing after the event, mixed up the two sessions in his memory.

II, c. 5), the penalties of which were appointed under this act, did no more than attack certain specified papal activities in England, namely provision to benefices. It was an attack on Rome's invasion of patronage rights, not an attack on Rome's whole position in England.[1] The Act against Appeals might quote laws made in the times of Edward I, Edward III, Richard II, and Henry IV, but its authors knew that this was idle talk, and that their attack was not directed against evils already legislated against. For they stated, in a phrase interlineated by Cromwell himself, that 'sythen the makyng of the sayde good holsom statutes and ordenaunces dyuers and sondry inconuynences and dangiers not prouyded for playnly by the sayde former actes . . . hathe risen and sprongen',[2] thus tacitly admitting that what they proposed to do was new, although they might represent their work as merely supplementary to earlier legislation. The Act against Appeals marked a revolution no less definite because in the manner of English revolutions it attempted to find justification in the past.

It remains to apportion responsibility. Parliament did little but endorse what was put before it. Henry, no doubt, kept himself fully informed of the progress of the measure, but he put his hand to it only once, and some of the corrections which he then made were dropped at the next stage.[3] Audley drafted the original bill which was to deal with Henry's case only. Riche may have had something to do with the drafting in a subordinate capacity. But the man who appears again and again is Cromwell. His clerks drew up the drafts, or most of them. He supervised the drafting, himself added some of the more important clauses, and shaped the provisions one by one by constant correction. He called the conference which was to approve the bill before it went to parliament. The act against appeals was his act. It embodied his political thought and marked the triumph of his policy in the counsels of the king, for it was only in April 1533 that he came before the world as Henry's chief minister.[4] He signalled his advent by the act which began his life's work – the separation from Rome,

[1] Cf. W. T. Waugh, 'The Great Statute of Praemunire,' *EHR* 37 (1922), particularly 174–5, 178–80. [2] C, fo. 58.

[3] Holdsworth (*Hist. of English Law*, xi. 368, n. 1) asserts that 'Henry VIII himself settled the preamble of the Statute of Appeals'; he based this view on the only draft known to him (H), the preamble of which was printed by the Ecclesiastical Commission on Church Courts of 1883 (Hist. App. I. 213–14). This contained the only examples of Henry's writing in the whole series, and the few corrections he made, especially when compared with Cromwell's, certainly do not bear out Holdsworth's statement.

[4] *LP* vi. 351 (p. 168). [*1973*. The progress of listing at the PRO has brought to light yet another draft of the Act of Appeals: E 175/8. This turns out to be the missing stage

and the subjugation of the Church in England to the sovereignty of the Crown. The Act against Appeals achieved the first of these aims; the other was to be attained in the next two years.

between B and the Act as passed; it embodies the corrections on the former and its text as corrected is identical with that of the enacted statute. Believing that B was introduced into the Commons, I conjectured above that these last changes were made in Parliament, but this must now seem doubtful. The newly discovered draft is in appearance like any of the preparliamentary official drafts of the period. Alterations were inserted in an unidentified hand, but one or two phrases could be in that of Lord Chancellor Audley. The probabilities, therefore, are in favour of the supposition that the new draft represents the final polishing of the bill before introduction and that neither House touched its wording during passage.]

25

THE COMMONS' SUPPLICATION OF 1532: PARLIAMENTARY MANOEUVRES IN THE REIGN OF HENRY VIII*

In the third session of the Reformation Parliament, which began on 15 January 1532, the Commons presented a petition against the misdemeanours of the ordinaries, the judges in ecclesiastical courts, and in particular against the way in which heresy trials were conducted; from this 'Supplication against the Ordinaries' and the answers produced by Convocation arose the demands of May 1532 which compelled Convocation to abdicate the independent jurisdiction and law-making power of the Church.[1] Thus the Supplication, an interesting document in itself, also marks the beginning of the real attack on the liberties of the Church, an attack which had been heralded by the *praemunire* fine of 1531 but had not before resulted in practical measures. The events of this third session – the passage of the first Act of Annates and the enforced submission of the clergy – ended the period of temporizing and hesitation, and ushered in the full revolution which dominated the history of the 1530s. While the policy pursued up to the beginning of 1532 shows great reluctance in high places to destroy all hope of a settlement with Rome and of obtaining the divorce with the pope's sanction, the session of that year introduced a new and active policy, one of whose first achievements was to reduce the clergy to impotent obedience.

I

The Supplication, which had such momentous consequences, has not had the study it deserves. Its importance has been recognized, but it has not been investigated. Ever since the fifth volume of the *Letters and Papers . . . of the Reign of Henry VIII* appeared, with its note of a copy of the Supplication and some extant drafts corrected by Thomas

* [EHR 66 (1951), 507–34. Attacked by J. P. Cooper, 'The Supplication against the Ordinaries reconsidered,' ibid. 72 (1957), 616–41. Cf. above, vol. 1, pp. 170–1.]
[1] The outlines of the story have been told frequently: e.g. H. A. L. Fisher, *Polit. Hist.* v. 311–13; J. Gairdner, *Hist. of the Eng. Church in the 16th Cent.* 113–22.

Cromwell,[1] it has been usual to assert that the document was clearly no more than a government manoeuvre, a palpable blind. The idea that Cromwell's corrections show the court provenance of the Supplication was first given currency by Gairdner who always hesitated to admit any wider or national support for Henry's and Cromwell's policy, and it has passed into the textbooks.[2] Merriman, as a biographer will, ascribed it entirely to Cromwell, but to Cromwell as the king's minister.[3] Pollard alone dissented, pointing out that Cromwell's corrections do not necessarily represent Court or Council deliberations as Cromwell was also a member of Parliament, and that the grievances expressed were nearly all more likely to be felt by the nation than by the king.[4] The latest study of the subject, while attempting to deal with the originals rather than the calendar, does so with more attention to a general thesis than to the details of diplomatic and development.[5]

It must first be noted that there are among the state papers not four but five drafts and copies of the Supplication, for one was misplaced in the calendaring. Internal evidence makes it possible to arrange them in due sequence; the reasoning underlying the process is too tedious to rehearse here, and it is hoped that the result may suffice. The first document (hereafter called A) represents roughly the first half of the points of the Supplication;[6] it is to be supplemented by B

---

[1] *LP*, v. 1016 (1–4).

[2] The manner in which the idea gained ground is an example of how a small misstatement may breed a big misconception. In his introduction to *LP* v, p. xix, Gairdner asserted: 'That the petition of the Commons against the spiritualty really emanated from the Court, is placed beyond doubt by the fact that four corrected drafts of it exist at the Record Office, the corrections generally being in Cromwell's hand'; yet his own entry at ibid. 1016 reveals only three drafts and one fair copy, and only two of the drafts are stated to be corrected by Cromwell, half the number so loosely suggested in the introduction. Gairdner repeated the allegation, as loosely, in his *Hist. of the Eng. Church*, 114. Fisher repeated the error that four drafts with Cromwell's handwriting on them exist, though he did not in so many words draw the conclusion from it (*Pol. Hist.* v. 311). Pickthorn, who does not mention Cromwell's hand at all and seems to think that the Commons' grievances were genuine enough, yet has 'no doubt that the Supplication against the Ordinaries was inspired and edited by the government' (*Early Tudor Gov.* i. 179 f.). The more recent pronouncements on the point by H. Maynard Smith revert wholeheartedly to Gairdner's position and mistakes: *Pre-Reformation England* (1938), 49, n. 1 ('The *Complaint* was concocted at court. Four drafts of it exist corrected in Cromwell's handwriting'), 52; *Henry VIII and the Reformation* (1948), 53.

[3] Merriman, i. 96: 'the first of a number of measures ostensibly emanating from Parliament, but in reality prepared by the King's minister and forced by him upon the very tractable Lords and Commons.'   [4] Pollard, *Henry VIII*, 291 f.

[5] A. Ogle, *The Tragedy of the Lollards' Tower: the Case of Richard Hunne and its Aftermath in the Reformation Parliament 1529–33* (Oxford, 1949), 297 ff.

[6] PRO, SP 2/L, fos. 203–4 (*LP* v. 1016 [3]).

which contains the remainder.[1] Further drafts of both parts were made (C_1 and C_2): they are separately written but belong together.[2] C_1 has all the matter and corrections of A though the wording has undergone considerable alteration, while C_2 is practically an accurate copy of B with its corrections. Both C_1 and C_2 were further corrected. The next draft (D) made one whole of the two sources of the Supplication; it is very different from its predecessors in phrasing and occasionally in meaning, but the points elaborated and the general tenor prove it to be a later development from C.[3] Finally, there is E, a fair copy of D with all the corrections embodied.[4] D alone of these drafts is in the form normal for draft acts of Parliament – written on one side of large sheets of paper, with spaces at least one inch wide between the lines, and in the standard round clerkly hand of the period; A is also fairly written but not in that typical clerical script, and its lines are much closer together; while B, C and E, though in script and setting out like D, are written on both sides of the paper.

The drafts, then, fall into two groups: A, B, and C on the one hand, D and E on the other.[5] The first group presents the document in two parts (A and B, and C_1 and C_2 respectively), while in the second the parts are combined into one. There is direct and indubitable descent from A and B to C, and from D to E, while the link between C and D is much less immediate. It is as though a complete revision and reconsideration had taken place before D was committed to paper. A further difference lies in the corrections. A, B, and C are plentifully corrected by one man only – Thomas Cromwell; the corrections in D are not by him (with two small exceptions which prove that he looked the draft over)[6] but in a number of hands, mostly in that of Thomas Audley.

The most important difference, however, between the two sets of drafts, is in their respective places of origin. The appearance and

---

[1] PRO, SP 1/56, fos. 40–3 (*LP* iv. 6043 [7]). This is the draft misplaced in the calendar.

[2] PRO, SP 6/7, arts. 21–2 (*LP* v. 1016 [4]). This is the draft printed by Merriman, i. 104 ff. It is not, as will be seen, the first, as Merriman thought (p. 104). As he points out there, there are two blank pages after fo. 113v; what follows from fo. 114v. was written by a different clerk. The same draft is the basis of the version printed by Gee and Hardy, 145 ff.; the editors rearranged the pages in the belief that they had become 'confused in the binding', an odd supposition in view of the different handwritings and blank pages.   [3] PRO, SP 2/L, fos. 193–202 (*LP* v. 1016[2]).

[4] PRO, SP 6/1, art. 22 (*LP* v. 1016[1]).

[5] The difference was noted by Ogle (*Lollards' Tower*, 310) who, however, sees two completed and separate versions, whereas I have no doubt that wording and content prove D to have been developed from C.

[6] He inserted 'or to lytell ponyshment' on fo. 196, and '& promocyon' on fo. 200.

wording of A are as conclusive proof as can be hoped for that it came from the Commons: it was not a draft made 'at court' or anywhere except in the House.[1] It is written in a hand not to be found in any of the many extant government drafts of acts of Parliament, in fact not in that typical round and clerkly hand of the period which we meet again and again in Cromwell's drafts, and which, moreover, we meet in every other draft of the Supplication.[2] Draft A is in effect a list of grievances, rather succinctly stated. The list begins with 'ffirst' and continues with 'Item', while Cromwell, who never employed this method in his parliamentary work, preferred the word 'also' to introduce new points, a practice significantly adopted in the other drafts of the Supplication. A, then, is alone in script and construction, being altogether different from B–E which have the mark of Cromwell on them. But A is very closely paralleled by the only other parliamentary petition of the time of which evidence survives, a petition to the king to ask the bishops what the law of the Church was on certain listed grievances: here, too, the draftsman began with 'ffirst' and continued with 'Item'.[3] There can be no doubt that this petition, dealing as it did with some of the abuses which Hall describes the Commons as discussing off their own bat in 1529[4] was produced by the Commons; the fact that it is in the same form as A, and in so different a form from all other known parliamentary papers of the period, goes far to prove that A came from the same place. It may further be said that A's petitionary preamble has much more the flavour of a genuine Commons' petition than have the later versions, after the draft had passed through Cromwell's hand. The preamble of A reads like the work of a lawyer, with its reference to the High Court of Parliament, and of a member, moreover, of that body, with its desire that the grievances be remedied in Parliament, while in the version of C the request for parliamentary action has disappeared and there is a distinct loss of assertive independence. C's preamble is long and detailed in the manner typical of Reformation statutes, and undoubtedly like those that Crom-

---

[1] Mr Ogle also argues for the Commons as the place of the Supplication's origin, but his arguments (*Lollards' Tower*, 313–16) do not seem to me to prove his point – in fact, they might be used against him. While agreeing with his major premise, I find surer proof in the appearance of the first draft.

[2] There is a facsimile of A in Mr Ogle's book (opposite p. 312) which may help to illustrate this point.

[3] BM, Cleo. F. ii, fo. 249. The dating in *LP* v. 721 (2) – 1532 – is wrong; the grievances mentioned (worldly activities, pluralism, and non-residence) were dealt with by the statute of 21 Henry VIII, c. 13, and the petition must belong to 1529.

[4] Hall, *Chronicle*, 765 – the points marked 3–6.

well loved to draft.[1] The other petition that has been mentioned has, like A, a short preamble which refers to the High Court of Parliament and mentions the device of 'articles' to which a reply is desired from the spiritualty. If allowance is made for the different target and scale of the two petitions, it is seen that they were both designed on the same pattern.

For all these reasons, and especially because it is so like the one known genuine Commons' petition of this Parliament, A may confidently be taken to have been the work of the Commons. D, on the other hand, was produced by the government. As has been said, it is corrected in a number of hands, but most of the work was done by Audley, the Speaker of the House of Commons. Had the draft been handled inside the House in a Commons' committee – and only a committee could have produced corrections in several hands – it would have been impossible for the Speaker's hand to appear on it: even in the Reformation Parliament procedure was sufficiently developed to assure us of that.[2] Audley, however, was not only Speaker; he was also chancellor of the duchy of Lancaster and, since 14 November 1531, a king's serjeant.[3] That is to say, he was one of the king's legal counsel who were the normal draftsmen of government legislation. In the previous year (1531) Cromwell had been instructed to see parliamentary bills prepared by the legal counsel,[4] and the fact that more than one hand corrected D suggests that a similar step was taken with the Supplication. The Council – that is, the government – prepared draft D.

---

[1] A, fo. 203: 'Your most lovyng and obedient subgettes the Knyghtes Citezens and Burgessez in this present parliament assembled shewen to your excellent highnes certen articles herafter ansuyng wher of they most humble besechen your grace to provide som remedy and reformacion in this your most High Court of parliament as to your most excellent wisedom shall seme convenyent.' C's version beginning 'In most humble wise Shewen vnto your excellent highnes and most prudent wisedom your faithfull louyng and obedient Subiectes The Commons on this your presente parliament assembled', may be read in Merriman, i. 104 f. For Cromwell's way with preambles, cf. above, p. 56.

[2] Cf. Neale, *Elizabethan House of Commons*, 393–402, for the Speaker's work in an Elizabethan Parliament. Though it would be folly to suppose that no changes had taken place in procedure since 1529, it would be equally wrong to assume that there was no ancestry to so well-developed a House of Commons as that of Elizabeth's reign (cf. Sir Thomas Smith's account, written as early as 1565, in *De Republica Anglorum*, ed. Alston, 49 ff.). The Speaker occasionally spoke to a bill, but even that was against strict rule, and unquestionably he could not sit in committee to do the detailed work of correction which was done on D. That was inherent in the office and as true of the Reformation Parliament as of later ones.

[3] *DNB.* [4] *LP* v. 394.

II

The Supplication, therefore, grew up in two separate stages. It was presented in 1532; there can be no doubt of that, and Froude was quite wrong in putting the whole business into 1529.[1] A good deal is known about this session of 1532, rather more indeed than about those preceding it. Hall tells a circumstantial story:[2] after much complaining in the Commons of the cruelty of the ordinaries and their heresy proceedings, 'at the last it was concluded & agreed' to draw up a petition, 'whiche by great aduyce was done', and on 18 March a Commons' deputation led by the Speaker presented the Supplication to the king. Henry proved reasonably gracious, though he had something to say about the concurrent petition for the dissolution of Parliament, and about his desire that peace be kept between the clergy and laity; but he also insisted that the Commons could hardly expect much consideration for their grievances as long as they refused their assent to the government's proposals concerning uses and primer seisin. Shortly afterwards Parliament was prorogued until after Easter (it reassembled on 10 April), and then the avalanche started by the Supplication got under way. Hall spares a bare word for the first Act of Annates; to him the Supplication was clearly the chief business of the session, together with the acrimonious debates on the Statute of Uses whose rejection at this time he deplores. He certainly gives the impression that the first two months of this long session were taken up with the discussion of grievances and the drawing up of the Supplication (this second step being taken right at the end), an unconvincing picture which, however, is necesary for the assumption that in 1532 the Commons themselves promoted the Supplication, an assumption Hall clearly makes and undoubtedly believed to be true.[3]

Fortunately the story can be filled out from letters of ambassadors

---

[1] J. A. Froude, *Hist. of Eng.* i, 207 ff. The copy of the Supplication which he printed is also C, but C mistranscribed and entirely rearranged. For his dating he was severely taken to task by R. W. Dixon, *Hist. of the Eng. Church*, i. 79 n., 81 n.; but, as will appear, there may have been some unexpected intuition in what was evidently only a mistake.   [2] Hall, *Chronicle*, 784–5.

[3] A complication is introduced by a paper in BM, Harl. MS 2252, fo. 34b (*LP* vii, 399), which describes how the Speaker made a 'preposyssyon' for reformation of certain grievances against the Church courts, but dates the Speaker's address 5 March; the writer (a contemporary, to judge from his hand) does not appear to have used or copied Hall's account, but his reliability is impugned by his ascribing the whole business to the session of February 1534 and including matter which did belong to that later session. Hall's date is more likely to be correct.

and others, though it should for once be pointed out that the chief witness, Chapuys, is unreliable where the government's motives and the strength of the opposition are concerned; he had persuaded himself that the government intended to legislate for the divorce in the 1532 session, and when nothing of the sort happened he was constrained to express constant surprise.[1] However, while his information was bound to be incomplete, biased, and often tardy, his statements of bare fact always deserve attention. His reports show that the first business of the session were the bill of primer seisin and the fifteenth; by the middle of February nothing else of moment seems to have been brought forward.[2] At this point a new note crept in. Shortly before 14 February, Norfolk called a meeting – we do not know of whom – which he sounded on the question of matrimonial jurisdiction: he alleged that it belonged 'to the King who is emperor in his kingdom, and not to the Pope'.[3] The meeting proved unhelpful, and nothing further was heard of this attack on papal jurisdiction until the session of 1533.

However, another line was now being tried, and on 28 February Chapuys reported the bill of annates in Parliament.[4] This took more than three weeks to get through, for it was not done with until 21 March,[5] and in the meantime the king's feudal claims disappeared from the record. The Commons had found something else to talk about – a matter more pleasing to themselves. On the same day that Chapuys for the first time reported on annates, the duke of Norfolk, writing to the king's envoy at Rome, had strange things to say: 'Notwithstanding the infinite clamours of the temporality here in Parliament against the misuse of the spiritual jurisdiction, the King will stop all evil effects if the Pope does not handle him unkindly. The realm did never grudge the tenth part against the abuses of the Church at no Parliament in my days as they do now.'[6] A few days later Chapuys had also woken up to the fact that something was afoot that affected the clergy, though he made a hash of it.[7] Towards the end of

---

[1] *LP* v. 737, 805, 832, 879.

[2] Ibid. 762, 805. *Span. Cal. 1531–3*, 383 (Chapuys to Charles V, 14 Feb. 1532): 'Nothing else [i.e. only the primer seisin bill] has been done in the said Parliament except the prohibition of importing new wines before Candlemas . . . They have also tried for some days to prohibit the importation of silk cloth . . .'   [3] *LP* v. 805.

[4] Ibid. no. 832. He added that since his last 'nothing has been done in Parliament' (*Span. Cal. 1531–3*, p. 390).

[5] *LP* v. 886.   [6] Ibid. no. 831.

[7] He reported that Parliament wished to abolish the archbishops' authority over the bishops and transfer it to the king (ibid. 850); just what he meant is doubtful. It is

February, then, and not earlier, the Commons began to discuss those grievances which Hall suggests were their main business from the start of the session, for Norfolk's letter – a palpable manoeuvre to put pressure on the pope – establishes the date with fair accuracy: if the attacks had started earlier, why was this useful argument not employed earlier at Rome?

It therefore seems that for the first four or five weeks of the session the government were trying in vain to push through financial measures distasteful to the House, and it was not until towards the end of February that the attack on the Church was resumed with two concerted moves: the pope was attacked through his revenues, and the English Church through its courts and canons. While the Act of Annates was obviously designed to increase the pressure on the pope, the Supplication applied more directly to the clergy in England and exploited grievances of the Commons, who had little interest in saving the bishop's pockets. It appears, then, that when the House had been put into a thoroughly bad temper the government shifted their ground by allowing the complaints against the ordinaries and heresy jurisdiction to go forward. Hall would have it that these were genuinely the Commons' complaints, but a doubt is raised by something he records himself: when Henry remarked on the incompatibility of the two petitions presented in March – one against the clergy and the other for an early dismissal of Parliament – he spoke justly, and it may be thought that the Commons were not really so much interested in the Supplication as the anticlerical chronicler would have us believe. Furthermore, it is difficult to see how a genuine Commons' complaint could have come to be embodied in an undoubted government draft; the final form of the Supplication was produced by the government, for E is merely a fair copy of D, and D, as has been seen, was not drawn up or corrected inside Parliament. Thus it appears that the agitation of 1532 must have been inspired by the king and Council.

There would be little difficulty in this view (the common view of the textbooks), were it not for that earlier group of drafts (A–C) which, as has been shown, began with a document produced by the House itself. It might be suggested that after a beginning had been made in the Commons, their draft was taken out of Parliament to be

interesting though not important to the argument that Chapuys did not become aware of the Supplication and its true import until after the Easter recess (ibid. 989, 1013); actually, he never mentioned the petition itself. How he came to miss the scene of 18 March it is impossible to say; that he did miss it is a comment on his information.

worked up by Cromwell and other councillors. Though possible, this is very unlikely; it is hard to see why the drafting should not have taken place in the Commons, under the supervision of the councillors there. The unlikely suggestion can, however, be shown to be impossible if it can be established that D was drawn up before the agitation in the Commons began.

In the first place, there is a draft act of Parliament, belonging to the session of 1532, which, being corrected largely by Cromwell, in a few places by an unknown hand, and in part by Audley who re-wrote the final clause, must have been a government draft for the same reasons as D was.[1] This draft, after an extravagant preamble asserting principles of political philosophy and the supremacy of the Crown, prohibited Convocation from legislating without the king's consent, thus embodying in a statute one of the most important points touched on in the Supplication. It looks very much as though the government was at first in two minds whether to proceed by act of Parliament or by direct action in Convocation reinforced by a Commons' petition, and if this interpretation is sound it would have to be taken that the action in the Commons was prepared – that D was prepared – before the Supplication came up in the Commons.

This is not conclusive, but D itself provides proof in a list of memoranda in Audley's hand on the back of its first folio (fo. 193v). They are difficult to decipher, for Audley's writing is never easy and here he scrawled more fragmentarily than usual, but eighteen of the notes can be identified as referring to acts of this session. The list cannot be of the acts passed of which sixteen are missing, including even the Act of Annates, while there is at least one bill suggested which cannot be identified in the statutes ('for Sc^t york'); it can therefore be only either a list of matters in the preparing and despatching of which Audley was concerned, or a list of bills received by the Speaker. The first alternative is supported by a few obscure notes which do not refer to legislation and may be other business of Audley's; the second by the inclusion of undoubted private bills (23 Henry VIII, cc. 29, 31), though Audley may have had a hand in them as a private lawyer. Whichever explanation is correct, they both make certain that D was drafted before the Commons began to discuss the Supplication. If these are Audley's private memoranda of matters he had to prepare, the inclusion of the act for the import of wine (23 Henry VIII, c. 7) proves the list, and with

---

[1] PRO, SP 2/L, fos. 78–80 (*LP* v. 721 [1]). A fair copy of this draft (SP 2/P, fos. 17–19) is misplaced in the calendar (*LP* vii. 57 [2]).

it draft D, to be earlier than 14 February: that act had passed by then.[1]
If the list is of bills received, it must have been made early in the session,
before that same bill came up. In any case, D precedes the first appearance of the Supplication in the House of Commons.

But if this is so, Hall's tale collapses: the government were very
likely working on the Supplication before ever Parliament met in
1532, and the existence of an earlier group of drafts beginning with one
made in the Commons raises a big question. It now seems impossible
that all the drafts of the Supplication should have belonged to the same
session of Parliament; while the petition, in a form worked out by the
Council, was presented in March 1532, it must apparently have arisen
in an earlier session in the House of Commons itself.

III

Here we must part company with certainty. The problem raised cannot
be solved by direct proof because there is no mention of the Supplication in any session but that of 1532. Nevertheless, an answer may be
suggested, and evidence can be produced which it is hoped may make
the suggestion very strong. If the first draft of the Supplication was
drawn up in a session earlier than 1532, that of 1531 may be excluded
on general grounds: the only important business of that session was the
praemunire charge against the clergy,[2] and the Commons appear to
have rested after their first onslaught in 1529. That, however, was the
session when grievances were loud against the clergy. After years of
clerical rule exacerbating long-felt resentment against the Church,
Wolsey's fall opened the floodgates to a fierce attack on ecclesiastical
abuses and pretensions, and abuse after ancient abuse, long and often
denounced but never effectively tackled, was assailed by the laity.
'When the Commons were assembled in the nether house', says Hall,
who was one of them, 'thei began to common of their grefes wherwith
the spiritualtie had before tyme greuously oppressed them, both
contrarie to the law of the realme, & contrarie to all right, and in
especial thei were sore moued with six greate causes' – the grievances
dealt with in the three great reforming statutes of that session.[3]

'In especial . . . with six greate causes', but not exclusively so. The
Supplication against the Ordinaries was a document concerned with
'grefes' against the Church, and there is reason to think that some of
its points, particularly the objections raised to the canons, were present

---

[1] Above, p. 113, m.2.   [2] *LP* v. 62, 124.   [3] Hall, *Chronicle*, 765.

to the Commons in 1529. Hall states that when the Lords and Commons met to discuss the proposed bills for mortuary and probate, 'the temporaltie laied to the spiritualtie ther awne lawes and constitucions',[1] a point which Strype elaborated into the view that matters were raised at this conference which later reappeared in the Supplication of 1532.[2] He seems to have had nothing to go on except Hall's brief phrase, and there is no denying that he made more of it than caution would approve, but Hall's words are at least sufficient evidence that other matters than those passed into statutes were in members' minds in this first session, and that these matters included points also mentioned in the Supplication.

It has further already been shown that the device of petitioning the king for replies from the clergy to the Commons' complaints (the device, that is, of the Supplication) was adopted or at least suggested on one other occasion, and that – since the points in question were settled by a statute of the first session – that occasion must have been in 1529.[3] If one petition was drawn up in 1529 concerning clerical abuses, the possibility is strong that the other petition – so like the first in drafting, concerned with those further grievances whose existence Hall hints at, and apparently bound to belong to either 1529 or 1531 – was also in hand in the first session. Perhaps the committees appointed to put the Commons' complaints on paper intended at first to proceed by such petitions rather than by bills.

The suggestion that the Supplication originated in 1529 can be further supported by internal evidence from the drafts themselves. One section of the Supplication deals with the exactions of the clergy: A enlarges on the excessive cost of process in the spiritual courts, while B mentions additional points – fees are taken for the administration of the sacraments which ought to be free, crowds of officials appointed by the ordinaries ('which like a sorte of Rauenous Wolues nothing ellis attending but there onelie Pryuate Lucres')[4] make the probate of wills excessively dear, the judges of the spiritual courts take bribes,

---

[1] Ibid. 766. It might be thought the laws meant were those made by the Church itself against the evils under discussion, and if I understand him aright, that is Pickthorn's interpretation (*Early Tudor Gov.* i. 136); however, this seems to be in conflict with the further statement that 'the spiritualtie sore defended' these laws 'by prescripsion and vsage', which leaves no doubt that the Commons were *attacking* the laws of the Church, not quoting them in support of their own views.

[2] *Eccl. Mem.* i, ch. 17 (ed. 1721, pp. 129 ff.).

[3] Cf. above, p. 110, and n. 3.

[4] Cromwell regrettably changed this phrase to 'which coueting somoche but there Pryuate Lucres'; B, fo. 40v.

and the ordinaries themselves take illegal fees for instituting and inducting new incumbents to benefices.[1] C repeats these charges, though the one about corrupt judges was later crossed out.[2] But in D there is an important change in the clause concerning probate. While B and C₂ state, in terms so indefinite as to amount to no more than a general grumble, that people bringing wills for probate find themselves mulcted of large sums of money by the great press of officials at the bishop's court,[3] D invokes the statute passed in 1529 which limited the fees for probate.[4] Here there is no general complaint against the malpractices of ecclesiastical court officials; instead, it is alleged that as regards the probate of wills, 'not withstondyng the last statute therof made', money is extorted by delaying the admission of a will to probate, and executors are made to travel far from their shires, 'though', as the corrector (Audley) was quick to add in anticipation of the defence later made by the ordinaries,[5] 'the probate therof belong not to the prerogatyff'. Moreover, 'sithen the estatute made for mortuaries', the clergy had found means of defeating the law by exacting greater tithes than was customary, or – refinement of chicanery – by bringing a suit for a mortuary due but not demanded and taking in costs sufficient to make up for the limited mortuary fee allowed by the statute.[6]

Twice statutes of 1529 are mentioned in D, while C and its predecessors have not a word about them. In C the complaint about probate fees is worded in a general and imprecise way that reflects general and imprecise grievances; after 1529 the law on the subject was definite, and if there were grievances they could no longer be so vague. Nor are they at all vague in D. The voice of scepticism might still claim that this only proves inefficient drafting at the start, but in view of what has already been said about the two groups of drafts the point gives great weight to the suggested date of 1529.

[1] B, fos. 40v–41v.   [2] C₂, fos. 114v–116.

[3] C₂, fo. 115: 'And also where in the spirituall Courtes . . . ben lymyted and appoynted so many Iudges Scribes Apparitours Sommonrs praysours and other ministres for the approbation of testamentes, Whiche coveting somoche their owne priuate lucres and satisfaccion of the appetites of the said prelates & Ordinaries that when any of your said loving subiectes do Repaire to any of the said Courtis for the probate of testamentes, they do in such wise make long delays and excessively take of theym so large fees and Rewardes for the same as is Importible for theym to beare, directly against all Iustice lawe equite and good conscience.'   [4] 21 Henry VIII, c. 5.

[5] The ordinaries denied that executors were forced to travel except when the will came under the prerogative court of Canterbury which dealt with wills affecting property in more than one diocese (PRO, SP 6/7, art. 24; the copy of the Answer printed by Gee and Hardy, pp. 154 ff., is accurate and will normally be quoted in this paper: pp. 168 ff.).   [6] D, fo. 198.

The argument can be buttressed with one last piece of evidence. The second paragraph of A complains that Warham, as archbishop of Canterbury, had made an ordinance 'lately devised' (C uses the words 'now of late') which limited the number of proctors practising in the court of the Arches to ten; it was alleged that in consequence there was no remedy against the judges or proctors there, that the course of justice was delayed and made unbearably expensive, and that the proctors, for fear of their office, would not 'disclose' any cause touching the Crown or the royal prerogative. Warham's ordinance, which incidentally only restored the 1295 statute of Archbishop Winchelsea,[1] was made on 8 March 1528,[2] and the Commons' language, in suggesting a recent grievance, seems more reasonable in 1529 than later. Another document dealing with the same problem, a reasoned exposition why Warham's ordinance should be overruled by Parliament,[3] was printed by Strype who thought it belonged to Cranmer's tenure of the see;[4] his mistake was pointed out by Pollard who, however, assigned it to 1532 and to Warham himself.[5] Brewer, realizing that the document was not drawn up by any archbishop, called it a 'Bill against Proctors' and placed it in the 1529 session of Parliament.[6] It is not a bill in the parliamentary sense, but simply a statement of reasons why Parliament should annul the archbishop's ordinance; it outlines the dangers of a small number of proctors on the lines of the Supplication though more fully, mentions that the prerogative might be involved in an action in the Arches as does the Supplication, and points out that the archbishop is powerless to alter his own statute because it has been confirmed by the chapter and convent of Christ Church, Canterbury. The writer therefore suggests that 'the present Parliament' take action. Together with the remark that the alteration in the number of proctors was 'lately procured', this phrase favours Brewer's conclusion that the document was drawn up at the beginning of this 'present Parliament' in 1529 when clerical abuses engaged the Commons' attention. As it was to all appearance the basis of the paragraph in the Supplication, it adds another link to the chain of speculation which ties the Supplication's origin to the session of 1529.

As far as circumstantial evidence will permit, this case appears now

---

[1] Churchill, *Canterbury Administration*, i. 436.
[2] Wilkins, *Concilia*, iii. 710 f.
[3] BM, Cleo. F. i, fos. 95–6.
[4] Strype, *Cranmer* (Oxford, 1812), 717 ff.
[5] A. F. Pollard, *Cranmer* (new ed. 1926), 95, n. 2.   [6] *LP* iv. 6045.

to be fairly strong. True, there is no contemporary statement pointing the same way, and Hall appears to think of the Supplication as belonging wholly to 1532. In 1529, all independent observers – the Imperial, Venetian, and Milanese ambassadors, for instance, who usually produce some valuable light on events in Parliament – as if by common agreement fail us; there is only Hall. Yet it may be claimed that even he is not so negative as he appears to be. He does note that the grievances he details are only the chief examples among others, and he does mention that the problem of the laws of the Church was in members' minds. Hall never concerned himself with parliamentary discussions unless they produced some result, either in the form of legislation or at least in that they provoked trouble with the king, as in the matter of the primer seisin bill of 1532.[1] His account of parliamentary history must not be taken to be complete, and at the same time, his version of events in 1532 has already been shown to be unsatisfactory.[2] His silence, then, does not stand very seriously in the way of the view that the Supplication originated in 1529. This view developed from the fact that it is virtually impossible for all the drafts of the Supplication to have belonged to 1532, and it was reinforced by stray hints in Hall's own account and by the existence of a 1529 petition remarkably like A in appearance. Evidence from the drafts themselves – their respective probate clauses and the complaint against Warham's ordinance – has gone far to turn supposition into something not so very unlike certainty after all.

The suggestion that the Commons were discussing clerical jurisdiction as early as 1529 also helps to explain Hall's familiar story of Bishop Fisher: how, in 1529, he complained in the Lords at the bill concerning probate, compared the Commons to Bohemian heretics, and alleged that with them it was 'nothing but doune with the Church, and all this me semeth is for lacke of faith only'.[3] No one ever seems to have wondered that Fisher of all men should have let himself go in this fashion.[4] What was at issue was probate and the clergy's profit from it; other bills coming from the Commons dealt with other abuses which the Church had long recognized as such, even if it had no wish to see them reformed by the laity; yet we are to believe that these attacks on worldliness and greed provoked an outburst – not from Warham the

---

[1] Hall, *Chronicle*, 785.   [2] Above, pp. 112–14.

[3] Hall, *Chronicle*, 766.

[4] Lord Herbert of Cherbury was worried, though his trouble was that he felt some defence necessary against attack from such a quarter where others would presumably have left him cold (*Henry VIII* [1672], 321).

lawyer, or Nix the persecutor – but from Fisher the saint. What right had anyone to talk of heresy when only recognized abuses were under discussion? But if the Commons were also denouncing ecclesiastical jurisdiction and especially heresy trials, Fisher's words become more understandable and some reason can be admitted on his side.

IV

It has been shown, then, that the Supplication as presented in 1532 was drawn up by the government, and that its final form was ready before the matter came up in the House. From that it has been deduced that the first group of drafts, which begins with a genuine Commons' draft, cannot have been made in the same session, and a case has now been suggested for putting the origin of the Supplication into the first session of the Reformation Parliament. The view is put forward that in that session grievances concerning Church courts and legislation got so far as to be embodied in a petition, though that petition was not then presented. Though this is a suggestion and not proven fact, it appears to be the only suggestion which can explain the known discrepancies and rest on circumstantial evidence both outside and inside the drafts. It is therefore proposed to reconstruct the history of the Supplication on the basis of this suggested interpretation, that is, on the assumption that A, B, and C belonged to 1529, while D and E belonged to 1532; in order to avoid overloading the account with reservations and qualifications the assumption will have to be treated as though it were certain.

If A was a Commons' draft of 1529, it disposes of the idea that the Supplication originated with the Court and Council. In that year Cromwell was not yet a member of the government, so that his corrections do not prove the official influence they have so readily been taken to substantiate.[1] Since A, with its preamble and list of 'Items', has so legal a flavour, it may well have been drafted in one of the committees of lawyers appointed to reduce the Commons' grievances into bills.[2] One side of their complaints – those that were brought to book

---

[1] Cromwell entered the king's service soon after the end of the 1529 session, probably as a result of his activities there (Hall, *Chronicle*, 769; *LP* v. 86; this letter belongs to 1530, not 1531).

[2] Hall, *Chronicle*, 766. The alleged parallels between the Supplication and Christopher St German's *Division between the Spiritualty and the Temporalty* (cf. A. I. Taft, *The Apologye of Syr Thomas More*, p. xxxvii; Baumer, *Early Tudor Theory of Kingship*, 66) are undoubtedly due in the main to this common origin in legal minds considering related problems. I have found no similarity in phrasing and nothing more than a not

in the act concerning pluralism and the like[1] – was first embodied in a petition to the king;[2] A was perhaps the work of a similar committee, not expressly mentioned by Hall because it never got round to drafting a bill. One member of the committee at least would be known, for only such membership could explain the corrections in Cromwell's hand which began the turning of A into C_1. Cromwell is likely to have sat on other committees in this session; there is evidence that he presided over one appointed to discuss a bill about 'protections'.[3] All this was part of his work in Parliament; his corrections on these drafts of 1529 prove not that they were officially inspired, but that Cromwell himself took up the idea of attacking the Church through its courts, and of doing it by means of a petition against their abuses. The very idea may have been his; there is no way of telling. At any rate, he supervised and shaped it from the beginning.

It was complained in A, (1) that Convocation made laws without the consent of king or Parliament, which laws bound the king's subjects though they were not published in English; (2) that process in the court of the Arches was rendered unjust by the recent limitation in the number of proctors; (3) that ordinaries summoned poor people *ex officio* and on frivolous grounds; (4) that people were forced to answer on oath sudden and unsupported accusations; (5) that excommunication was overfrequently and unjustly used; (6) that the fees charged in the spiritual courts were excessive.[4] The draft kept strictly to the grievances against practices in the Church courts without enlarging in detail on those complaints of the conduct of trials, especially heresy trials, on which posterity has fastened as perhaps the most significant point of the Supplication.

What appeared significant to Cromwell is quite another matter. The first sheet of A is endorsed in a hand frequent on Cromwell's

very close kinship in matter between the treatise and the petition; St German had nothing to do with the latter. [Cf. Reform and Renewal, p. 74, n. 21.] It is of interest to note that in describing evasions of the Statute of Mortuaries by fraudulent priests he adduced not one of the examples given in D but a new and less likely one: curates, he claimed, extorted money from sick men before they would give them hope of recovery, providing in that way for the reduced mortuary to follow (Taft, *Apologye*, 227). It is, of course, possible that the tract, published in 1532, was designed to popularize the views underlying the revived Supplication, but even for this the parallels are slender.

[1] 21 Henry VIII, c. 13.   [2] Above, p. 110, n. 3.

[3] *LP Add.* 663. The endorsement has been largely destroyed since the document was calendared but enough can be made out to confirm Mr Brodie's reading.

[4] This interesting scale of fees has been printed several times in copies of the Supplication; A (fo. 204) adds the fact that the *significavit* into Chancery, which cost 12*s*., was for 'the Kynges writte de excommunicato capiendo'.

papers, and therefore belonging to one of his clerks,[1] as 'how ordynaries do make lawes without the Kynges Royall assent'. This not only abstracts from a body of grievances affecting the laity of the land the one matter of interest to the king – the one solitary point which touched the royal prerogative; it turns this more plainly still into a royal concern by laying the stress on the absence of the king's assent (mentioned in passing only in the draft) and not on the troubles and vexations of the Commons. Cromwell was quick to seize on this point which would on the one hand incline the king to give a hearing to the petition, and on the other would attack the independence of the Church; in this part of one complaint lay the seeds of the three demands of May 1532 which secured the submission of the clergy and Convocation's surrender as a legislative body of moment.

Cromwell's corrections show a similar preoccupation with the first paragraph which he completely redrafted, essentially in the form in which it remained to the end, while there is only one minor correction in the rest of the document. The first grievance was not only restated in better and more forceful language; Cromwell also altered one point. The original complaint had been that while the lords spiritual had a voice in the making of laws in Parliament, they and the clergy yet claimed to make further laws in Convocation without consulting anyone.[2] Cromwell knew better than to let stand a roundabout attack on the bishops' place in Parliament, and in redrafting the passage he concentrated attention on the point that 'the prelattes & ordinaries with the Clergy of this your most excellent Realme[3] have in thayr Convocacyons hertoffore made ordeynyd and Constitutyd dyuers lawse and also do make daylye dyuers lawes and ordenaunces[4] without your Royall assent or knowlage or the assent or consent of Any of your laye Subiectes'. That was the thing that mattered, the accusation

---

[1] This clerk's hand is found in December 1529, e.g. on *LP* iv. 6117 (a letter to Cromwell) and 6043 (3) (a paper in Wriothesley's hand and belonging to Cromwell).

[2] The fine grumbling, it may be suggested, of the House of Commons man, and more particularly of the secular lawyer M.P., who does not see why the bishops should have a say in lay legislation at all, and certainly not why they should repay the concession by preserving Church legislation from lay interference.

[3] 'and Empyre' is here struck through. I agree with Mr Ogle on the significance of the concept of the imperial crown of England in Cromwell's political thought (cf. above, p. 86), but I think he makes too much of 'the first appearance of . . . Cromwell's "Big Idea"' (*Lollards' Tower*, 312); for one thing, there is a reference to the king's 'Imperiall pour' in the body of this very draft for which we cannot even be sure that Cromwell was responsible.

[4] With its accumulation of terms and phrases, especially the unnecessary trilogy, this is typically Cromwellian style; the original had said simply 'make lawes and ordynaunces'.

that could be turned to account, and Cromwell saw its possibilities as early as November 1529 when Henry was still looking to Rome for his divorce without thought of making himself pope over a submissive clergy. Such hints in Reformation statutes (and others could be found) forcefully support the evidence offered by the history of the attack on the Church (the hesitancy of 1529–32, the new and powerful policy beginning in 1532) that Cromwell, seeing from the first where Henry's actions were leading him, prepared a plan which he put into practice as soon as he had convinced the king of its efficacy; the matter is clinched by the testimony of a contemporary who assures us that Cromwell's thought was running along such lines before ever the Reformation Parliament met.[1] Everything suggests that the mind behind the measures which broke the bond with Rome was the minister's, the king, supreme opportunist that he was, looking no further than his immediate hopes and desires, though always ready to take advantage of the helpful ideas of others.

It is probable that before anything further was done the beginnings made in A received the closer attention which produced C_1. This contains a greatly enlarged preamble regretting the hatred and hostility between laity and clergy which had grown because of the heretical opinions spreading among the former and the 'vncharytable behaueour' of the latter; a new and lengthy conclusion asked the king to intervene and establish peace. It is therefore a finished document in itself, which suggests that the additional complaints outlined in B and transcribed in C_2 were brought forward afterwards. Although C_1 and C_2 make up between them the end of the Supplication's first stage, they were not written at the same time.

Where A had been little more than a list of heads, C_1 elaborated greatly. As already noticed, a long preamble and longer petitionary conclusion were the main improvements; furthermore, though no new point was actually added, some of the old ones were so far enlarged that the whole balance of the complaints appears to have shifted. The draft embodies the issues of law-making in Convocation[2] and the proctors of the Arches without material alteration, describes the grievances concerning frivolous summons and excommunication

---

[1] Cf. Cardinal Pole, 'Apologia ad Carolum Quintum Caesarem,' cap. xxvii–ix (*Epistolarum Pars Prima*, Brescia 1744). Pole outlines the political plan underlying the Henrician Reformation and categorically affirms (pp. 123–4) that he had often heard the ideas informing it from Cromwell and his circle. Pole left England in 1531, and his first and most memorable encounter with Cromwell was in Wolsey's day (p. 133).

[2] I.e. Cromwell's redrafting of A's first point.

along much the same lines as A though at greater length, and copies the scale of fees complained of. For the rest, however, some four pages are spent in detailing the abuses common, it is alleged, in trials in the spiritual courts which had found only bare indication in A.[1] They are arranged under four heads: arbitrary summons and imprisonment without bail or mainprise, use of perjured witnesses without remedy to the accused, subtle and unfair interrogation on charges of heresy,[2] and credit given to disreputable witnesses for the prosecution even if the accused can produce better witnesses on his side.

There may be some significance in a caret mark of Cromwell's placed against this virtually new section of the Supplication,[3] and there is more in the fact that script and appearance of C_1 hint strongly at an origin in Cromwell's own office;[4] together with the history of A and the few and immaterial corrections (all by Cromwell) in C_1,[5] these facts show who was behind the redrafting of the petition. Retaining the vital point of Convocation's law-making, Cromwell had now turned the Supplication into a full exposition of the main grievance genuinely entertained by the Commons against the Church courts: their fear of heresy proceedings conducted in an arbitrary and vindictive manner, the scales weighted against the accused, and the innocent unable to defend himself either because false witness was preferred to true or because the judges' subtlety led simple and harmless men to incriminate themselves in despite of the truth. These charges do not read like the trumped-up pretences of propaganda or the fruits of lawyers' rivalry for briefs; they read like the true feelings of men confronted with the technicalities of a machine which they could not understand but knew to be deadly in use.[6] It matters little whether

---

[1] C, fos. 109r–111r. The whole of C, can, of course, be read in Merriman, i. 104 ff.

[2] This is point 4 of A, much developed and much clearer.

[3] C_1, fo. 109r.

[4] As far as one can be certain with these rather impersonal clerkly scripts, it seems likely that C_1 was written by Ralph Sadler, at that time Cromwell's confidential clerk. This would tend to show that Cromwell personally took over the further development of the Supplication. Merriman also thought that the copy he printed (C) was written by Cromwell's 'chief clerk' (i. 104), but he appears to have overlooked the difference between the handwritings of C_1 and C_2.

[5] Of all Cromwell's corrections in C_1 only one seems to do more than slightly define or elaborate the meaning: on fo. 109v he added the words 'and that Secretlye and not in oppen placys' to the charge of arbitrary proceedings.

[6] [M. Bowker, 'Some Archdeacons' Court Books and the Commons' Supplication against the Ordinaries', *The Study of Medieval Records: Essays in Honour of Kathleen Major*, ed. D. A. Bullough and R. L. Storey (Oxford, 1971), 282–316, argues that the complaints were not justified, and that the Commons' main concern was with the danger that gentlemen might justly incur humiliating penalties.]

heresy trials were usually conducted in the fashion alleged; what matters is that men believed they were, and that in these complaints we hear the authentic voice of the Commons of England, as interpreted by the man who, through his activities in the 1529 session of this Parliament in which he had intended to make himself 'better regarded',[1] was quickly becoming their spokesman and leader. With that sense of the larger issues and of the value of concrete detail which is typical of all his work, Cromwell turned the Supplication into a comprehensive catalogue of genuine and legitimate grievances supporting the fundamental issue of the clergy's legislative authority.

In his search for weight and pressure Cromwell decided to include further grievances not necessarily connected with the courts of the Church but to be brought home to the hated ordinaries for the sake of uniformity. B, in a hand very different from that of A and much more fully corrected by Cromwell, appears to be a product of his office. That it was to be added to A is clear from the first words – 'Also where the said prelatis and ordynaries do permyt . . .' It discusses the fees for sacraments, bribes in court, and fees charged for institutions in the manner outlined above,[2] and complains further of nepotism and the bestowing of livings on minors,[3] and of the excessive number of holidays, detrimental both to the true observance of Church feasts and the prosperity of 'your comen welthe'. This last point, always one of the chief concerns of the English reformers, was to recur in Cromwell's Injunctions of 1536.[4] In 1529 he deleted the reference to the commonwealth and instead provided for 'the brekrs of the said contrary to such ordenaunce as shalbe deuysed for that purpose to be punysshed accordinglye' – quite a characteristic touch.[5] B with its corrections was copied into C$_2$ which was further corrected by Cromwell; these alterations are most of them of little importance, but it may be noted that Cromwell deleted the accusation that spiritual judges took bribes, presumably because it was rash and unprovable, a step which makes the charges left standing the more convincing.[6]

---

[1] George Cavendish, *Life of Wolsey* (ed. of 1852), 180.   [2] P. 117.

[3] '. . . the said Spirituall Ordynaries do dayly conferre and yeue sundry benyfices vnto certen young folkes calling them their nephewes . . .' (B, fo. 42). Despite this dry remark the real grievance was apparently not the immorality proved by these ostensible nephews, but that the ordinaries thereby acquired the profits of the livings, and that the 'poure selie sowles' of people in such parishes were deprived of the spiritual provision due to them.

[4] Burnet, *Hist. of the Reformation* (ed. Pocock), iv. 309.   [5] B, fo. 43.

[6] Apart from minor alterations, Cromwell's corrections in C$_2$ made more concrete the complaint of fees taken for sacraments, added 'or kynffolkes' to the alleged nephews

At this stage, then, the Supplication consisted of two parts, but for the moment no attempt was made to weld them together. The Supplication was laid aside, not to reappear for over two years. The first session was short – only six weeks;[1] the Commons spent all their time and energy on getting their three bills against ecclesiastical abuses through in face of strenuous resistance from the spiritual peers, and there was no time and probably little inclination to stir up a worse hornets' nest by attacking in the Church's jurisdiction one of its most cherished strongholds. Bishop Fisher's attack in the Lords may also have contributed to the dropping of these wider issues: the Commons' desire to forego none of that reputation for orthodoxy which Englishmen valued so much may explain why, after the charge of 'lacke of faith' and their indignant rejoinder, they could hardly go on with these quasi-heretical grievances. The accusations against the ordinaries were shelved, but not before Thomas Cromwell had realized the value of a line of attack which, starting from popular grievances, led through one of the king's tender points to the very heart of ecclesiastical liberties. At this time Cromwell was not yet connected with the government, far less the man behind the throne.[2] But he had his ambitions, and he had made a position for himself when such major issues could be entrusted to him; as he filed away the abortive drafts the thought of future use may well have occurred to him.[3]

of the ordinaries, and reinforced the point about holidays by inserting 'and specyall suche as shall fall in the heruest' (fos. 114v, 116v, 117r). This last section was altered a little from B before being committed to paper: in the place of the invocation of the commonwealth and Cromwell's substituted suggestion of penalties, C$_2$ hopes a reform in the matter would cause remaining holidays to be better observed 'to the laude of almyghty god and to thencrease of your high Honour and fame' – perhaps a better line to take with Henry.

[1] 3 November to 17 December 1529.

[2] This is not the place to discuss at length when and how Cromwell came to be the man behind the government's policy: analysis of his correspondence, together with some surviving evidence of his activities in Parliament and the general trend of events between 1529 and 1536, indicates that he did not gain the king's ear much earlier than the end of 1531 and was not in full control of events until about a year later. [Cf. *Tudor Revolution*, 71–98.]

[3] The fact that these drafts of the Supplication were kept by Cromwell is proved by endorsements on A and C$_2$ in the known hands of Cromwellian clerks; Cromwell's correspondence shows that the endorsing of papers kept by him was one piece of office routine he insisted upon. A document endorsed in the identical words used on A, and therefore A, is listed in a catalogue of his archives (*LP* vi, 229, ixD); it is unfortunately impossible to determine from the catalogue the date at which any item came into Cromwell's possession, such dates as are mentioned being quite unreliable.

v

There is no sign that the Supplication played any part in the session of January 1531; an autumn session had been intended that year,[1] but preparations for it had not included any matter connected with the Supplication.[2] However, the fact that a draft was to hand soon after the session opened, as well as the hint that an act rather than a petition was at one time contemplated, suggest that the final preparation of the Supplication was undertaken in readiness for the session of 1532. To judge from its appearance, D was drawn in Cromwell's office, for it is the only draft in the series which looks like all his parliamentary drafts; it may therefore be supposed that Cromwell submitted for consideration a version he had had drawn up from the drafts lying among his papers since 1529. This was then passed to the king's counsel learned in the law for final revision, the lead being taken by Audley who as Speaker would have to play an important part in steering the petition through the House. E, the Supplication as presented, was no doubt made up soon after; its exact date matters little. It must have been ready by the end of February when – as has been shown – discussion of grievances began again in the Commons. Hall remarked casually that the Supplication was drawn up 'by great aduyce'[3] and this is highly significant. In the use of the time the phrase cannot have meant anything except 'by the suggestion of the great and important men' – the king's councillors who sat in the House and guided its actions. It would have been easy for a councillor with one judicious speech to revive the whole complaint and then at the right moment to produce the draft Supplication, and while this is necessarily conjecture it fits in with everything we know of the history of the Supplication and the methods of management practised in the Tudor House of Commons.[4] Nor need we seriously doubt that if things happened in this way the man who handled it was Thomas Cromwell who had supervised the first stage of the Supplication and had brought it with him into the king's service.

[1] *LP* v. 559 (5).
[2] Ibid. no. 394; cf. *StP* i. 380 ff. Many of the bills and exchanges of land there mentioned took effect in the session of 1532.   [3] Hall, *Chronicle*, 784.
[4] Cf. W. Notestein, *The Winning of the Initiative by the House of Commons* (1924), 5 ff. Prof. Notestein recognizes the difficulties produced by insufficient evidence, but even his cautious account makes plain the influence of councillors in the Commons. Prof. Neale (*House of Commons*, esp. ch. xx) gives a full picture of the councillors' work in an Elizabethan Parliament; in this case it is permissible to argue that they would be even more influential in the less mature Parliament of Henry VIII's reign.

It may therefore be suggested that the whole course of the 1532 session had been planned in advance: the king's financial demands were introduced while the attack on the Church was held back, to be unleashed when the Commons had talked themselves into a bad temper; it did not prove difficult to start them off on the new (and old) track, and in the end they may well have believed, as Hall did, that they were again acting on their own initiative. The king could then offer to comply with their wishes against the Church if they complied with his wishes regarding wards and primer seisin. That purpose failed, for the bill did not pass in that session, but the government had sufficient use of their own for the Supplication to be content with pressing it home and securing the submission of the clergy. The man – whether it was Cromwell or Henry – who could hold a useful, important, and fully prepared measure back until it should be doubly useful by also relaxing hostile tension in the Commons, had nothing to learn about the arts of parliamentary management.

At least the argument shows that, when the second stage of the Supplication appeared in 1532, the Commons had no hand in it;[1] the document was now – though not in origin – but a skilfully used instrument in the government's campaign against the Church. What mattered in the end was that first paragraph which had immediately attracted Cromwell's attention in 1529, the paragraph accusing the clergy of making laws without the king's consent. Convocation was at the last compelled to face that accusation alone and to surrender on it, while the Commons' grievances concerning the spiritual courts were quietly dropped. However, while the Supplication was deliberately revived in 1532 as part of the government's programme, its contents were little different from those of the 1529 document which had represented the grievances of the laity fairly enough without any interference from the court.

The new form of the Supplication combined the two parts of which C had still been composed.[2] It began with the identical preamble, alleging that heretical literature and the uncharitable dealing of the ordinaries were causing much strife in the realm and asking the king to provide a remedy. It went on to the fundamental point of ecclesiastical

---

[1] This goes counter to Mr Ogle's theories about the Commons' watering down of the Supplication, designed, he thinks, to make it acceptable to the king (*Lollards' Tower*, 318). If watering down there was (which is by no means certain), it did not take place in the Commons' debates.

[2] In this discussion of C and D small differences affecting only a word or two and of no importance to the meaning will be ignored.

law-making, and while the general import of the complaint was unaltered there were some significant changes in the wording. The prelates and clergy 'beyng your subgettes' – an aside not to be found in C – made laws which not only affected the king's lay subjects, but (and in such force this is new) 'extende in certen casez to your excellent person, your libertie, and prerogatyf Roiall, And to the interdiccion of your londes and possession'; the king's interest in limiting Convocation's powers is much more stressed than before, and the subjects' troubles, though still fully set out, do not bulk so large.[1] Another new point is the mention of heresy, supposed to be the consequence of enforced ignorance of the law: the tone of the revised Supplication with its emphasis on unjustifiable accusations of heresy (which is a 'detestable cryme and synne') is set from the start.

This comes out most clearly in the second section of the new draft. One long paragraph sums up the detailed and diffuse complaints of C against the conduct of ecclesiastical courts, especially in heresy trials; every point previously alleged is included – frivolous or unjust summons and imprisonment, the *ex officio* procedure, traps set for the unlearned, use of false witness – 'So that euery your Subgettes vpon onely will and pleasure of the ordynaries, their Commyssaries and substitutes, may be infamyd vexid and trobled to the perill of their lifes, their shames costes and expenses.'[2] This, of course, was the true core of the Commons' genuine complaint, and the version of D, despite its concise brevity, was quite as complete as the several paragraphs of C.[3] But D was not content with this; it continued the point with a new and interesting assertion that 'it is not intendid . . . by this article to take away from the said ordynaries their auctorite to correct and ponysshe synne and especiall the detestable cryme of heresy'; if present legislation was insufficient, the Commons petitioned that 'ther may be devised and made more dredfull and terreble laws' to define heresy, as well as some regular means of summons, so that summons and trial for heresy might cease to be determinable at the 'only Will and pleasur' of the ecclesiastical judges.[4] This eager desire to see heresy suppressed,

---

[1] D, fo. 194. When D was drawn up C was not discarded; in correcting the paragraph the reviser brought back the phrase 'vnder the supportacion of your mageste' which had been in C but was dropped from D. [2] D, fo. 195.

[3] It will be convenient, in order to avoid burdening this paper with lengthy quotations, to point out that a comparison may now be made in print: the relevant parts of C are in Merriman, i. 106 ('And where . . . Lay Subiectes'); 106–8 ('And Furthermore . . . shame and vtter vndoing'); while Mr Ogle has printed E (though not D) in modernized spelling, the section concerned being that marked by him as II (*Lollards' Tower*, 325 f.).

[4] D, fos. 195–6.

if necessary by new and fiercer laws, reflects more accurately the mind of the king who was always ready to assert his orthodoxy and must have been particularly eager to do so at a time when he was at last seriously intending to attack the pope, than it reflects the secular temper of Cromwell; as for the Commons, who thought themselves orthodox enough but were the last persons deliberately to strengthen the hands of the spiritual courts, they – we know – did not insert this clause. The first hint at heresy in the Supplication actually occurs in Cromwell's preamble to C_1: as early as 1529 he knew well what manner of argument was likely to prevail with Henry.[1]

The attack on the independence of the Church was thus combined with an assertion of popular grievances suitably decorated to proclaim the unshaken orthodoxy and horror of heresy which, the king liked to declare, the nation shared with him. The remaining points can be dealt with briefly. The problem of the proctors of the Arches came next, to be followed by a new clause attacking citation out of a man's proper diocese.[2] The complaint against excessive fees charged in the courts was taken over from C, but then D went on to the breaches of the statutes concerning probate and mortuaries which have already been noticed.[3] The remaining paragraphs, dealing with money taken for induction to benefices, the conferring of livings on minors, and excessive holidays, were taken virtually without change from C_2, with Cromwell's corrections to that document now embodied in the text.

Finally, the concluding paragraph of C_1 was placed at the end of the whole document, with only one alteration worth noting. The king was now asked to provide a remedy for the evils complained of 'by the assent of the seid prelattes and other temporall noblez of this your

---

[1] C, fo. 105 ('new fantastycall and erronyous opynyons'); cf. above, p. 124. It is possible also – if I am right about the effect of Fisher's attack (above, pp. 120–1) – that this stress on heresy was designed to help the Commons over that particular hurdle.

[2] This clause (D, fo. 197) embodied and elaborated part of clause 3 in C (fos. 108r–v) which had discussed frivolous summons and the proctors' unpleasant way of getting money for absolutions from charges they had engineered, but citation out of the proper diocese was an addition. The inclusion of this complaint is interesting because in this same session of 1532 an act was passed against the abuse (23 Henry VIII, c. 9); nevertheless the complaint was retained, an inconsistency which Warham in his reply was not slow to point out (Gee and Hardy, 167). The word 'Citacon' in Audley's list of bills on the back of D proves that the act was ready while the Supplication was still drafting. The fact is that the paragraph in the Supplication, though partly concerned with the question of citation, was mainly directed against the malpractices of practitioners in the Church courts, and was possibly therefore allowed to stand although in part the complaint had already been covered by legislation.

[3] Above, pp. 117–18.

Realme with the comenz in this your most hy Court of parliament assemblide',[1] an addition which by asking for statutory enactments practically restored the request of A which had been altered so noticeably in the drawing up of C.[2] In a document not drafted by the House this cannot have been a sign of parliamentary independence, but reflects rather the new policy of Henry VIII and Cromwell who intended to put through the attack on Rome and the Church by means of acts of Parliament.

The corrections on D were many, but most of them merely added precision to points already stated: they were the corrections of lawyers dealing with a document they had not themselves conceived and did not really control, and the virtual absence of Cromwell's hand is significant. The Supplication was in fact finished when he handed it over to the king's legal counsel, though improvements in detail were still necessary. Two further complaints were added to those against individual priests and curates (the section dealing with probate and mortuaries): in some parts, it was alleged, double tithes were exacted 'ouer & besides the tythe for the catell that pastureth the same lond', and secondly, 'yf eny spirituall person hath opteyned the possession of any profites for the terme of xxx or xl yeres ageynst eny lay person . . . it ys seyd that prescripcion in ther lawe of suche litell terme of xxx or xl yeres makyth for them agood title ageyn eny lay person'.[3] In this latter complaint one seems to hear the voice of the common lawyer; the words 'in ther lawe' especially suggest the indignant query whether thirty years' possession really constituted a good title in the canon law, and if it did why the common law should put up with it.

One major alteration was made in D: the paragraph dealing with the proctors of the Arches was struck through and 'vacat' written against it, possibly by Cromwell. At first sight it is difficult to see why this effective argument, combining popular grievances with a defence of the prerogative, was jettisoned, but the explanation is perhaps to be found in the ordinaries' Answer. The charge concerning citations out of a man's proper diocese and frivolous excommunication on proctors' certificates only was answered by Warham in person, as touching him alone: he pointed out that he had reformed some of the things alleged twelve months earlier and others within the last ten weeks, 'as it is I suppose not unknown to your grace's Commons'.[4] Did he perhaps also relax his order limiting the number of proctors

---

[1] D, fo. 201.   [2] Above, p. 110.
[3] D, fo. 198.   [4] Gee and Hardy, 166.

in the Arches, thus anticipating the Commons' complaint and causing it to be dropped? Unfortunately it has proved impossible to discover any positive evidence,[1] but the correctors' action seems most readily explained in this way.

D having been drawn up and corrected, a fair copy was made (E) which it is reasonable to suppose was the Supplication as – if the interpretation here put forward is right – it was introduced by the government after discussion of the grievances had been deliberately revived. Whether further changes were made in the House it is impossible to say,[2] but any such thing is very unlikely in view of the fact that the ordinaries' Answer replied point by point to a document, which was either E or extremely like it.[3] Any changes made by the Commons must have been very minor ones, and the document prepared by the king's legal counsel before the opening of the session was to all intents the same as that submitted to the king as the Commons' petition on 18 March 1532.

VI

This is as far as we propose to follow the history of the Supplication in detail. Documents survive which make it possible to trace to some extent the gradual weakening of opposition in Convocation,[4] but

---

[1] No orders for the Arches between 1527 and 1532 are to be found in the 'Black Book of the Arches' at Lambeth Palace, or elsewhere there. The records of the court itself are well-nigh unapproachable, but I have been assured by Miss I. J. Churchill that they consist only of proceedings and the like and contain no administrative regulations.

[2] There is one correction in E (the few others merely correct writing errors) which deserves a little attention. In the section dealing with holidays complaint had been made that their excessive number led to 'many grete abhomynable and execrable vices, ydle and wanton Sportis', and in E the catalogue was continued by the interlineation of 'and plaies of the staige'. There is no sign of this addition in the ordinaries' Answer which quotes the rest of the passage (Gee and Hardy, 172). The handwriting, which resembles that of the rest of the document, is cramped, as though the writer had tried to imitate someone else's script, the ink is different, and the spelling – especially 'es' in place of the usual abbreviation for the plural ending – surprising: may it not be that the interlineation belongs to a later age – to that puritan attack upon the theatre which broke out in the early seventeenth century? It is, at least, not incredible that someone interested in giving his hatred of the stage respectable ancestry may have tampered with the document. The earliest date given by the *OED* for stage in the present sense is 1551 (s.v. 'stage', i. 5. a).

[3] The Answer (P RO, SP 6/7, art. 24) is printed by Gee and Hardy, 154 ff.

[4] Apart from the ordinaries' Answer (see previous note) there are the submission of 16 May 1532 (Wilkins, *Concilia*, iii. 755; Gee and Hardy, 176 ff.) and several drafts of replies to the king's demands (BM, Cleo. F. i, fos. 101 ff.) which are noted in *LP* v. 1018, and printed in F. Atterbury, *Rights, Powers and Privileges of Convocation* (1700), App. III, 464–71. Strype printed some documents concerning the submission in considerable confusion (*Eccl. Mem.* i, ch. 17).

the result was really determined once the king's three demands had been presented. Although Henry received the Supplication on 18 March, it did not come up in Convocation until 12 April, with a request for a speedy answer: this was produced by the 19th.[1] In the circumstances it was hardly fair of Henry to maintain that he had been unable to get a reply within three days before he passed the answer to the Commons on 30 April.[2] To the king it appeared 'very slender', and to Hall 'very Sophisticall and nothing auoydyng the greues of the lay people';[3] it hardly surprises to find that Gairdner thought it 'certainly a temperate and dignified reply'.[4] Temperate it may be called, and Henry's adjective seems inappropriate for a document which greatly exceeded the Supplication itself in length. However, it was sophistical: in a number of points the reply to specific charges confined itself to saying that such things, if practised, were illegal, but the writers were not aware of anyone so offending – a disingenuous attitude which it is not easy to describe as dignified. The ordinaries' request for cases and names was reasonable, but their reply often betrays an uneasy awareness of the truth of a general charge which nevertheless has somehow to be turned.[5]

At any rate the Commons took the royal hint and declared themselves dissatisfied, and Convocation resumed the discussion. On 8 May it was proposed to beat the Commons at their own game by presenting a clerical petition to the king for his kind favour, as hitherto shown to his lay subjects, and a deputation was sent to see Henry. But Henry had a different measure for his clergy; the mission failed miserably, and on the 10th Edward Foxe, one of those despatched but also a leading supporter of the royal policy, returned to present the famous three demands to Convocation. They were to agree to enact no constitutions without the king's assent, to allow a mixed commission of thirty-two to examine the existing canons, and to accept those left standing as the law of the Church, with the king's assent. With that skill in manoeuvre of which Henry and his Council had given such proof throughout the session, the king reinforced the impression made by Foxe and helped waverers to decide: on the next day, the 11th, he called the Speaker and twelve of the Commons to meet him, and after informing them of the bishops' oath to the pope which made the clergy 'but halfe our subiectes, yea, and scarce our subiectes', asked the

---

[1] Wilkins, *Concilia*, iii. 748.
[2] Hall, *Chronicle*, 788.
[3] Ibid.
[4] *LP* v, p. xix.
[5] Cf. e.g. Gee and Hardy, 169, 170, 171.

Commons 'to inuent some ordre, that we bee not thus deluded, of our Spirituall subiectes'.[1]

The threat worked, and despite some flickers of resistance, reflected in defiant drafts of replies to the king's demands, it took Convocation only a few days to make up its mind. On 16 May 1532 the Submission of the Clergy, a document embodying their complete surrender on the question of legislative independence, was presented to the king at Westminster.[2] There were present George Lord Abergavenny, John Lord Hussey, John Lord Mordaunt, Sir William Fitzwilliam, and Thomas Cromwell – an interesting group. The first two were old servants and soldiers of Henry VII's day and honorary household officials, Abergavenny as chief larderer and Hussey as chief butler; the first was to associate himself with Cromwell, while Hussey was to lend his support to the Pilgrims of Grace. Mordaunt, a younger man, was also closely connected with the household and a friend of Cromwell's.[3] Not one of the three was among the leaders of the Council, the king's chief ministers. The other two were men of the future – Fitzwilliam already an important man as treasurer of the Household, Cromwell only just an office-holder.[4] None of the great were there: More, who resigned the chancellorship that very day, Norfolk, or the earl of Wiltshire; only a few old associates, a leading household official, and the man who had brought with him, as part of a greater plan, the Supplication of whose workings he now witnessed the last scene. Cromwell had gained the king's ear, and for the next eight years he was to be, next to Henry, the most powerful man in England.

The history of the Supplication against the ordinaries is thus nothing like as simple as has been thought, and an attempt has here been made to solve the various problems set by the extant drafts. If the views put forward in this paper are right, it was in the first place the product of genuine grievances of the laity against the courts of the Church, and discussion of it began in 1529 when the matter was committed to Cromwell. Nothing came of it then, but he kept the drafts, and when the preparations for the third session were being made he brought them forward as a suitable weapon for bringing the clergy properly to heel. The draft he provided already laid more stress on the king's interests and the nation's orthodoxy than the earlier Commons' drafts had done, and the legal counsel who finished off the drafting

---

[1] Wilkins, *Concilia*, iii. 748–9; Hall, *Chronicle*, 788–9.
[2] *LP* v. 1023.   [3] For details cf. *DNB*.
[4] He was appointed master of the king's jewels on 12 April 1532 (*LP* v. 978 [13]).

added nothing of moment. Skilful manoeuvring in the Commons produced the right moment for reviving the subject of ecclesiastical jurisdiction, and after suitable debate a petition was resolved on and produced ready made. Just under a month after receiving the Supplication from the Speaker, Henry was gratified by the sight of Convocation surrendering their independence to him, and Cromwell's methods had proved triumphantly successful. The work of the 1532 session laid the foundation for that new polity, that new view of the jurisdictional authority of the Crown and the relations of state and Church, which was to find its clearest expression a year later in the preamble of the Act in Restraint of Appeals to Rome.

26

AN EARLY TUDOR POOR LAW*

While the secularization of poor relief was one of the outstanding achievements of the sixteenth century in most of Western Europe, England stood out because she developed machinery for administration and enforcement to which there was no parallel elsewhere. The basic problems were much the same everywhere: economic causes were producing unemployment and in consequence vagrancy, and traditional methods of relieving the needy were proving insufficient. Since the problem was a general one, the solutions put forward and adopted also had many points in common. The need to relieve the real poor, the desirability of putting the unemployed to work, insistence on organized collection of alms (whether voluntary or compulsory), in short, the responsibility of the lay power for the less fortunate of its subjects – all these appear in the legislation of continental towns like Augsburg or Rouen or Ypres, in the thought of reformers like Luther or Zwingli, in the schemes of theorists like John Major or Juan Luis Vives.[1] This general and natural agreement makes it very difficult to trace the influence of one scheme on another, or even to speak with much confidence of influence being exercised. Like problems tended to produce like answers, and English thought often arrived independently at much the same ideas as those evolved on the Continent.

In the end England produced the only really effective national system of poor relief – the great Elizabethan code of 1597 and 1601. It is generally agreed that nothing much was done until the reign of that queen, though acts were passed under the early Tudors. Some municipal authorities produced workable schemes in the first half of the sixteenth century, but the government took no serious action beyond repressing vagrancy by savage punishments.[2] Severe censures have

---

* [Econ. Hist. Rev., 2nd Series, 6 (1953), 55–67.]
[1] For continental poor relief, cf. F. R. Salter, Early Tracts on Poor Relief (1926); W. J. Ashley, Economic History and Theory (1888–92), ii. 340 ff.; R. Doucet, Les institutions de la France au XVIe siècle (Paris, 1948), ii. 810 ff.
[2] E. M. Leonard, Early History of English Poor Relief (Cambridge, 1910), 61: 'Before 1569 no effective system of poor relief had been established, but many experiments had been made.'

been passed on the statesmen of the reigns of Henry VIII and Edward
VI for their apparent failure to realize that a man might be poor and
workless through no fault of his own; as Professor Tawney has put
it: 'After three generations in which the attempt was made to stamp
out vagrancy by police measures of hideous brutality, the momentous
admission was made that its cause was economic distress, not merely
personal idleness.'[1] The indignation behind this view deserves respect,
even though it probably ignores the existence of the genuinely workshy
whom temporary experience of the easier life of the roads taught the
permanent advantages – such as they were – of vagrancy; that famous
Elizabethan underworld of cozeners and coney-catchers was not entirely populated by the innocent victims of economic distress.[2] Nor
should it be forgotten that theorists and statesmen were aware from
an early date of the part played in the creation of wandering bands of
beggars by such phenomena as enclosure, depopulation, and industrial
slumps. Legislation against these evils, however, proved ineffective,
and relief measures were slow in coming.

There were two stages in this legislation for relief. From the reign
of Richard II to 1531, little more was done than to punish vagrants and
talk piously about the need for charity to the genuinely poor. Begging
was to be controlled, not prohibited or replaced by organized relief.
The act of 1531 marked an advance of sorts.[3] It is still not admitted
that vagabondage and poverty may be due to anything but idleness
('the mother rote of all vyces'), but the body of the act makes a clearer
distinction between those able to work (who are to be whipped) and
those unable, and for the first time attempts to regulate the relief due
to the latter by allowing them to beg under licences enrolled by the
justices of the peace. But this licensing system was likely to break down
over the simple impossibility of keeping a constant check on beggars;
nothing had been laid down about the way in which work was to be
found for those capable of doing it, and opinion was altogether
turning against public begging. Thus another act was passed in 1536[4]

[1] *Religion and the Rise of Capitalism* (repr. 1948), 262 f.
[2] Cf. F. Aydelotte, *Elizabethan Rogues and Vagabonds* (Oxford, 1913).
[3] 22 Henry VIII, c. 12. It is possible that at this time, or a little earlier or later, poor relief
provisions of some interest (including the setting up of poor boxes and the collection
of an assessment) were put into a draft act 'for spiritual causes'; unfortunately, the document listed in *LP* v. 50, cannot now be traced at the Record Office, while the abstract
is quite insufficient. [Cf. above, p. 80, and *Reform and Renewal*, 71–7, for descriptions
of this document, discovered soon after this paper was written.]
[4] 27 Henry VIII, c. 25. Miss Leonard stated that this act 'was probably drawn up by the
king himself' (*Poor Relief*, 54). She gives no evidence for this assertion, and I think it

which has generally been taken as marking the beginning of the real Tudor poor law.[1] It was framed on new principles of which the three most important were these: work must be provided for those who cannot find it; begging is wrong and the helpless must be a charge on the community; the parish is to be the organization responsible for the task, and the justices of the peace must supervise it. The subsequent history of the poor law down to 1834 is the development of these principles and their application in practice.

However, at the outset of this new era there stood, not the somewhat ineffectual act of 1536, but a discarded draft of vastly greater scope, ingenuity, and originality.[2] It is the chief purpose of this article to rescue from oblivion a document which includes matter so revolutionary that it was never put into practice, as well as points which found their way into immediate and later legislation. It was written after the appointment of the commission which compiled the *Valor Ecclesiasticus* (30 January 1535);[3] indeed, the words of the draft, in speaking of the 'late Comyssioners appoynted for the valuacion of spirtualties',[4] are strong suggestion that the return had by then been made. This would put the date of composition into the autumn of 1535.[5] That it was intended for the session of 27 Henry VIII, which opened on 4 February 1536, is twice mentioned in the document itself.[6] Nothing except a full transcript could altogether convey its special air of competence and completeness, but its length – thirty-three folios written on front and back – precludes an operation which would also involve much tiresome repetition. It is hoped that relevant quotations, lengthy at times, will supply an acceptable compromise.

The preamble must be given in full. It represents a thorough and

---

must be wrong. It cannot be shown that Henry drew up any acts at all in his reign, though very occasionally he corrected one. That the statute emanated from the government need not be in doubt, but we know from many a draft who the man in charge of government legislation was at this time. Thomas Cromwell perhaps was behind this act, but certainly not the king.

[1] Cf. W. S. Holdsworth, *History of English Law*, iv. 392 ff.

[2] The draft is in the BM, Royal MS 18 C. vi (hereafter cited as 'draft'). It is not calendared in *LP*; the Royal MSS were first properly catalogued in 1921, and the draft was not listed in the older catalogues. Its only mention, as far as I am aware, before this is in Schanz, *Englische Handelspolitik*, ii. 478 n. Schanz describes the draft well enough, but his deductions and comment are sadly astray; he also misled Ashley (*Econ. Hist.*, ii. 358), who added some imaginative embroidery of his own.

[3] *LP* viii. 129 (1).   [4] Draft, fo. 6v.

[5] The *Valor* was generally completed by June, though some returns did not come in till September (J. Hunter, in his introduction to the *Valor Eccl.*, Record Commission, p. 25). Draft, fos. 10, 10v.

logical classification of the poor, and its language is remarkably free both from the sentimentality which sees only innocent victims and the brutality which sees nothing but idle knaves.[1]

Forasmoche as the Kynges Maiestie hathe full and perfite notice that ther be within this his Realme aswell a right grete multitude of strong valiaunt beggers, vacabundes, and idle persones of bothe kyndes, men and women, which – though they myght well labour for ther livyng if they wolde – will not yet put themself to it as dyuers other of his true and faithfull subiectes do, but geue themself to lyue idlely by beggyng and procuryng of Almes of the people to the high displeasure of almyghty god, hurte of ther owne soules, euyll example to other, and to the grete hurte of the comen welthe of this Realme; as also dyuers other olde sicke lame feble and impotent persones not able to labour for ther livyng but ar dryuen of necessite to procure thalmes and charite of the people. And his highnes hathe perfite knowlage that som of them haue fallen into such pouertie onely of the visitacion of god, through sickenes and other casualties, and some through ther owne defaulte, whereby they haue come fynally to that poynte that they coulde not labour for any part of ther livyng, but of necessite ar driven to live holy of the charite of the people. And that some haue fallen to such mysery through the defaulte of ther maisters which haue put them out of seruyce in tyme of sickenes and left them hooly without relief or comforte. And some be fallen therto through default of ther frendes which in youthe haue brought them vp in ouermoche pleasure and idlenes and instructed them not in any thyng wherwith they myght in age gett ther livyng. And some haue set such as haue ben vnder ther rule to procure ther livyng by open beggyng euen from childehod, so that they neuer knewe any other waie of livyng but onely by beggyng – And so for lacke of gode ouer-sight in youthe many live in grete mysery in age. And some haue comen to such myserie through ther owne defaulte, as through slouthe pride negligence falsehod and such other vngraciousnes, wherby ther maisters louers and ffrendes haue ben driven to forsake them, and fynally noman wolde take them to any seruyce, wherby they haue in processe of tyme lyen in the open stretes and fallen to vtter desolacion. And dyuers other occasions haue brought many to such pouertie, which wer very long to reherse here. But whatsoeuer thoc-casion be, charite requyreth that some waie be taken to helpe and socour them that be in such necessite, and also to preuent that other shall not hereafter fall into like mysery.

Here, for once, we see the sixteenth century looking with open eyes at the failures of its society. The workshy are separated from the willing and helpless, and the latter are classified into the victims of circumstance (and act of God), of a faulty or vicious upbringing, and of their own

---

[1] Ibid. fos. 1–2v. Throughout I have modernized the punctuation and extended abbreviations; the spelling remains unchanged.

folly. There are points missing which are obvious to the modern student, surveying the business four hundred years later, but at least there is here no moralizing on idleness; this preamble reveals a thoughtful economist of common sense and compassion.

Diagnosis was one thing – later statutes were to be nearly as plain about it as this draft; but no statute ever succeeded as this did in evolving machinery for dealing with sturdy vagabonds. That those who can work should be set to work was and is a commonplace, and the great Elizabethan statutes provided for such employment locally and on local responsibility. But this draft was much bolder. It proposed to solve the problems of unemployment by a comprehensive, though short-term, scheme of public works. A body called the 'Councell to aduoide vacabundes', consisting of eight members, five at least to be a quorum, was to be set up to superintend

certeyn comen workes, aswell for makyng of the Hauen of Douer, renouacion and reparacion of other hauens and harbours for shippes, as for makyng of the comen high waies and ffortresses, skowryng and clensyng of watercourses through the Realme.

The council was to take up its duties on the first day of the coming Easter Term (1536), 'and to contynue foreuer'; the works which it appointed were to start on 1 March 1537 and to stop, in the first instance, at Michaelmas 1540. Later clauses empowered the council to make ordinances concerning the works and the administration of relief, to appoint salaries for subordinate officials, and to punish offenders against its orders. Such wide powers of delegated legislation were unusual in scope, though they did not differ in principle from those enjoyed, for instance, by the court of Augmentations. What was exceptional was that this council's orders were to be proclaimed in like manner as proclamations made by the king and Privy Council.[1] Each piece of work was to be in the charge of a deputy appointed by the council. A week before the work was to start, proclamations would be made, and all able-bodied unemployed were to report for duty. They were to receive 'reasonable wages', and the money due ('besides mete and drynke') was to be kept until enough had accumulated to clothe the man. Vagabonds failing to report were to be arrested and brought to the place of work. If the man proved obdurate he was to be taken before a justice of the peace, and being there convicted, on the word of three lawful witnesses

[1] Draft, fos. 29–30v.

of his refusell to labour, or of his contynuall loitryng, or of any sedition, vnlawfull meane, corrupt councell, or practice to make murmuracion grudge insurrection in and emong the rest of the laborers,

he was to be gaoled until the next market day. Then he was to be publicly burned in the ball of the right thumb, 'as Clerkes that take ther bokes for felonye ben on the lefte honde', and discharged. If branded vagabonds were apprehended who could not prove that they had been engaged on the public works during the preceding four weeks or could not show some just impediment, they were to be indicted for felony at 'the next Sessions'.[1]

The basis of the draft was, then, a great and astonishing scheme of labour, to be administered by a central board through the direction of local officers responsible to it. The remarkable vision and enterprise of such an idea early in the sixteenth century does not need stressing. Hardly less remarkable is the comparatively mild treatment of strikers, agitators, and incorrigible rogues. They would, in fact, be given two chances of mending their ways, with nothing worse than forcible rounding up and a little light branding to jog their obstinacy; and only if they refused what must, in sixteenth-century conditions, be called the authorities' long-suffering kindness, were they to suffer the rigour of the law. They would not even be proceeded against unless three good witnesses bore testimony, two more than were required to swear a man's life away for treason.[2] For the device of public works to cure unemployment there was no precedent in England, nor has such a step ever been taken under the direction of the central government; the thought proved sterile. No genuine foreign influence seems to be discoverable, either, and one feels that the scheme was the author's own.

That these public works would have to be paid for was not overlooked.

And for the bearyng of the charges of theseid workes and for the relief of theseid vacabundes, *The Kynges* grace, of a speciall zeale and loue that he hathe to the welthe of all his subiectes, will geue to the furtheraunce of theseid workes as by his highnes shalbe thought conuenyent.[3]

But, realizing no doubt that to rely exclusively on the royal benevolence would hardly be sound policy, the draft went on to decree an

---

[1] Ibid. fos. 3–6.

[2] It was only in 1551–2 that *two* witnesses were demanded in treason trials, and even this remained not incontestable until 1696 (Holdsworth, *Hist. of Eng. Law*, iv. 499).

[3] Draft, fo. 6. The words 'his . . . conuenyent' were substituted for 'theseid Councell shalbe appoynted and thought convenyent' – i.e. that the council would fix the king's contribution! Probably this was only a slip of the pen.

annual[1] levy or graduated income tax. It lists six separate groups affected, though unfortunately the sums to be paid by each are left blank: ecclesiastical dignitaries[2] with an annual income of £100 or over; the same with £20 or over; all temporal lords and laymen with £100 annual income from land ('of enheritaunce or by ffees'), or worth £1,000 in moveables; the same with £20 in income; the same with £5 in income or £20 in moveables; all the rest except some exempt persons – femes covert, apprentices, 'such as live of the charges of ther frendes without wages', and any certified by the churchwardens of their parish as unable to pay. It was a comprehensive catalogue, and one would gladly know what percentage of the national income this radical reformer was proposing to distrain for his scheme of social relief.[3] In addition, there was to be a collection of contributions in parish churches appointed for the purpose, a box being set up in the church 'before the sacrament there as nygh as can be reasonably deuysed', with three keys – one to the parson, one to the churchwarden, and one to the local deputy who took charge of the money and gave a bill of receipt to the other two.[4]

The next clause is so extraordinary that it deserves quoting in full.

It is also enacted by thauctorite aforeseid that if any such vacabunde and idle persones be sicke, which of likeliod myght well labour if they were hoole, that then theseid deputies shall assigne certeyn Phisicians and Surgeons to loke vnto and remedie ther diseases; And that thesame Phisicians and Surgeons shalbe paied for ther labour and paynes in and about the curyng and helpyng of the sicke and sore vacabundes and idle persones, as is aboueseid, of theseid moneye and of thother charite of the people; And when such sicke and sore persones ben cured and heled, then they to be put to labour in theseid workes vnder the paynes before expressed.[5]

The poor were to have free medical attention, at the public expense. With its stress on the cure of unemployment and wholesale income taxes and this last amazing provision, the draft would almost seem to have anticipated much of very recent happening, though admittedly its concern in curing the poor was to make them fit for work. But even that was much better than leaving them in diseased idleness.

---

[1] That these sums were to be levied every year and not only once appears solely from a chance remark on fo. 9v.

[2] 'Euery Archebisshop, Bisshop, Abbot, Abbesse, priour, priouresse, Master or warden of College, Maister of hospitall, Archedeacon, Dean, prouost, prebendary, parson, vicar, and euery other persone that hathe office, dignyte, or promocion spirituall . . .' The dignitaries with £20–100 naturally do not include bishops or archbishops. The *Valor* was to be used in assessing income.

[3] Draft, fos. 6v–7v.   [4] Ibid. fos. 8–8v.   [5] Ibid. fo. 9.

A few more clauses concluded this part of the draft. Unlicensed departure from the works was to be felony. The collection of the annual levy was to cease at Michaelmas 1540, 'as the workes aforerehersed do'. All commissions of the peace were to be renewed before 24 June 1536, with an additional clause (given in full and in Latin) ordering the carrying out of the present act and all ordinances to be made 'per Senatum siue Concilium selectum et ordinatum per idem Parliamentum'. (The council was to be appointed by Parliament inasmuch as the names would be listed in the proper act; in the draft they are represented by the letters A to H only.) The document further recites the oath to be taken by all local government officials in shires, cities, boroughs, and towns, swearing to enforce the act and the council's ordinances.[1]

So much for the first and most striking part of the draft. In order to deal with those vagabonds and valiant beggars who were strong enough to work but either could not or would not find employment, the state was to provide useful public works much needed at the time;[2] a special department of state – for that is what it amounts to – was to be set up to administer the scheme, with powers to make administrative orders and appoint local officials; the nation was to pay for it by a graduated income tax; the local magistrates and police officers were to assist in enforcing the duty to work on recalcitrant beggars; and labourers in ill health were to receive attention at the public expense. The scale and scope of the plan are breath-taking, even if they must raise immediate doubts as to its practicability. But there can be no question that the author of this draft believed in going to the root of things and in applying drastic remedies; that he limited the operation of his scheme in the first place to three and a half years does not mean that he did not intend to prolong it before it expired. Possibly, however, he may have hoped to cure unemployment in a few years, or doubted the capacity of the state to find enough roads and harbours to supply work for a longer period. Or again he may have had prudent doubts about his ability to persuade Parliament to vote heavy taxation for more than a few years.

The draft next turned to the other class of poor – those too old, weak, or sick to work, and therefore in need of relief. It recognized that legislation as such would do little good unless it were consistently

---

[1] Draft, fos. 10v–11.

[2] The repairing of harbours and defences, in particular, is a point that often comes up in Thomas Cromwell's notes of things to be attended to (e.g. *LP* vii. 420; viii. 527, 1077).

enforced, and that the justices, mayors, and the like, whom previous acts had made responsible for the little that was attempted, were likely to be too busy on other matters. They were therefore enjoined to meet once a year, starting before Michaelmas 1536, in such convenient places within their jurisdictions as they thought best, and there to appoint two 'Censours or Ouerseers of pouertie and Correctours of Idlenes' for each parish, choosing them from four men presented by the relevant constables.[1] These censors were to be the essential element in the system. To ensure their attention to the work they were to hold no other office and were even freed from jury service.[2] They were answerable to the justices in quarter sessions who could imprison them for neglect, to await punishment by the council to avoid vagabonds.[3] Their duties were many and heavy. Once a month they were to search out all idle vagabonds in their parish and bring them before the justices for punishment.[4] They were to discover and report all the impotent and sick poor whom the justices would then convey to a hospital or other suitable place, if necessary at the public expense.[5] Thirdly, their monthly search was to include all those in misfortune – honest men who cannot live on their earnings 'by reason of multitude of children or other honest cause', or who have come to extreme poverty through 'sickenes, fyre, water, robberie, or otherwise'; these were to have assistance in the form of public alms by order of the justices acting upon the censors' certificates.[6] They were to take all healthy begging children between the ages of five and fourteen and apprentice them to masters, first clothing them suitably out of the poor box; children between twelve and fourteen who proved refractory were to be 'whipped with roddes' at the justices' orders, as often as was necessary.[7]

The money obtained by the general levy and the triple-locked chest in the parish church was only designed to pay for the public works; as regards the needs of the sick and unfortunate, the author came out strongly against indiscriminate charity as an encouragement to open begging. He made it an offence punishable by a fine of 40s. to give, 'in money, mete, drynke, or clothyng', to sturdy beggars, though apparently he permitted some assistance to the genuine poor.[8] Since men were in any case averse to charity towards vagabonds and only

---

[1] Draft, fos. 11v–13v.
[2] Ibid. fos. 26v–27v.
[3] Ibid. fos. 28–28v.
[4] Ibid. fo. 14.
[5] Ibid. fos. 14–15v.
[6] Ibid. fos. 15–15v.
[7] Ibid. fos. 20v–21.
[8] Ibid. fos. 19–20. He excepted 'the power sicke sore aged impotent and feble neighbours, and such as be not able to get ther livyng holy by labour'.

paid them blackmail under duress, a clause which punished the victim rather than the source of intimidation was not likely to prove effective. Ordinarily, however, alms were to be administered by the authorities. Every week the censors were to appoint one to three poor men, to go round the parish 'with a Maunde or basket and a Tankerd or pot, knockyng at euery doore', to collect spare food and drink for the poor. Even these men were given an official title – 'bedelles of the pouertie within the parisshe of A'. The stocks, bread and water, and finally the withdrawal of the dole and compulsory labour – by these means the overseers were to make sure of their beadles' honesty and efficiency.[1]

As for alms of money, there was first to be some vigorous encouragement of charitable feelings among the people. To this intent, the 'Ordynaries of euery Diocesse' (the bishops, that is) were to supply to every parson, before Michaelmas 1536,

a compendious sermon or collacion wherin the manyfold vertues of charite, and how meritorious it is in the sight of god, And what guardon or rewarde is prepared for such as vse thesame; And also the manyfold vertues of labour and occupacion, and howe highly it is commended by scripture, And how holsome it is for the body, and on thother side how odious the vice of slouthe and Idlenes is in the sight of god, And how pernicious it is to the carnall body [are set out].

This sermon the parish priest was to read on Sundays and holidays 'in the high masse tyme', improving the occasion as best he could, and exhorting the people to almsgiving. He was to appoint two 'honest persones of the parisshe' to collect alms in the church; they were to hand them for immediate distribution to the overseers (who had charge also of all money left to charity by testament), and provision was made for failure on anybody's part to carry out these complicated instructions.[2] Ordinary alms would never, therefore, have to be accumulated, since it was thought that the censors would make assignment on each occasion; yet there was to be an alms box in the church, doublelocked with a key each to parson and overseers, to store the half of each 40s. fine levied on those who continued to practise private charity towards the undeserving poor.[3] The draft has no inkling of a compulsory poor rate to replace all private charity; compulsion is applied only to the financing of the public works, while poor relief proper continued to depend on private conscience and voluntary alms, even though much organized pressure is exerted.

There now remain only a few odd points to mention. Shipwrecked

---

[1] Ibid. fos. 17v–18v. [2] Ibid. fos. 16–17, 18v–19.
[3] Draft, fos. 20–20v.

mariners[1] were to be given food and lodging for one day and one night, after which (unless they wished to find work locally) they were to return to their place of birth or proper residence, being passed from town to town at the expense of 'the comen Treasure or Chamber of euery such Citie borough or Towne'.[2] Justices, mayors, and so forth, were empowered to permit the victims of natural disasters, robbery, and sickness 'to make and procure asmany games of shotyng for his & ther relief and furtheraunce as shalbe thought expedient'; all other such games were forbidden, unless a justice of the peace was present.[3] The last clause but one seems to have wider application than the relief of poverty. It orders that

euery persone and persones that hereafter shalbe before any whatsoeuer Iusticiar delyuered for suspicions of felonye by proclamacion, or be acquyted of any felonye by verdyt or by the Kynges generall pardon

shall be discharged immediately and without payment of any fee to any officer, sheriff, clerk of the peace, or anyone else.[4] While it is possible that only such people were meant as were charged under the ordinances of the council to avoid vagabonds, the clause suggests that a remedy was provided for a more general grievance; bribery may often have been necessary before even an acquitted man could regain his freedom.

The draft concludes with a list of various kinds of people to be included among the vagabonds punishable under the act, a list which is both so interesting in itself and so strikingly phrased that it deserves extended quotation:

seruyng men comenly called Ruffelers which be retayned in no man his wages but lyve idlely in Cities and Townes (and namely in the Citie of london), procuryng and makyng assaultes and affraies, hauntyng and frequentyng the Tauerne and vicious places; Scolers of the vnyuersitees of Oxforde and cambridge that go about beggyng without sufficient authorite; Shipmen pretendyng naufrages or hurt in the Kynges wares or seruyce . . . ; proctours and pardoners goyng about and not autorized by the Kinges highnes; and all other persones . . . vsyng and practisyng dyuers and subtyll craftes and vnlawfull games, that is to seye, dise, cardes, bowles, Closshe, tenes, or other new inuented or to be inuented games,[5] which cannot dispende yearly of fee, inheritaunce, or by his wages, fyue poundes, or is not worthe in mouable goodes xl li'; And such as

[1] Victims of 'naufrage'.   [2] Draft, fos. 21v–23.
[3] Ibid. fos. 23–23*b*. I confess that I do not understand how a game of archery (if that is what it was) could assist in poor relief, unless a man could earn money by arranging one.
[4] Ibid. fos. 31–31v.
[5] Similar lists of forbidden games are found in earlier legislation, e.g. 12 Henry VII, c. 12.

147

pretende knowlege and conyng in physik, surgery, phiysnamye, palmestrie, destenyes, or other craftie sciences wherby the poore rude and innocent people is disceived; Syngle women livyng by thabomynable vice of Lechery which shalbe founde loitryng in the Contrey; And generally all and euery persone and persones which shall contynue out of seruyce by the space of xl daies . . .

What a picture, not unfamiliar though it is, of the roads of Merrie England – with its brawlers and drunkards, its wandering but far from innocent scholars, its pardoners, its cheats and quacks and prostitutes! No one can deny them colourfulness, but to-day, when we are no longer in danger of having our heads broken or our purses cut by them, it is fatally easy to grow sentimental over these ruffians. One may prefer to take a contemporary's word for it, believing that the criminal classes at least existed before 'the rise of capitalism'.

It is plain, of course, that even this draft made no attempt to deal with the deeper economic and moral evils from which pauperism sprang – evils it so competently diagnosed in the preamble. But that could hardly be its purpose: other legislation was required (and existed) to prevent depopulation and the like, and this act was intended to cure symptoms only. Apart from the notable scheme of public works, it is the administrative machinery provided in the draft which strikes one as most impressive. Through the whole of it there runs a deliberate preoccupation with organization and the means of enforcement, and the author is in no way afraid of creating office after office. At the head of the whole scheme he puts his council, a virtual ministry of social welfare, empowered to legislate and enforce its decrees, and charged with the supervision of both public works and public relief. Under them there are, on the one hand, the deputies commanding individual works – purely administrative officials, these. On the other hand, there are the justices of the peace and equivalent borough officials who have to see to the local enforcement of the orders received from the council as well as of the act itself. Furthermore, as there are executive officers in charge of the works, so permanent executive officers are required for the relief of the impotent poor and the searching out of vagrants. Thus we have the censors or overseers on whom in practice the effectiveness of the act depends even more than it does on the other officials mentioned. They in their turn appoint the beadles who collect spare food and drink, while they are associated with the clergy responsible through collectors (sidesmen) appointed by them for the collection of alms which the overseers distribute.

The creation of suitable machinery has already been mentioned as the specific achievement of the English poor law. This draft sets the tone very determinedly, inventing much more boldly than the Elizabethan acts were prepared to do. It also embodied all the rest of the principles which were to govern future action – the responsibility of the lay power, the need to provide work, the prohibition of begging, the parish organization. Its general levy foreshadowed the later poor rate which was also in the first place intended to make possible the purchase of materials for the unemployed to work on. In nearly all its provisions it either went as far as the completed poor law was to go, or very much farther than any English government ever found itself able to go. The appointment of parish overseers and the effective supply of work, which are supposed to make the acts of 1572 and 1576 a new departure,[1] are here worked out; the least one can say is that the statesmen of Elizabeth's reign are more likely to have learned these principles from this draft than from the practice of local authorities or the precepts of continental reformers at work in Edward VI's England, both of which have been invoked for this purpose.[2] Some of the phrases listing classes of rogues, which close the draft, recur almost word for word in the Elizabethan poor law;[3] it does not look as though the draft failed to attract notice in the second half of the century.

Of more immediate importance, however, is its relationship with the act actually passed in 1536, the act which apparently took the place of the draft and therefore needs a little closer attention. Although ostensibly passed to deal with the question of men out of work, it devotes little time to them, only declaring that local officials must find work for the unemployed. Its main concern is with a new way of relieving the needy: open begging is forbidden, town officers and churchwardens are to make a collection of alms every Sunday and holiday, and the money is to be put in 'common boxes' in the parish church.[4] The sole exceptions to the general rule against private alms-giving are private charity within a man's own parish and alms to prisoners (sect. xxi); the exceptions added in a separate schedule (sects. xxiv–xxviii) must be ascribed to changes made in Parliament under pressure from the Houses since they make mention of friars and monasteries who were already condemned to extinction in the plans of the government. On the large lines, therefore, the act as passed is very similar

[1] 14 Eliz., c. 5; 18 Eliz., c. 3. Cf. Leonard, *Poor Relief*, 70 ff.
[2] Ibid. pp. 61 ff.; C. Hopf, *Martin Bucer and the English Reformation* (Oxford, 1946), 116 ff. (for a cautious view). [3] E.g. 39 Eliz., c. 4, sect. ii.
[4] 27 Henry VIII, c. 25, sects. iv, xiii, xvii–xix.

to the draft: work is to be found for the unemployed, and voluntary charity is to be organized in each parish so as to abolish indiscriminate almsgiving. The resemblance of act and draft appears even more clearly from some of the details. Sect. vi orders local officials to apprentice pauper children to masters and to give them 'a raiment to entre into suche service' from the alms; older children refusing to work are to be whipped. This clause is so like the corresponding provision in the draft that it seems to be based upon it. In sect. ix the clergy are exhorted to take every opportunity to preach in favour of alms; the draft is more specific, but the idea is the same. Vagabonds found idle a second time are punished with whip and ear-cropping; a third offence makes them felons (sects. x–xi). The details vary a little from the draft; the principle is the same. Every week some of the poor are to be appointed to collect surplus meat and drink (sect. xvi); these are the beadles of the draft. There are, of course, differences, and in one or two points the act is more precise than the draft.

The poor law of 1536, the law which inaugurated the era of real poor relief legislation, was thus based on the draft which we have discussed at such length. From the draft the act took all that was new in its principles, but it dropped all the new machinery which alone gave reality to good intentions. Not only did it discard altogether the scheme of public labour, contenting itself with vague phrases, and the council which would have given to poor relief a more constant and effective attention than the Privy Council could spare time for; it even discarded the parish overseers. It was naturally this absence of machinery, no less than the voluntary nature of the alms, that rendered the act ineffective. However, it retained enough of the draft to have made it appear ever since the first of a series of enactments which, partly by reincorporating details dropped in 1536, were in the end to give England her remarkable system of poor relief.

Thus this draft is very important in the history of the attempts made by Tudor governments to solve the problem of pauperism. Yet it does not look in the least like a government draft. I have discussed the characteristics of such 'proper' drafts elsewhere;[1] this manuscript, with its small pages, its writing upon both sides of the paper, its clerkly but unfamiliar script, is quite unlike the real thing. Striking proof of its unofficial origin is found in small points like the use of 'senatus' to describe the council for vagabonds, or of 'censors' as an alternative

---

[1] Above, pp. 64–5.

title for parish overseers. These terms suggest the mind and tongue of the humanist; there is nothing like them in the known work of government draftsmen. Yet the document is among the British Museum's Royal Manuscripts and very probably belongs to those which entered that collection from Thomas Cromwell's papers; that is, it found its way into government circles.[1] It was used in preparing the official act of 1536, and its influence can be traced in later legislation. Though it, therefore, came from outside the government, it was known to it; does this offer a clue to its author? The man to fill the bill must be a pamphleteer with an interest in social reform; he ought to be a humanist and – because of his opposition to indiscriminate charity – a reformer in religion;[2] he must have had a connection with the government, for his plan was either communicated and in part adopted, or (which is more likely) was commissioned when the need for another poor law became apparent. In a shadowy manner the author shows signs of belonging to that circle of clients, servants, and remote followers which grew up round Thomas Cromwell in the 1530s – men who were to him both propagandists and planning staff.[3]

As it happens, there was a man among them who answers the requirements listed to a satisfyingly complete degree. In 1535, Thomas Godfray, printer of London, brought out, under the title *The maner of Subuention of poore people*, a translation of the relief ordinances made in 1525-9 by the town of Ypres. The translation was by one William Marshall, himself a printer on occasion, but like so many of his profession at the time also a pamphleteer and ardent reformer.[4] His chief claims to fame are the reformist *Primer* of 1535 and the translation which he made and printed of Marsiglio's *Defensor Pacis*. This latter work

---

[1] Cf. *Catalogue of Western MSS. in the Old Royal and King's Collections* (1921), i. p. xvi, for the fact that some of the volumes in the collection 'evidently' once belonged to Cromwell. Like our draft, the volumes thus identified were omitted from the old catalogues.

[2] Cf. Salter, *Early Tracts*, 33, 76 ff., on the orthodox judgment of the Sorbonne in 1531. Admittedly the doctors made exceptions to the rule of no organized almsgiving, even as the draft does; but they started from the premise that it is lawful and not punishable to give at any time and anywhere, while the draft adopted the 'reformed' opinion that this is not so and allows exceptions only as necessities. On the Lutheran and Calvinist views, cf. Tawney, *Religion*, 92, 114 f.

[3] Cf. for some light on this group, W. G. Zeeveld, *Foundations of Tudor Policy* (Cambridge, Mass., 1948). Mr Zeeveld errs, it seems to me, in seeing in these men originators of ideas rather than disseminators – a source of inspiration for action rather than of comment upon it. [I now think Zeeveld was right rather than wrong in this: cf. below, no. 32.]

[4] Marshall's translation is conveniently reprinted in Salter, *Early Tracts*, 36 ff. On the man himself, cf. *DNB*, and E. G. Duff, *A Century of the English Book Trade* (1905), 99 f.

was commissioned by Cromwell who advanced Marshall £20 for the production.[1] That the printer was certainly well acquainted with the minister is also confirmed by another of Cromwell's correspondents who, deploring Marshall's extremism in religion, remarked that 'ye know what Marshall is'.[2] The pamphleteer was something of a stormy petrel. In 1534 he corresponded with a discontented Oxford scholar on the iniquities of heads of houses and the lack of learning in the University, while in 1535 he tried his eager hand at persuading the recalcitrant Carthusians to the right way by distributing copies of Marsiglio.[3] In August 1536, at a time when the government were cautiously advancing towards Lutheranism, Marshall wrote a sententious letter to Cromwell in which he bewailed the fate of poor people persecuted for heresy, warned the lord privy seal against flatterers, and sent him a sermon for edification;[4] Cromwell's patience must have been greater than he is usually given credit for. Marshall was, then, a man who held advanced views in religion, translated and published propaganda material, and was employed by Cromwell in his most enterprising pamphleteering venture.

To cap it all: in the very year (1535) when our draft was written, Marshall proved his interest in matters of poor relief by translating a recent continental ordinance on the subject and publishing it with a dedication to Queen Anne Boleyn. It would be convenient if easy parallels could be drawn between the Ypres *Forma Subventionis Pauperum* and the draft, but matters are not arranged with such admirable simplicity. In any case, two points rob such arguments of much force. As has already been said, progressive ideas on poor relief were much the same in a number of places; while, secondly, Marshall especially stressed that he was not putting the Ypres scheme forward as the best available:

Nat that my meaninge is . . . so highly to esteme this maner and forme of subuention and helpynge that none coulde be deuysed so good or better or that I wold haue it obserued and kepte of ineuytable necessytie bycause it lyketh me or yet that I (beyng baren of wytte lernynge and experience) wolde to ostente and bost my selfe and take vpon me to be a prescriber and teacher yea of any man in this behalfe.[5]

---

[1] *LP* vii. 422–3; xi. 1355.   [2] *LP* ix. 345.

[3] *LP* viii. 600; ix. 283, 523. Mr Zeeveld's doubts of this story (*Foundations*, 133, n. 13) are due to an error he makes in his dates. Marshall's activities did of course take place before the executions, and the evidence offers no difficulty on that score. [We were both wrong: *Policy and Police*, 210, n. 2.]

[4] *LP* xi. 325.   [5] Salter, *Early Tracts*, 32.

He was only publishing the ordinance in order to draw the attention of king and Council to the problem. Though deeply interested in the whole question he held no special brief for this particular solution; may one not suppose – despite, or even because of, his mock-modest disclaimer – that his interest was also finding expression in ideas of his own? If Cromwell was engaged upon the preparation of a poor law, either because it was in any case necessary or because the forthcoming Dissolution made it an urgent matter, would he not most likely commission a draft from that one of his pamphleteers who had recently proved his special knowledge by printing a book on the subject?

These are conjectures, though of a kind that ought to carry some weight; unfortunately, little positive evidence is forthcoming to support them. It has already been pointed out how difficult it is to trace influence and derivations in this field. The most one can say is that this draft, which in any case has a good many highly original ideas of its own to contribute, does suggest a general acquaintance with continental solutions of the problem, and that the only Englishman known to have been actively interested in continental poor relief at this time was William Marshall who also had close contacts with the government of Thomas Cromwell. Handwriting is no help: it is neither impossible nor certain that Marshall wrote the draft. Perhaps one had better prevent one ever intrusive King Charles's Head from entering the discussion: there is not the slightest link between this draft and More's *Utopia*.

We cannot, then, be certain of the author of this remarkable document, though Marshall's name is the most likely one to attach to it. However, this after all is not a very important matter. What is certain is that the draft was not written by the official draftsmen – either by Cromwell himself (let alone the king) or by the king's legal counsel – but originated in the fertile brain of a private individual. It is also certain that the draft was written for the government and formed the basis of the official legislation of 1536. In the event, its most striking details were dropped. There is no scheme of public works, no income tax, no council to avoid vagabonds, in the act of 27 Henry VIII. There are not even parish overseers of the poor, though these were later to be appointed. With all the new machinery excised, the act proved ineffective. It followed the draft in organizing the relief of the impotent, in acknowledging the need for employing the sturdy, and in fully recognizing the essential difference between the two. But it would not take the necessary steps even to ensure relief. Neither the act nor the draft can be blamed for insisting on voluntary alms rather than a poor rate: it was axiomatic at this time that alms had to be freely given to do good to the giver's soul, a position only reluctantly abandoned when it was seen that most men preferred other ways of doing good to their souls. But the failure to provide effective machinery is surprising, especially because the government of the 1530s did not usually fail when administrative reforms were called for. Yet if it is remembered what the chief business of this session early in 1536 was to be, the explanation suggests itself. A government which was about to embark on the vast and delicate operation of dissolving the monasteries had enough administrative problems on hand without installing new machinery for poor relief. Like Parliament, the author of the draft was not aware of these plans; Cromwell, however, knew well what was coming, so that he found himself forced to substitute for Marshall's plan (if it was his) a mere stop-gap measure of good intentions.[1]

All this allowed for, the achievement of the draft still remains remarkable. It was not still-born: much of its detail became law at once, and more found realization later. It originated new principles and practice; it stood at the beginning of serious and effective legislation to deal with the great social problem of the day. That its most revolutionary suggestions were always to prove beyond the capacity of government is perhaps a pity. But what ought to stay in the mind is that a scheme of such magnitude and precise detail, so much practical humanitarianism and sound common sense, so much immediate and so much more ultimate effect, grew up in 1535 in the circle of advisers and thinkers who surrounded the government of Thomas Cromwell.

[1] [No: the draft bill was introduced into Parliament, to be replaced by the enacted bill when the Commons rejected it. Cf. *Reform and Renewal*, 173–4.]

27

THE STUART CENTURY*

Of all the centuries of English history, the seventeenth probably seems the most crucial to most students. It is generally regarded as the period when state and society were shaken apart and put together again, a revolutionary era with powerful consequences for the future, the foundation of modern England. Not only did it witness – or so we are told – the end of the medieval constitution, the establishment of parliamentary monarchy, and the acceptance of a secular state harbouring any number of Churches and denominations; it was also the time when England's imperial expansion began, when capitalist organization took its modern form, and when developments in science and philosophy replaced a whole inherited body of thought about the world by one that may fairly be called modern. Many would regard it as *the* formative century in the experience of England: an age of fascinating and fruitful turmoil.

One would therefore naturally expect to find an abundance of good books on this century; good minds and able writers must surely be falling over each other in their zeal to make the age their own. Now it is quite true that many of the ablest English historians have in fact been so attracted, but it is surprisingly difficult to find a good, up-to-date, single account of the whole period. Maurice Ashley's contribution to the *Penguin History of England* (1952) is the weakest volume in that series. Christopher Hill's remarkable *Century of Revolution* (1961) offers more a number of sharp vignettes and idiosyncratic discussions of problems than a real survey and account. Necessity still forces the teacher, in school and university, to refer the student to G. M. Trevelyan's *England under the Stuarts*, first published in 1904, and while this was once a very fine book it is now little more than a serious obstacle to real understanding. No textbook can possibly live for sixty years, especially not in an age in which historical research has become a major industry. The two volumes in the *Oxford History of England*, different in quality though they are, can also do little to

* [Review of G. E. Aylmer, *The Struggle for the Constitution 1603–1689* (1963), in *Annali della Fondazione italiana per la storia amministrativa*, 2 (1965), 759–65.]

satisfy the needs of the 1960s: Godfrey Davies's *Earlier Stuarts* (1938) is not only singularly uninspiring but also adds virtually nothing to the sort of interpretation enshrined in Trevelyan, and G. N. Clark's *Later Stuarts* (1934: 2nd ed. 1955), which does recognize the existence of new questions and answers, is by now thirty years old. The initiation of yet another series of textbooks on English history thus offered Professor Aylmer a chance to take the field for himself. Admittedly, the conditions of the series worked against him. It is intended for the schools rather than the universities or the reader of history, and its volumes are relatively short. Allowing for this, Professor Aylmer has done well enough. He has provided a readable, straightforward account, embodying most of the recent work on the period, including his own important researches in administrative history. Perhaps he has been a little too conscious of his probable audience: an air of patient exposition pervades too many of his pages. But the reader will get a solid and searching description, judicious and balanced at the points of controversy, thorough and suggestive in the earlier part of the century, rather more conventional in the latter. What he will not get is any sort of shock, pleasurable or otherwise. He is not, to be frank, being made to think.

That this is not because Professor Aylmer has not some important things to say about the meaning of his period is plain enough. There are plenty of significant sentences in the book. The style may not be exciting, but neither does it begin to bore. Why, then, is one at the end left with a feeling of an opportunity missed? Is it not because Professor Aylmer's seventeenth century is in the last resort still Trevelyan's seventeenth century – still the age described by S. R. Gardiner, Macaulay, Ranke, Hallam, Hume, even Rapin? Naturally, a consensus so long established must represent a large measure of the truth: or so one would normally think, though no historian is wise to allow ancient assurance and frequent repetition to carry conviction with him, especially when that conviction seems to reflect largely the partisan views of the age discussed. And while no one wants to see mere originality for originality's sake, it may yet be suggested that the accepted framework for that century needs to be thought about very critically indeed. Is it really the case that the massive work of the last few decades, while deepening understanding and adding new points here and there, has left the outline story and the interpretative scheme untouched? Or is it time that we radically rearranged our instinctive reactions to the seventeenth century? A lot of things have assumed a new appearance in the two centuries surrounding this one: has this no meaning for the one encapsuled? At least it might lead to fruitful and exciting reconsiderations if we could deliberately attempt to look at the age with a mind prepared to question not the detail but the larger whole.

Moreover, this new look can be achieved without shifting the old angle of vision. Traditionally, the central events of the century are those touching the nature of the state, the constitution and government: it is quite rightly treated as an age of political revolution, even if that revolution is now seen to have derived in great part from social, economic and intellectual changes. Professor Aylmer has chosen a title for his survey which shows that he would agree with this main concentration. And it is by looking again at the facts about state and government that, I believe, we can most readily gain a new light upon the Stuart age. If we follow fashion and write its history round 'the origins of modern science', or the development of trade, or the decline of religious uniformity, we shall only by-pass the central questions and retain the traditional framework. We shall do least good by being most fashionable: the difficulties encountered by the methods of social analysis in noticing or explaining change are here aggravated by the fact that in the seventeenth century social structure changed remarkably little. This in itself, however, gives a clue to the reassessment which seems to be necessary. Was this century in fact so manifestly dominated by revolution?

The traditional, and still accepted, story is straightforward, though minor variations have of course been offered, usually in the cause of allotting praise and blame. It runs as follows. When Queen Elizabeth died, she left a system of government much debilitated by recent change. A price inflation had seriously weakened the Crown; the Church faced an insidious and fundamental attack from the Puritan party; the House of Commons had recently grown in power and independence; the ambitions of rising classes (the gentry, the bourgeoisie) were threatening the ascendancy of monarch and aristocracy. Altogether, the traditional power of the Crown was failing in the face of a variety of discontent and criticism. All these strains – which expressed themselves in a conflict between king and Commons – became increasingly obvious in the reign of James I and exploded in the first years of his successor. The country was heading for civil war, and after Charles I's ill-conceived attempt, in the 1630s, to govern without Parliament, that is what it got. The war led to constitutional and religious revolution, though social revolution was prevented by the triumph of an army controlled by that characteristic member of the solid gentry,

Oliver Cromwell. Though the revolution collapsed in 1660 and the king returned, the Restoration 'restored' a system of government which had lost the conciliar machinery of the Tudors, admitted the ascendancy of the classes represented in the Commons, and tilted the balance against the Crown. Government had now to be more parliamentary, for the king could no longer rule without the revenue granted by the Commons, and the experience of the Interregnum had given that House a conviction of predominance. Charles II and James II, however, handicapped by their adherence to Roman Catholicism, determined to restore absolutism to monarchy, and so the battle had to be fought once more in 1688. The outcome of that second revolution was constitutional monarchy, with the king now effectively only the servant of the state and in practice subject to the control of the propertied classes in Parliament. The new mechanism for the control and promotion of government was party, and the two major political parties (Whigs and Tories) formed the foci of political activity from the reign of William III onwards. Even those who recognize that the party names are hard to attach to organized interests still tend to discuss the reign of Queen Anne as though those parties existed.

Within this established framework, the arguments and controversies have been brisk. The 'causes of the civil war', especially, have provoked much heat and some light from historians. Was James I responsible for the deterioration of the position, or could no one have triumphed over the consequences of inflation, sectional ambition and bigotry? Was Charles I a tyrant, or did he attempt to provide good government in the interests of the nation as a whole? What lay behind the move towards war – social divisions, religious convictions, constitutional conservatism, or all of these and other 'factors' as well? The extent of the Restoration, and the real aims of the last two Stuart kings, have also been debated, though much less so. But the main guide-lines remain undisturbed. This was a century of conflict between king and Parliament, working out the several strains incorporated in the Tudor system of government and the consequences, in religion and in matters economic, of the Reformation and the 'rise of capitalism'. What emerged at the end was a markedly different society and constitution. Despotism was dead. So was uniformity in religion. Society was secularized, its behaviour and attitudes recognizably different from those of 1603. The setting of political structure and life was revolutionized by the establishment of constitutional monarchy.

That there is much to be said for this interpretation is obvious not only from the well-nigh universal consensus on its main lines, but also from some of the facts. Yet there are also manifest weaknesses in it which recent work (and some not so recent) has surely brought out. Here we have room only for a few of the main points that must raise doubts about the tradition. The whole interpretation depends on one basic conviction: that king and Parliament are naturally opponents, that therefore the Tudor peace was a temporary aberration, and that the early Stuarts were bound to run into trouble which inescapable weaknesses in their position as well as some mismanagement made certain should lead to civil war. Everything follows from this – but nothing in that last sentence seems to me to be valid. The conventional notion starts from a false premise because it quite misunderstands the Tudor situation. It does so in two ways. It supposes that under Elizabeth Parliament – that is, the Commons – were 'loyal' and therefore amenable and no trouble to the Crown, at least until the 1590s, for to the traditional interpreter the Commons could never do anything but approximate closely to either extreme, subservience or opposition. Sir John Neale has shown how mistaken this view is: queen and Commons clashed frequently throughout the reign, but this did not prevent equally frequent co-operation. Secondly the conventional view supposes that serious conflict on the parliamentary stage is somehow normal: that 'the Commons' misbehaved unless they opposed the Crown. This is nonsense. Parliament was part of the king's government, called to assist him by making grants and laws, but also designed to keep the Crown in touch with opinion and an accepted occasion for complaint and protest. It was, and is, a talking institution, a place for debate. The historian who supposes that debate must mean 'inevitable conflict' had better investigate his subconscious. Elizabeth's difficulties with her Parliaments, the frequent clashes of views in the Commons, did not make those Parliaments any the less 'loyal', nor did their basic agreement with government make them incapable of argument and opposition. At least from Henry VIII's time we discern a 'modern' Parliament, an arena of politics in which all opinions are liable to be expressed on given issues and where decisions and ultimate attitude depend on effective leadership from one or another such body of opinion. All the talk of accommodating Parliaments and hostile Parliaments badly misleads because it does not see the past in a real light but in the light of doctrine. It is in any case time that historians cured themselves of the habit of referring to the Commons as a body, as though those more than 400 men were as single-headed and single-purposed as the king himself.

Once generalizations of this kind are properly absorbed – once, that is, the early seventeenth century is treated as a sequence of events rather than the working out of a destiny – the parliamentary history of 1603–28 ceases to be the record of the 'inevitable' accentuation of inherent strain and becomes comprehensible as a series of political crises, complicated by personality, in which the outcome may be idetnified but cannot be presumed from the start. In the context it is worth notice that James I's last Parliament was the only one in which Crown and Commons worked in a measure of harmony, and that even in 1628 the opposition leadership carefully avoided any proposals which could be read as an invasion of prerogative rights. The ineffectiveness of the Petition of Right, as futile a document as even constitutional struggles have ever thrown up, neatly demonstrates the absence of revolutionary strains in the difficulties encountered up to that point. Before Charles I's experiment in the 1630s, war was not so much inevitable as totally improbable; and the failure of Charles's government was not rendered 'inevitable' by deep divisions in society or inherited stresses in the constitution, but was conditioned by the inability of the king and his ministers to operate any political system.

Or take the question of Puritanism. The traditional view is buttressed by the notion that from the reign of Elizabeth onwards something called the Puritan movement grew steadily from general dissatisfaction through a presbyterian programme to sectarianism, till it amalgamated with the constitutional opposition to produce the 'Puritan revolution'. Of course, many more knowledgeable historians modify this crude scheme, but none has effectively discarded it. Yet it is in no way in accord with the facts. Puritanism has no continuous history. Throughout James I's reign the dominant note of what called itself by the name was moderate, reformist, co-operative, quite unlike the militancy of the 1580s; and both were quite unlike the fragmentation of the 1650s. Presbyterianism as a native growth vanished before Whitgift's attack, and even Parliament's victory in the civil war did not manage to revive it. The sects remained a small, insignificant manifestation, distrusted as socially and spiritually disruptive by all the governing sort, until they became important in the later 1640s when war and victory released all manner of forces hitherto suppressed. The so-called Puritan leadership of the Long Parliament (and Pym certainly was a Puritan) had no programme for the Church; indeed, Pym spent much of his time avoiding and sidetracking discussion on this topic because he, at any rate, knew that the 'Puritan party' he led was neither properly Puritan nor anything so solid as a party. Bishops, much attacked under Elizabeth, became the enemy again only when Laud attempted his own ecclesiastical revolution in the 1630s. There is no continuous or 'inevitable' development here. And the same is true of those other allegedly divisive issues – the place of the common law, the problems of prerogative jurisdiction, the doctrine of divine right. On all these, political opponents shared more essentials than they differed over. The history of England between 1603 and 1640 is not the history of a growing disease in the body politic, but of conflict – some of it healthy, some morbid – within a setting of agreed essentials: or rather it was this until the impatient attempt at a drastic solution on the king's behalf persuaded his opponents that the essentials were no longer agreed.

Thus the prehistory of the civil war should certainly be read as the breakdown of a system of government. But it did not break down because it had been unworkable from the first. It had depended for its working on the recognition that political conflict – disagreement over interests and issues – is a natural state of affairs, requiring detailed, day-by-day management from those charged with the conduct of affairs, that is the Crown and its ministers, as well as some mutual accommodation to other people's views and desires. It broke down because the early Stuart governments could not manage or persuade, because they were incompetent, sometimes corrupt, and frequently just ignorant of what was going on or needed doing. This is not to deny the existence of difficult and critical problems (every age has those), nor the often factious and bigoted and ill-conceived opposition which those governments encountered. Certainly they had quite a job on their hands, but that is what they claimed to be there for. What matters is their repeated inability, for reasons also often factious, bigoted and ill-conceived, to find a way through their problems.

What of the later Stuarts? Did their failure produce the end of a particular system of government, as is usually supposed? Certainly, in so far as Charles II and James II looked to absolutist and Catholic France as a model, they failed, and the loud though unconvincing doctrines (non-resistance, passive obedience) were heard no more from the pulpits. That is to say, the royalist revolution came to grief in 1688. But to suppose that this failure resulted in a profound reformation of the political structure is, again, to mistake externals for realities. It is not true that 1688 produced a system in which the Crown was controlled by the Commons and the Commons were controlled by a majority party elected by the nation (however that last term may be qualified); no respectable historian would nowadays suppose so, though the interpretative scheme still in use depended on the notion. All the work of the last thirty-five years, stemming largely from Namier's original researches, has tended to show us a very different picture by stressing how very unlike those parties of the seventeenth and eighteenth centuries were to what developed after 1800. But the consequences of what by now is a commonplace still do not seem to have been drawn. We know that after 1688 the king continued to be in control of 'the Executive', continued to govern in person or through ministers whom he chose. We know that he required reasonably regular support in the Commons and endeavoured to obtain it through the use of a Crown interest in the House round which temporary government 'parties' were constructed by the amalgamation of ministerial connections.[1] We know that the formal organization of opposition 'parties' was intermittent and inconsistent, and that the bulk of those not connected with government behaved according to the name of independents on which they prided themselves. In other words, after 1688 (and in great measure also between 1660 and 1688) constitutional peace and the carrying on of the king's government depended on the reasonable co-operation, in Parliament, of king, Lords and Commons, and this co-operation was achieved by the management of opinion and business provided by the government. Yet this last sentence is also entirely true of the reign of Elizabeth, or even of Henry VIII. Of course, methods of management had altered (though less so than some might suppose) and the business of managing Parliaments had become a much more regular part of ministers' preoccupation (though, again, not as regular as conventional history would lead us to suppose: there were still many months every year when Parliament did not sit). Changes in emphasis and techniques there had certainly been; but where, in this question of the constitution, is the change in fundamentals, in principles of government?

I should therefore like to suggest that historians of the seventeenth century would do well to turn their eyes from the appearance of revolution at every turn to the realities of affairs. I am not ignoring the civil war and Interregnum. I am not concerned to deny the importance of ideas, the part played by passion and faith. I am sure that society

[1] [For the reign of Anne, recent opinion (especially Geoffrey Holmes, *British Politics in the Age of Anne* [1967]) again asserts the existence of 'real' parties. But even in this interpretation governments were not strictly party-based.]

changed somewhat, as well in its organization as in its attitudes, though I am not sure that it did so more in the Stuart century than in most others. But I think that the bluster and tempest of conflict have distracted historians too readily from asking some really searching questions about the outcome. Perhaps it is too much to ask that they should look upon this 'century of revolution' as an age in which many ups and downs – a civil war, the execution of a king, several complete upsets in government – produced in the end only an adjustment in the methods by which the inherited constitution was made to work. But, at any rate, there is quite a lot to be said for this point of view, and an attempt to see the age afresh with this supposition in mind may well lead to some important new insights and a more vigorous reinterpretation, on whatever lines, of what at present looks to be one of the most ossified sections of English history.

28

A HIGH ROAD TO CIVIL WAR?*

Why was there a civil war in seventeenth-century England? The question continues to exercise historians, especially as the coherent explanations of S. R. Gardiner, echoing in reality only the partisan account of the Grand Remonstrance of 1641, no longer command easy acceptance. Of late, discussion has mostly concentrated on social analysis, on the supposition that the division which became manifest in 1642 reflected definite and ascertainable groupings within the nation. This paper is not going to treat once more of the much battered problem of the gentry; that controversy has found enough summaries, of varying degrees of sympathy, to deserve the decent rest and respect accorded to old age (if not old hat).[1] Those who took part in the war believed themselves to be defending opposing views on Church and state; they thought – or often said – that religious and political convictions divided them from one another. This interpretation has taken some bad knocks from historians investigating what was actually said and done in the years before 1640. Even the existence of a distinguishably Puritan point of view in the Church of England has been called in doubt,[2] though it should be said that such arguments lead more properly to the conclusion that within the Church there existed both high and low streams of opinion, and that at least before the age of Laud these did not represent a conflict between Anglican and Puritan

---

* [From the Renaissance to the Counter-Reformation: Essays in Honour of Garrett Mattingly, ed. C. H. Carter (New York, 1965), 325–47. Copywright © 1965 by Random House, Inc.]

[1] The most famous review of the problem is J. H. Hexter's 'Storm over the Gentry,' *Reappraisals in History* (1961), 117 ff. His convincing reluctance to see much value in the debate is to some degree shared by Willson H. Coates, 'An Analysis of Major Conflicts in Seventeenth Century England,' *Conflict in Stuart England: Essays in Honour of Wallace Notestein* (1960), 15 ff. C. Hill, 'Recent Interpretations of the Civil War,' *Puritanism and Revolution* (1958), 3 ff., and P. Zagorin, 'The Social Interpretation of the English Revolution,' *Journal of Economic History* 19 (1959), 376 ff., are more inclined to believe in the reality of the discussion, though they disagree with the particular answers offered.

[2] C. H. and K. George, *The Protestant Mind of the English Reformation* (Princeton, 1961). Their views receive some support from such studies as R. A. Marchant, *The Puritans and the Church Courts in the Diocese of York* (1960), and I. Morgan, *Prince Charles's Puritan Chaplain* (1957).

so much as a struggle for ascendancy between two sections of the English Church. This is also the interpretation to be placed on Mr Haller's and Mr Hill's demonstrations of the emergence of identifiably Puritan attitudes in religion and society;[1] neither work produces proof that the Puritanism of the prewar period was bound to lead to an irreconcilable conflict until Laud decided to believe that it must. As for political thinking, it is only necessary to remember Miss Judson's revelation that Crown and Parliament agreed far more than they differed in their views of the constitution.[2] One of her important suggestions still awaits proper exploration: the idea that in the age of James I there was some profound conflict between king and common law persists in a shadowy way,[3] even though common law was king's law, common lawyers composed a main part of the king's assistants, and James himself expressed pleasure at the advantages offered to kings by the law of England. Sir Edward Coke no doubt identified the common law with himself, but we are possibly ill-advised to follow him in this and to mistake his personal battles with James or Bacon for titanic conflicts of principle.

In this welter of negatives there may be some danger of concluding that the civil war cannot be properly explained, though the more common reaction is to shrug off the criticisms and continue to hold, in attenuated form, the simpler views of the past. Most historians remain convinced that social divisions created the parties of the civil war. Some would follow Mr Trevor-Roper into his refinement of his original thesis and divide the political nation before 1640 into 'court' and 'country' sections upon which rested the sides of the civil war, even though the evidence for such identifiable categories is doubtful enough.[4] Mr Hill, on the evidence of his latest book, continues to adhere to a much subtler but essentially unchanged version of his earlier views concerning the bourgeois and urban revolutions against the economic and social structure of a gentry-run rural society.[5] Most historians

---

[1] W. Haller, *The Rise of Puritanism* (New York, 1938); C. Hill, *Society and Puritanism in Pre-Revolutionary England* (1964). However, Michael Walzer has reminded us of the existence of more drastic elements in Puritan thinking than the dominant note of reform within the Church: 'Puritanism as a Revolutionary Ideology,' *History and Theory* I (1963), 59 ff.

[2] Margaret A. Judson, *The Crisis of the Constitution* (New Brunswick, N.J., 1949). And cf. R. W. K. Hinton, 'Government and Liberty under James I,' *CHJ* II (1953), 48 ff.

[3] Or not so shadowy: Ogilvie, *The King's Government and the Common Law.* [Cf. now W. J. Jones, *Politics and the Bench* (1971), for an important revision.]

[4] Cf. my remarks in *Past and Present*, 20 (1961), 79 ff.

[5] His *Society and Puritanism* is pervaded by a general and sometimes explicit acceptance of this interpretation.

seem also convinced that there was something seriously wrong with the system of government inherited by the Stuarts: it is thought that when James I came to the throne nothing could have prevented conflicts with Parliament so serious as to call in doubt the whole survival of the structure. The Tudor constitution is considered ramshackle. 'The problems of James I' remain a favourite topic of undergraduate study, a fact which reflects not only the conservatism of examination papers but also the quite real, if very curious, belief that somehow only James I ever had problems. Even the emphatic demonstration that he either created his own or was responsible for making existing ones insoluble[1] has not disposed of the general notion that in some way the situation was past praying for in 1603. There is a marked reluctance to realize that Sir John Neale's work on the Elizabethan Parliament has made it impossible to see the position in the traditional light. Elizabeth was not dealing with a co-operative, even subservient, Commons, till things changed in the 1590s and an impatient, new generation of 'mature' parliamentarians came to make things too difficult for her successor. She faced a troublesome House throughout her reign, and the fact that she had advantages denied to James should not obscure the difficulties she had which he was spared. Thus in the years before 1590 she was confronted by a militant and often revolutionary Puritanism of which there is very little trace in the age of Bancroft and Abbot.

What these views have in common is a sense of inevitability, a feeling that so profound a disturbance as a civil war must have had roots so deep, causes so fundamental, that analysis can be expected to discover them clearly enough. The history of the years 1603–40 remains understandably dominated by what came after; the breakdown in the constitution colours all interpretations of the time when the constitution was either breaking down or failing to adjust itself. But is this readily comprehended approach in fact the right one? No one will deny that in the society, economy, Church and government of England there were strains (as there always are), even real conflicts of interest and opinion which the outbreak of war brought into the open, and which in turn helped to determine the alignments and developments of the years after 1642. The question is whether they had to lead to such results. The mistake is one of logic: to suppose that because the

[1] E.g. D. H. Willson, *James VI and I* (1956); R. H. Tawney, *Business and Politics under James I* (Cambridge, 1958); R. Ashton, *The Crown and the Money Market 1603–40* (Oxford, 1960), and 'Deficit Finance in the Reign of James I,' *Econ. Hist. Rev.*, 2nd ser., 10 (1957), 15 ff.

civil war happened therefore it was bound to happen, and that because the war gave arms and voice to rival groupings therefore rival groupings made the war inevitable. Unconsciously ruled by these convictions, historians have run either into an absence of explanation or into explanations somewhat violently fitted to theories not very well borne out by the facts. Such a situation suggests some error in method. Progress would seem to depend on deliberately abandoning the notion that the reigns of the first Stuarts not only led to war but were somehow certain to lead to it. We must stop reading the age back from its drastic end and try to read it forward through vicissitudes which, though serious enough, were not notably different from those that beset any political situation. This involves a better understanding of the true springs of Tudor government and an end to the idea that somehow it was much easier to govern in the sixteenth than the seventeenth century. It is not, of course, suggested that the civil war was just an accident, or that real and serious divisions did not exist which in retrospect may be seen to have made smooth the road to war. The anger of the 'country' against the 'court', the ambitions of gentry, merchants and what Mr Hill calls 'the industrious sort'; Puritanism of one kind and another, authoritarian government, differing interpretations of prerogative and privilege – all these respectable topics of discussion were real enough. But we shall get nowhere even with them, not to mention the war itself, if we keep studying them so determinedly with the known end in view.

This essay is manifestly not going to attempt anything like a comprehensive attack on all these problems. It will confine itself to some general points which cast doubt on prevalent attitudes, and to one particular event which has been generally read as underlining the inevitability of conflict. Under James I and Charles I, says Mr Hill, the political nation 'was rent by political disagreements which led to civil war'.[1] But is this strictly accurate? Assuredly, the nation was rent in those years, but in 1640 the one thing quite out of the question was a civil war. When the Long Parliament met, the gentry – the political nation – were remarkably united, and the king had no party to speak of.[2] Certainly there were strains in the unity, and divisions of opinion and interest, which would show themselves soon enough; but the fact remains that in 1640 the Commons displayed quite unwonted

---

[1] *Puritanism and Revolution*, 14.

[2] To my knowledge this point is recognized only by Mr Coates, op. cit., 25; recognition is, however, also implied in B. H. G. Wormald, 'How Hyde became a Royalist,' *CHJ* 8 (1944–6), 65 ff.

unanimity. The thirty-seven years since Queen Elizabeth's death produced a united political nation, not one lined up in opposing parties and divided for war, and no account of those years can be acceptable which does not remember this.[1] Whatever part larger social movements or bodies of opinion may have played in the ultimate outcome, the fact is that between the supposed growth of a split and that later stage when the nation was unquestionably split there intervened the immediate product of the prewar years: a nation united, a king isolated, no chance whatever of political conflict, let alone civil war.

The importance of looking closely at events is underlined by a curious paradox. In considering the Long Parliament, the only one under the early Stuarts which for a time justified the conventional collective noun of 'the Commons', historians are usually concerned to distinguish the parties of the future. When, on the other hand, they look at earlier Parliaments, there are only too ready to suggest a unanimity which never existed by treating 'the Commons' as a unit opposed to the government. In no Parliament before 1628 was the king without sizable support, even if his men rarely succeeded in gaining an ascendancy. However, they did so, in a way, in 1624, in one of James's Parliaments (and that the last), when for once government took the sensible step of working with the Commons instead of against them. It is an error to see Buckingham's alliance with the 'Puritan' war party of Eliot and Preston as nothing but surrender to popular attitudes; a more fruitful analysis would consider him as for once understanding the essence of the English system of government – the procuring of support in the Commons by adjustments in policy and by the managerial enterprise of creating a strong Crown interest in the Commons. The mixed sovereigns of Tudor England required compromise and flexibility on all sides, but above all it required Crown leadership in the Commons, and in the context the fact of Buckingham's haphazard foreign policy is less significant than the fact that a negotiated peace was still possible after over twenty years of quarrelling and estrangement. It throws a strange light on the common opinion that the reign of James I, in a series of increasingly clangorous chords, produced of necessity the sound of war trumpets in the offing, as king and Commons drew further and further apart.

[1] It is worth notice that all the true later crises of the century (1673, 1678, 1688) witnessed the same phenomenon. It is this fact and not even the event of civil war which provides the best comment on Stuart political skill.

If in 1624 it was still possible to organize a Crown interest, it should be clear that policy and not inevitable necessity destroyed that interest in 1626–8. Even when this point has been realized, it does not usually seem to have been understood that in consequence any interpretation which sees the situation as so difficult from the start as to be virtually hopeless will not stand up.

Probably no single document had done more to persuade historians of the inevitability of the conflict than the Commons' *Apology and Satisfaction* of 1604, that 'lecture to a foreign king on the constitutional customs of the realm which he had come to govern but which he so imperfectly understood'.[1] The usual view of it may be summed up in the words of Godfrey Davies:

> It deserves the closest study both because it reveals the position the Commons took up and maintained for the next forty years . . . and because it was an authoritative pronouncement of the reforms and changes deemed necessary at the beginning of the new reign.[2]

The second half of this sentence calls in question the closeness of Davies's study, for the one thing hard to find in the *Apology* is a statement of 'reforms and changes': the document is much more noticeably concerned with preventing change. But it is a striking memorial, and close study would certainly seem to be called for. However, such study should surely involve the circumstances as well as the product, and this has not been offered anywhere so far. That the address was composed but never delivered might at once start doubts about the ready way in which the Commons, as a body, are nowadays associated with it. The history of the document is itself curious. Though not unknown in the later seventeenth century,[3] it was effectively dis-

---

[1] J. R. Tanner, *Constitutional Documents of the Reign of James I* (Cambridge, 1930), 202; hereafter cited as Tanner.

[2] *The Early Stuarts* (2nd ed., Oxford, 1959), 6 ff.

[3] The bibliography of the *Apology* is difficult and in part remains obscure; this note is based on a comparison of verbal differences which it would be impossibly tedious to detail here. Only one contemporary MS copy is now known (PRO, State Papers Domestic, James I, vol. 8, no. 70) which Gardiner appears to have been the last historian to use; however, another copy, vouched for at a later date (cf. below, p. 175, n. 2), may still exist somewhere and may turn out to be contemporary. It was apparently this missing copy, known from the transcript in the MS Commons' Journals, on which the first printed version rested: in Sir Matthew Hale's posthumous *Original Institution, Power and Jurisdiction of Parliaments* (Jacob Tonson, 1707), 206–40. William Petyt (1636–1707), keeper of the records in the Tower, had the *Apology* transcribed into his collection of historical materials (Inner Temple Library, Petyt MSS, 538, vol. 19, fos. 99–104v); this was further copied for him in a form apparently edited for printing (BM, Lansdowne MS 512, fos. 119–32), and it was probably this last version which was

covered by Hallam who was very proud of the fact, noting that Hume and Carte had ignored it and that even Rapin gave it only the briefest mention.[1] Hallam also at once jumped to the conclusion, which has ever since been reiterated, that 'it was the voice of the English Commons in 1604, at the commencement of that conflict for their liberties, which is measured by the line of the house of Stuart'.[2] Gardiner set his magisterial seal on this view which makes the *Apology* one of the profoundly important constitutional documents in a century full of such things:[3]

Such was the address, manly and freespoken, but conservative and monarchical to the core, which the House of Commons was prepared to lay before the King. In it they took up the position which they never quitted during eighty-four long and stormy years. To understand the Apology is to understand the causes of the success of the English Revolution. They did not ask for anything which was not in accordance with justice. They did not demand a single privilege which was not necessary for the good of the nation as well as for their own dignity.

Here is the full mystical concept: an identifiable single body, 'the Commons', preserving that unity for eighty-four years on a stand taken from the first. Whether Queen Elizabeth would have called a document conservative and monarchical which preached Peter Westworth's extreme doctrine of free speech, or whether one may suppose that the Commons 'never quitted' the position of 1604 when they passed the Militia Ordinance or the Test Act, may perhaps be doubted. Gardiner's authority is not what it was, but even today criticism concentrates on his politics when it would do well to attend to his

used when the document was published in his posthumous *Jus Parliamentarium*, 227–43 (1739). Unfortunately it was this printed version, easily the worst available, which was used by both Tanner (pp. 217–30) and G. W. Prothero, *Select Statutes and Other Constitutional Documents Illustrative of the Reigns of Elizabeth and James I* (Oxford, 1894), 286–93. The transmission involved a lot of deterioration. Hale's printed version is slightly better than that of the Petyt MS; although Petyt corrected his transcriber's labours, he left many misreadings standing. Both rest on a common ancestor which does not, however, seem to be the surviving State Paper MS, but rather another copy very close to it. The worst damage was done in printing Petyt's book when masses of often confusing errors were introduced. Even the State Paper MS includes one or two improbable readings, but wherever the versions conflict it seems to me so clearly the best that (quite apart from its contemporaneity) I have decided to accept it as authentic. Quotations here are from it, in modernized spelling. [This note is inadequate. More copies of the *Apology* exist than I was aware of, and the document was called for – without success – in the 1621 session. William Hakewill had a copy. All this requires more research, but does not affect the argument of this paper.]

[1] H. Hallam, *Constitutional History of England* (1827), i. 329.
[2] Ibid. 331.   [3] *History of England* (1883), i. 185 ff.

scholarship and his predilection for rather flat rhetoric. James I's latest biographers accept the *Apology* in the full sense of Gardiner's dictate, though Mr Hill, less interested in constitutional issues than social, reverts to pre-Hallam days by ignoring it.[1]

The first session of the first Stuart Parliament was certainly a troubled one. Right at the start there had been a muddle in the Parliament Chamber when the negligence of a gentleman-usher kept 'a great part of our House from hearing your Majesty's speech', and soon after some yeoman of the guard distinguished himself by addressing some members in 'opprobrious' terms more suitable 'to the peasants of France and boors of Germany' than the 'whole power and flower' of the kingdom present in the Commons.[2] There followed the more familiar troubles over Shirley's Case, the Buckinghamshire Election Case, James's proposal for a union between England and Scotland, and the Bishop of Bristol's book in favour of the union which the Commons regarded as unwarranted interference. Religion and money also played their part in exciting the Commons, and it had become painfully clear that the government's control was poor. Altogether, a very disturbed session, though not perhaps much more so than a session in many an Elizabethan Parliament. All these troubles were rehearsed in the *Apology*, but the immediate cause of its composition was more specific. This was the bitter dispute over the whole problem of wardship which a Commons' committee had long and fruitlessly debated with the Lords in April–May 1604.[3] The Crown, using the Lords in their traditional role as a check on the Commons,[4] had beaten off the attack on prerogative and resources; but in an address to the Commons, summoned to Whitehall, which he delivered on 28 May, and 'wherein many particular actions and passages of the House were objected unto them with taxation and blame', James had made it very plain how much he resented their attitude to his rights and what he regarded as the general wasting of time. The Commons might

---

[1] Willson, *James VI and I*, 249: 'a bold declaration of right, a lecture to a foreign king upon the constitution of his new kingdom'; W. McElwee, *The Wisest Fool in Christendom* (1958), 153 ff. (who even alleges that the Commons presented the document to the King, which no one else has supposed); C. Hill, *The Century of Revolution* (Edinburgh, 1961). The *Apology* is accepted as 'great' and truly important in the latest study of James I's first Parliament: Theodore K. Rabb, 'Sir Edwin Sandys and the Parliament of 1604,' *Amer. Hist. Rev.* 69 (1964), 646 ff.

[2] These parts of the *Apology* are left out in Tanner and Prothero.

[3] H. E. Bell, *Introduction to the History and Records of the Court of Wards and Liveries* (Cambridge, 1953), 138.

[4] Hist. MSS Commission, *Portland MSS*, ix. 11 ff.

well have remembered the much more conciliatory reaction of the late Queen in 1601, to franker attacks on the prerogative of granting monopolies.

On 1 June, Sir Edwin Sandys, who had led the committee that conferred with the Lords, reported on the abortive negotiations and reminded the House of the king's rebuke. 'Much dispute followed this report'. In the course of the debate, Sir Thomas Ridgeway, one of the knights for Devon, moved 'that a Committee might be named to take a Survey of the Proceedings of the House, and to set down something in writing, for his Majesty's Satisfaction; and to exhibit it unto him'. The Speaker rephrased the motion to read: 'A Petition to be framed, with Reasons of Satisfaction for the Proceeding in Matters of Wardships, &c.' It would appear that both motions were voted on and agreed, and the Commons then appointed a committee

to take a Survey of all the Acts and Proceedings of the House, which have been excepted unto, or whereof any Misinformation hath been given unto his Majesty, from the beginning of the Session; and to advise of such Form of Satisfaction to be offered to his Majesty, either by writing or otherwise, as may inform him of the Truth and Clearness of their Proceedings; thereby to free them from the Scandal of Levity and Precipitation, so often imputed to them; and particularly to consider of some Satisfaction touching the Proceeding in Matter of Wardship &c. This being done, to make Report to the House, and from thence to receive further Direction.

According to the form of words 'conceived by the clerk, being so directed', wardship remained foremost in the Commons' minds, but it was also felt that the business of self-explanation 'so advisedly and gravely undertaken . . . might not die or be buried in the Hands of those that first bred it'. There is certainly so far a powerful suggestion that the whole House, or an overwhelming majority of it, felt strongly about the criticisms they had received and meant to defend themselves.[1]

The committee appointed was enormous, consisting of the more than sixty-six members of the committee on wardships with six additions,[2] a body, one would have thought, more likely to founder than succeed in the task. Not until the 5th did the House receive a message from the king, softening the blow of 28 May and expressing his willingness to hear their explanations.[3] Barely a fortnight later – a

[1] For the whole story so far, cf. *CJ* i. 230b.
[2] For the wardships Committee see ibid. 222. It included 'all the serjeants at law', apart from sixty-six named members.   [3] Ibid. 232b.

time, at that, filled with the drafting of another address and the burdensome business of dealing with the Crown's financial needs[1] – the committee reported their document, now for the first time called *The Form of Apology and Satisfaction, to be presented to his Majesty*.[2] There is no denying the remarkable quality of the paper, which runs to over five thousand words. In fact, it is still a better piece of writing than the familiar version, taken from Petyt's *Jus Parliamentarium*, would suggest, for this contains an average of perhaps twenty-five errors per page of Tanner's printing. Most of these, though tiresome, are not serious, but the capricious paragraphing and messing about with sentence structure, as well as various omissions and transmutations, do much to impair the grammar, organization, and effect of the *Apology*. Some of Petyt's coinings puzzled Tanner who laboriously provided explanations for non-existent neologisms: 'seemingly', glossed as fittingly, is really seemly (223, l. 20);[3] 'evert', interpreted to mean upset, is reject (224, l. 19); 'deface', which Tanner took to mean discredit, is really refute (225, l. 28); where Tanner, remarking that the text read 'party', emended to 'parity', the manuscript has purity, which makes good sense (226, l. 26). The picturesque 'eye' of the King's grace and the obscure 'affiance' of his disposition (218, ll. 2, 22) are more commonplace but more comprehensible as acceptance and assurance; the 'poor united minds and readiness', with which the Commons credit themselves (219, l. 3 from foot), were really their 'power, united minds, etc.'[4] Sometimes the sense got distorted, as when the 'lawful knight' elected for Buckinghamshire becomes the Commons' 'lawful right' (225, l. 8). The omission of 'just' before 'burdens' (228, l. 15) makes nonsense of the concessionary addition, 'for so we acknowledge them'. Some errors are really serious. When the *Apology* says that in every previous Parliament complaint as well as claim had been made of 'your' rights (of purveyance), the transcriber introduced a different basis of discussion by reading 'our' (227, l. 6 from foot); and when it is pleaded that a new law

---

[1] On 13 June the Commons considered a petition for easing the burdens on Puritan ministers, proposed by Sir Francis Hastings's Committee (ibid. 238); Hastings was on the *Apology* committee. On the 14th they passed the bill for tunnage and poundage (ibid. 239a), but they had to deal with Lords' amendments to it after the 18th (*LJ* ii. 322–3). All this time the negotiations for a subsidy went on, until on the 26th the king made a virtue of necessity by graciously remitting all grants that session (*CJ* i. 246–7).

[2] Ibid. 243b.

[3] References are to page and line in Tanner's printing.

[4] Though eighty years earlier, in the early sixteenth century, poor was often spelled power, it is quite clear that power was here intended.

concerning purveyance could hardly be agreed to until members had sought their constituents' 'counsel', the printed version invented a dangerous constitutional principle by reading 'consent' (228, l. 8). And would Godfrey Davies have been so sure that the *Apology* reveals the Commons' attitude 'that their privileges were the general liberties of England',[1] if he had known that in the manuscript the phrase concerning 'the right and liberty of the Commons of England' (223, l. 5 from foot) is followed by 'in Parliament'? Lastly, we may note that the hitherto rather obscure allusion to the late queen (222, ¶ 2) was made so only by the omission of a few lines; these also point a contrast with the previous reign which historians have of late tended to ignore:

For although it may be true that in the latter times of Queen Elizabeth some one privilege now and then were by some particular act attempted against, yet not obscurely injured; yet was not the same ever as by public speech nor by positions in general denounced against our privileges. Besides that in respect...

However, these errors have not prevented the *Apology* from being recognized for what it is: a powerful, formidable justification of parliamentary claims and an equally solid attack on James's handling of the situation. It asserted without reservations some notions on privilege which in the previous reign would have had short shrift not only from the queen but (if Peter Wentworth's fate is anything to go by) even from a majority of the House, and it offered a definition of constitutional principles which, while never less than respectful, was also firmly directed at all manifestations of autocracy. The logic of its structure – running easily from general propositions to particular discussions and missing never a point – is clearer in the original paragraphing, but can be recovered from Tanner's version. But the important question, of course, is whether all this really represented the Commons' views, or only the committee's – or those of some part of the committee. For anyone who has ever taken part in the drafting of a paper in committee may well doubt from the first whether any such document could possibly have emerged, in less than two weeks, from the labours of more than seventy men.

On 20 June, Ridgeway presented the draft. Gardiner, introducing the *Apology*, said that 'the Commons, in whose name it was drawn up, began by explaining . . .'[2] The *Commons' Journal* says that the draft was 'twice read, debated and argued, *pro et contra*, whether

---

[1] *The Early Stuarts*, 7.
[2] *History of England*, i. 180. For the course of events, see *CJ* i. 243b.

the Matter and the Manner fit, or what was fit to be done with it'.
The clerk noted that seventeen members spoke in the debate; of
these no fewer than ten had been on the committee. We know a
little of what was said. Of the committee, Francis Bacon certainly
spoke against the document, and Sir Henry Beaumont and Sir Herbert
Crofts as certainly for it; Sir Edward Stafford was probably against,
while a member not on the committee, Dudley Carleton, certainly
opposed. Mr Fuller (of the committee) either argued that the draft
constituted a 'Precedent, that the Laity may censure the Clergy',
in which case he sounds to have been hostile; or he produced such a
precedent from the past, which would probably place him on the side
in favour. Mr Kyrton, who said something about the king's message
'within Two Days', would appear to have been warning the House
against going too far; Sir William Strode was provoked into inveighing
against noisy interrupters of debate. Where the others stood cannot be
told, except that the general statement quoted above makes certain
that they did not all speak on one side; in any case, the fact that a
member of the committee felt compelled to move that 'this Dispute
to cease, without further Proceeding, for this Day', indicates that all
was far from plain sailing in the House.[1] The clerk began transcribing
the *Apology* into the Journal, but, stopping after half a page, left several
sheets blank.[2] The reason the task was never completed becomes
apparent if, disregarding Gardiner's eclecticism, we read the last
Journal entry touching the *Apology*. On Friday, 29 June, Sir William
Strode moved

that the Frame of Satisfaction, touching the Proceedings of the House, penned
by the Committee, and by them reported, and read in the House, might be
re-committed, and some more Committees [committee members] added;
and such of the first committee, or others, as found any Cause of Exception,
or were not present at the former several Meetings, might be commanded to

[1] See the rough diary probably kept by the clerk of the House, printed ibid. 995b. Mr
Rabb, referring to the same passage, claims to identify nine speeches as *pro* and three
as *con*, with five unknown (op. cit. 660 and n. 53). His calculations bewilder me: he
seems to identify groups of speakers with the remarks attributed by the diarist to only
one of them. Even so I cannot quite see how he arrives at his figures.

[2] Or rather, eight pages were blank between fos. 316 and 317 when the editors of the
printed *Journals* looked at them, sometime in the eighteenth century. In 1804 these
pages were filled with a transcript of the *Apology* from 'a MSS. of Speaker Williams
communicated by Charles Williams Wynn, Esq., Member of Montgomeryshire, to
me, Chas. Abbot, Speaker' (MS Journal in the Record Office, House of Lords). Speaker
Abbot's well-known antiquarian instincts here got the better of him. It is interesting
that Sir William Williams, Speaker in the Exclusion Parliaments of 1680 and 1681,
should have had a copy of the *Apology*.

attend; that they might receive Satisfaction from the rest, or otherwise yield their reasons of Difference; so as, upon Report to the House, some Resolution may be taken for further Proceeding or Surceasing in the said Business.[1]

This was agreed to, and the afforced committee ordered to meet on Monday (2 July); but on the 7th the Parliament stood prorogued, and no more was heard of the *Apology*.

What happened is therefore plain. The famous form, or draft, which ever since Hallam has been interpreted as a worthy pronouncement from the embattled Commons, seemed less pleasing to the House than it has to historians. It was drawn up in a committee a number of whose members did not bother to attend; some of these absentees, it appears from Strode's motion, spoke against it on 20 June. The debate turned on two fundamental points: was it right to present the king with a document containing so much contentious argument, and even if it was, had the committee found the right tone? Some, it seems from the clerk's summary of the debate, were at once for dropping it; the mood of the House had changed since, on 1 June, it had resolved to put the Commons' side of the story on record. No sort of decision was arrived at on this occasion, and it took nine whole days to revive the discussion. Strode's motion carries a suggestion of annoyance, particularly at members of the Committee who, not having shared in the deliberations, had then attacked the proposal in the House, and it explicitly mentions the possibility of abandoning the whole idea. Though it may be true that the *Apology* received its quietus from the prorogation, this sequence of events strongly suggests that, if not dead before 7 July, it was also not very alive. One thing is beyond dispute: the *Apology* was never presented to the king because it was never adopted by the House. All the praise bestowed on its manly language and assertion of profound principle misses the mark. Faced with these excellences, many of the Commons had the gravest doubts, and it was the doubters, not the promoters, who won the day. The Commons not only never got around to endorsing the draft; they may, in all fairness, be said to have deliberately rejected it.

One would naturally like to know whether this difference between the committee and the House reflected any kind of factional division; was there perhaps a group of opposition men who dominated the committee but could not carry the House?[2] The answer is com-

---

[1] *CJ* i. 248b.

[2] I may say that I am not convinced by the simple assumption, made by Mr Rabb in his article, that a true opposition group can be identified in the 1604 Commons. That

plicated by the fact that though we know there were objectors among the committee men, we know of names only Bacon's and probably Stafford's. However, even the briefest glance at the committee suggests that it would be dangerous to regard it as either composed of or led by a specifically oppositionist group.[1] True, Sandys was on it, and Sandys had by this time sufficiently demonstrated his views of the government. But over the *Apology* he does not seem to have taken the lead, and it is doubtful whether he contributed to it at all.[2] John Hare was in 1606 described by Speaker Phillips as 'an inconsiderate firebrand' whose attacks on purveyance went too far even for the House.[3] Thomas Wentworth (the lawyer, who died in 1628) counted throughout this Parliament as a steadfast opponent of the court. Sir Francis Hastings, the passionate Puritan,[4] Sir Robert Wingfield, who attacked the king over Goodwin's Case,[5] and Sir Nathaniel Bacon, who in 1610 spoke against the Great Contract,[6] may also safely be put on that side. The same is less clearly true but still probable of such men as Sir Robert Wroth, Sir Henry Neville, Sir Edward Montague (who was to speak up for the Commons' privileges in 1610),[7] Sir Jerome Horsey, Sir Peter Manwood the antiquary, Sir John Scott, Sir William Burlacy (foremost against purveyors in 1610),[8] and Sir Thomas Beaumont and Sir Herbert Crofts, prominent in the tussle over the Great Contract.[9] Crofts and Sir Henry Beaumont had spoken for the *Apology* in the debate on 20 June.

certain individuals stood out in opposing the court is true enough, but not even they have ever been proved to have adhered consistently to an 'opposition' line. Williams M. Mitchell, *The Rise of the Revolutionary Party in the English House of Commons* (New York, 1957), 40, believes that a letter of Bacon's, in 1614, about new attitudes on the part of recent opponents of the court, 'lays to rest the question whether there was an opposition party' in the whole Parliament of 1604–10. It is difficult to know what to do with arguments of this order.

[1] The Parliament of 1604 awaits its Namier. The following attempt to assess individuals' attitudes, based on *DNB* unless other references are given, does not pretend to be more than a suggestion of probabilities.

[2] Mr Rabb (pp. 659 and n. 50) rightly disposes of the suggestion that Sandys was the moving spirit behind the *Apology*. His suggestion that Sandys was responsible for the section dealing with wardship may well be true.

[3] *Calendar of State Papers Domestic, James I,* i. 289, 292.

[4] Hastings had Court contacts but used them, behind a pretence of co-operation, to block such Court concerns as the need for a subsidy (Hist. MSS Commission, *Hatfield MSS,* xvi. 132 ff.).

[5] *Cal. S. P. Dom. James I,* i. 90.

[6] *Parliamentary Debates of 1610,* ed. S. R. Gardiner (Camden Soc. 1862), 135.

[7] Ibid. 51.   [8] *Cal. S. P. Dom. James I,* i. 593.

[9] *Parl. Debates of 1610,* 55.

However, over against a possible opposition group of this kind, the committee contained a large number of apparent courtiers. The sole two privy councillors in the House, Sir John Herbert and Sir John Stanhope, were, as was customary, members of it; and though, as we know, their influence was 'practically at zero,'[1] such as it was it must have worked against getting too tough with the king. In any case they might draw support from other present and future office-holders, like Sir George Moore, chamberlain of the Exchequer and for many years one of the few who seem to have spoken regularly for the Court;[2] Sir Thomas Aston and Sir Edward Hoby, gentlemen of the privy chamber; Sir Edward Stafford, career diplomat and from 1603 chancellor of the duchy; Sir Daniel Dunn, the civilian and commissioner for ecclesiastical causes; Sir John Doddridge, appointed solicitor-general a few months after the close of the session; Sir Lawrence Tanfield, elevated to the bench in 1606; Sir Robert Mansell, appointed treasurer of the navy, at the height of the argument between king and Commons; Henry Montague, whom James had in 1603 recommended for the office of recorder of London. Sir Francis Bacon we know was against the *Apology*, and Lord Treasurer Dorset's son, Robert Sackville, may with confidence be placed with the Court. Sir Francis Popham, son of the lord chief justice, and Sir Hugh Beeston, who in December 1604, was given a profitable minor office in North Wales,[3] are probables. Sir John Hollis, who in 1603 disliked Scotsmen, ended up as comptroller to Prince Henry, friend to Robert Carr, and enemy to Sir Edward Coke; his adjournment proposal on 20 June probably makes him a supporter of the *Apology*. Even more problematical was that thoughtful weather-vane, Sir Henry Yelverton, in and out of Court favour throughout his career; but in 1604 he would seem to have abandoned opposition over Goodwin's Case for support of the Court. Though from details such as these it is no doubt not possible to be sure of people's attitude to the *Apology*, the committee manifestly contained many men far from determined in opposition.

The oddest case is presented by the only two members of the committee specifically known to be associated with the *Apology*. Sir Thomas Ridgeway, who moved for it and reported it, was in no

---

[1] D. H. Willson, *The Privy Councillors in the House of Commons* 1604–10 (Minneapolis, 1940), 56.

[2] *Parl. Debates of 1610*, 55 (advocated two subsidies and tried to pour oil on troubled waters); *Debates in the House of Commons in 1625*, ed. S. R. Gardiner (Camden Soc., 1873), 16, 89, 121.   [3] *Cal. S. P. Dom. James I*, i. 175.

sense a leader of opposition. A new boy among some very old hands – this was his first Parliament as against Sir George Moore's seventh, Robert Sackville's fifth, Sir Henry Neville's sixth, Sir Nathaniel Bacon's eighth – he was out for a career which in the end, abandoning Parliament, he pursued in Ireland to the consummation of an earldom. What is more, even as he was taking the lead over the *Apology* he was being used to support Robert Cecil's private interests in the House: shortly before the prorogation, Stanhope wrote to his lordship that a certain private bill would be backed by Ridgeway, 'strong with his Devonshire crew', who had given assurance of 'a good party'.[1] But his promotion of the *Apology*, as well as his good standing with the Devon members, suggests that he was willing to take up causes in order to make a mark: it would be wrong to infer from his later life that the *Apology* owed its drafting to a staunch royalist. At the same time, he was no Eliot or Pym.[2] Sir William Strode, responsible for having the document referred back, was generally reckoned a courtier;[3] but then it is not clear whether he made his motion on 29 June in order to kill the *Apology* or revive it.

The best that can be said after this partial analysis of part of the committee is that the *Apology* did not represent a specifically opposition point of view, or (to put it in a more useful way) that the drafting of the *Apology* does not prove the existence in the House of an organized or systematic opposition to James I as early as 1604. We ought probably to see the situation in a less clear but more realistic light. Resentment at the king's ham-handed dealings and peevish outbursts was not confined to men of fixed opinion: the presence, in the House and the committee, of many old parliament men made certain that attacks on privilege and interference in the Commons' business would wound feelings in courtier as well as anti-court breasts. It was this general dismay which the *Apology* was intended to embody,

---

[1] *Hatfield MSS*, xvi. 264.

[2] Mr Rabb thinks that the opposition 'cleverly chose an inconspicuous and seemingly impartisan spokesman' in Ridgeway (op. cit. 658). He gives no shred of evidence for an argument which associates Ridgeway politically with Sandys solely because his aunt was Sandys's second wife!

[3] Willson, *Privy Councillors*, 109. Mr Mitchell (*Revolutionary Party*, 40) puts Strode in the opposition. His reason is that he spoke against the government. Of the three speeches in 1604, to which Mr Mitchell refers (two of his references are to wrong columns in *CJ*), one shows Strode speaking for the government, one has him join in the almost universal resistance to more taxation at that juncture, and one (a broken half sentence only) cannot be assigned. This example will perhaps act as an apology and satisfaction for my failure to use Mr Mitchell's book.

but it did so in terms so uncompromising and occasionally so intemperate that the House got cold feet. The mood of the Commons illustrated by the history of the *Apology* is familiar to any student of the Elizabethan Parliament: touchy, rather pompous, convinced of their rights, but entirely loyal and notably reluctant to start serious trouble with the king. High-sounding speeches on privilege and liberty were one thing; actually presenting a long and singleminded written defence of them was quite another. As far as can be judged from this story, there was nothing in the parliamentary situation of 1604 to prevent reasonable co-operation between king and Parliament, provided that James changed the disastrous tactics he had hitherto employed.

Indeed, what effect did the *Apology* have on the king? Did he ever see it, as Gardiner claimed, without citing any evidence?[1] Perhaps he was thinking of Hallam's assertion to the same effect.[2] This in turn is based on an alleged letter from James I, 'written to one of his ministers about the same time', which, discussing the prospect of a subsidy, mentions the Commons' expectation of an answer 'to their petition'. It is an odd-sounding letter, and the sceptic is not helped by Hallam's bland reference to an '*MS penes auctorem*', which makes the document untraceable. In any case, the *Apology* was not a petition, had not been presented, and required no answer; if the letter is genuine, the king may well have had in mind the petition concerning religion agreed to by the House on 13 June.[3] Or was Gardiner thinking of the fact that a copy of the *Apology* is among the state papers? He would be extremely daring who would suppose that the presence of a paper in that archive proves that this particular king had seen it. Robert Cecil was informed of the *Apology:* among his papers there is a long report on the whole affair concerning wardships which includes a perfectly accurate account of Ridgeway's motion and the reading of the *Apology*, with a long quotation from it.[4] The surviving copy is much more likely to have been sent to the secretary and read by him than by the king. The evidence of James's extraordinary speech to the Parliament at the end of the session is no less ambiguous.[5] As the king let himself go in a general diatribe of abuse and resentment, many of his listeners must have regretted that they

---

[1] *History of England*, i. 186: 'there can be little doubt that a copy of it reached his hands'.
[2] *Constitutional History*, i. 331.
[3] *CJ* i. 238. [4] *Hatfield MSS*, xvi. 142 ff.
[5] PRO, State Papers Domestic, James I, vol. 8, no. 93. Mr Willson also thought that this speech was meant for an answer to the *Apology* (*James VI and I*, 249).

had not after all told him his business in Ridgeway's *Apology*. Those who remembered the 'golden speech' of 1601, at the end of an equally troubled session, may well have stood astonished: the legend of Good Queen Bess's glorious days could not help but take wing from this contrast early in the new reign.

In the course of his speech, James did say something that sounds like an allusion to the *Form of Apology*: 'The best Apology-maker of you all, for all his eloquence, cannot make all good. Forsooth, a goodly matter, to make Apologies when no man is by to answer.' But this proves little enough, and the second sentence would hardly apply to the history of the *Apology*. The king had been aware of Ridgeway's motion and, on 5 June, had expressed his interest in a statement from the Commons: the words quoted could easily rest on no more knowledge than that. The rest of the speech makes no attempt to answer the *Apology* or even to refer to it in any particular; the king's complaints of the Commons' doings are not placed in the order of the *Apology* and are confined to the union with Scotland, religion, and purveyance; nothing is said about wardship, the immediate cause of the *Apology*, or parliamentary privilege, its major concern. In all probability, therefore, James knew that an *Apology* had been drafted but not agreed to, and Cecil may have told him something of its tenor. If the king, a man who could never resist displaying both his reading and his cleverness, had read frank remarks about his lack of experience and understanding, it seems very unlikely that he could have refrained from specifically replying to them.

Thus the *Apology* came to nothing at the time. So far from embodying a position taken up in 1604 and firmly maintained thereafter for forty or eighty years, so far from being a constitutional programme finally triumphant in 1688, it represented a minority opinion rejected by the House as too extreme. The king almost certainly never saw the 'lecture' addressed to his inexperience. The views of the Commons in 1604 cannot be deduced from it. Hale and Petyt, taught by recent history, recognized its importance as a statement of the Commons' claims, but it was virtually forgotten until Hallam raised it on the flagpole of Whig history. So much for the negative side of the story; positively, it may be suggested that, with the *Apology* out of the way, and in view of what by now is known of Tudor Parliaments, it ceases to be necessary to think the Parliament of 1604 any different from its predecessors, or the Tudor constitution already doomed before the Stuarts came to reign. The co-operation, more or less easy, of king, Lords, and Commons on which in the last resort government under Elizabeth had rested, was not shown to be no longer possible by a House of Commons displaying views of its functions and privileges with which no Tudor sovereign would have agreed. The system of parliamentary management perfected by Henry VIII and Thomas Cromwell, and further refined in the more difficult days of Queen Elizabeth, would no doubt have required tactful and sensible adjustment as the seventeenth century developed; but there is nothing in the story of 1604 to suggest that it had already ceased to be practicable.

29

THE UNEXPLAINED REVOLUTION*

Among the unsolved puzzles of English history, the Civil Wars of the seventeenth century stand high. There we have, on the face of it, a series of enormous events – war in England, between Englishmen, a king publicly beheaded, twenty years of violent upheaval. Something, surely, was badly wrong with the body politic, or so it would appear. Revolutionary situations and civil wars do not happen without good cause, and the good causes of those events have been passionately hunted ever since. But the hunt turns up more mythical unicorns than usefully edible prey. Did the factions divide over the true nature of the constitution: was it a conflict between royal absolutists and parliamentary constitutionalists? A supposition hallowed by tradition: but it has been shown that the leaders and spokesmen of all shades of opinion really held fundamentally identical views.[1] Was it a war for puritanism, for liberty of conscience against a repressive anglican uniformity? Such issues grew prominent as the war advanced, but revolutionary puritanism is rarely found before 1640, and in the early years of the Long Parliament the one thing that prevented Pym's party from breaking up was his careful avoidance of the religious issues.[2] Or was it, as all major revolutions are supposed to be, the outcome of a deep-rooted social split, between classes or within the governing class? The volumes which have been written around this supposition do not need listing here; yet in the end, neither the old Marxist view (bourgeois Parliament v. feudal king), nor a neo-Marxist view (the revolt of the 'industrious sort'), nor an anti-Marxist social classification of falling and rising gentries, have supplied the answer because in every case the facts stand awkwardly to the theory. At present it looks as

---

* [*Encounter*, July 1970.]
[1] Margaret A. Judson, *The Crisis of the Constitution* (New Brunswick, N.J., 1949); R. W. K. Hinton, 'Government and Liberty under James I,' *CHJ* 11 (157), 48–64.
[2] Recent analyses of puritanism have made it ever more difficult to know what the thing was, but they agree in showing that mainline puritanism was non-revolutionary, that until 1626 it looked like winning anyway, and that if there was a revolution it was not puritan. E.g. C. H. George, 'Puritanism as History and Historiography,' *Past and Present* 41 (1968), 77–104.

though only two kinds of historians can be satisfied that they know why the Civil War happened: those content with their ideologies, whatever the facts may say, and those content to believe that the wickedness of this man or that will serve for an explanation.

It is into this situation that Professor Zagorin has stepped forth with yet another attempt to tell why those dire events occurred.[1] His approach is not entirely original, but he employs it more consistently and fruitfully than anyone since Clarendon. In short, he sees the years leading to war as marked by the growth of two groups identifiable in and out of Parliament – one clustered round the king and his Court, the other clustered round a parliamentary leadership and characterized in the main by a comprehensive dislike of all things connected with the Court. The second (the Country) he regards as the bearer of revolution, or at least as the essential instrument for preparing the ground for revolution by destroying the power of the first. He rightly dismisses the various determinist interpretations and can find no applicable social categories into which to divide supporters and opponents of the Court: both groups were composed of men of the same stamp, standing, convictions and attitudes. Even religion does not define them, though extreme high-Church men leaned always to the Court and extreme puritans to the Country. Using these categories, he investigates the structure of parliamentary and, in the end, also extraparliamentary conflict, and though perhaps he does not get very far in uncovering the grass roots of either sector he scores some excellent points. He is especially good on the disastrous effects of Buckingham's regime which 'sowed disaffection in the Court and was the prime cause of enmity on the political scene' (p. 59). He handles the tricky question of puritanism with becoming care and wisely avoids identifying it with sectarianism.[2] His treatment of Pym's party – its triumph and decline in the first two sessions of the Long Parliament – is highly illuminating, a long overdue descriptive analysis which will do nothing but good. His refusal to be tied by theory, and his attempt to deal through real people, are both admirable. He has unquestionably made an important contribution to the debate which should be heeded by all. But if precedent is anything to go by, this account is likely to be swallowed rather than criticized, as all the explanations of the revolution have been when they first appeared. Therefore: is he right?

[1] Perez Zagorin, *The Court and the Country: the beginning of the English Revolution* (1969).
[2] But he grossly exaggerates when he speaks of puritanism 'tenaciously' preserving its identity for seventy years (p. 157). Historians' lives would be easier if this were remotely true.

Despite the rejection of theory, he depends in the last resort on his schematic categories which he treats as real and solid. There is not much question about the Court: it existed. Zagorin defines it as the 'throng of ministers, courtiers, officials, and servants' which clustered round the king and, at the centre as well as in the localities, governed for him. He excludes the unpaid local officials, such as sheriffs and justices of the peace, a distinction just worthy of acceptance (p. 41). Altogether, this is an adequate first definition, but for the purposes served here it needs a great deal of refining. A fuller understanding of administrative history and its problems might have led to some distinctions in all this welter. A secretary of state and a feodary of the court of Wards may both be called members of the Court, but they are so in very different ways. Working stiffs and sinecurists, administrators and household officers and lawyers, cannot really be so readily thrown into one great bag and never be distinguished again. Differences of employment, security and standing affect political attitudes and actions, the one thing that matters here; and so do personal preferences. And even if the crude definition were enough, it says nothing about party; many men with Court office found themselves at times in opposition to Court policy. There is no need to go into detail; the case of John Pym will suffice to call the category in question. We are told that he must not 'be classified as an official', even though he held a receivership of revenue for close on thirty years (p. 97) and that very office is explicitly included among those which 'the Court swept out to include' in the localities (p. 41). Clearly the definition may be too simple – especially a failure to hold office may, as we shall see, be read quite another way. And lastly, Zagorin's use of Court as equal to the king's political party hides a fundamental fact of the history of the time: the fact that a great deal of the political conflict occurred among the Court factions. Throughout, the members of the governing clique were usually more troubled by one another than by any regular opposition from the alleged 'Country'.[1]

The difficulties caused by the notion of the Court are child's play compared with the doubts that must hang about any attempt to classify the Country. The author is, in fact, aware how thin the ice is that he skates on. Again and again, he is careful to stress that the Country is

---

[1] Zagorin makes no reference to the outstanding recent treatment of Jacobean politics, Menna Prestwich's *Cranfield* (Oxford, 1966). Patrick Collinson's important study of *Elizabethan Puritanism* (1967) is said to have come out too late for use (p. 160, n. 2). In a book which itself reached the public eye towards the end of 1969 these are surprising omissions.

not really a party, a coherent body of men pursuing consistent political ends. But in fact he does regularly treat it as just such an entity, an agent of positive action 'doing' this or that, nor is it easy to see that if he had heeded his warning he would have been able to do anything at all with a thing that becomes manageable only when its elusive reality is overlooked. His definition begs all the questions: 'The Country was the first opposition movement in English history whose character transcended that of a feudal following or faction' (p. 74). But was 'the Country' really an 'opposition', and was it a movement at all? He has not shown it to be any of these things, and has indeed pointed out that it was really an exculpatory concept in the mind. The term, as he demonstrates, was used from the 1620s onwards to signify a general position of doubt in the face of government, and it is true that the dominant group of 1640 embodied a coalescence, under a leadership, of oppositionist particles that can be traced variously through the previous twenty years. But as against this, Zagorin has not succeeded in showing that the party of his dreams – the identifiable body of men promoting opposition to an equally solid Court group – ever existed at all. The jump from a discussion of the term to the description of a party in action is only, one fears, a jump. What Zagorin has proved (and this is important enough) is that the term was currently employed by those who wished to claim the respectability of a patriotic interest for their often very diverse resistance to the king's doings. To go beyond this is to fall back into the morass of 'whig' history, a point brought out when he slips casually into identifying this partified Country with Parliament itself (p. 90) – the Parliament, which of course, supplies his evidence for a struggle between two parties.

That the notion of a consistent 'Country' opposition will not do is well illustrated by the actions of its alleged leaders. Some of them may well be thought of as 'Country' by any definition, especially (and significantly) the puritan peers like Say and Bedford. But the men who opposed the Court in the Commons do not fit so well. We had already noted the puzzle posed by Pym. Was Coke, that old official, 'Country' – he who switched to opposition in Parliament only halfway through the 1621 session when the coveted treasurership went to Cranfield? Was Wentworth, promoter of the Petition of Right, who came to terms with Buckingham and took long-sought office as soon as the 1628 Parliament rose? Noy, the notorious attorney-general of the 1630s, had been another leading supporter of the Petition. Even Eliot, most passionate of 'opposers', held local office, was a Buckingham client, and was rightly thought to be looking for advancement. I am not suggesting that these men, and others like them, did not often oppose Court politics or advocate moves to counter the king's line of action, but nothing in their behaviour was as consistently and fundamentally 'oppositionist' as the scheme of Zagorin's book demands (and gets). Their position has been subtly misinterpreted: what moved them was not adherence to a County opposition to the Court, but a sincere and proper desire to improve the Court by joining it; as so many of them proved at the first opportunity, from Wentworth's misunderstood 'apostasy' to the wholesale elevation to office which accompanied the calling of the Long Parliament. They rightly believed that political life involved the exercise of power, and they believed with equal justice that they would manage the power of office better than the creatures the king delighted to honour. If they were 'Country', this was only because for one reason and another the 'Court' was closed to them; but this sort of 'Country' is no use to Zagorin's purpose of discovering 'the beginnings of the English Revolution'. Court and Country are useful concepts in defining certain attitudes and occasional positions, as well as offering political poles for ambition and opinion to gather round. But they were not movements or parties, not entities by means of which the political battles were fought. The Country, as it appears in Zagorin's book, did not exist at all, and his Court oversimplifies the realities. What we are really faced with is politics – the rivalries and differences among the monopolizers of power and those seeking to break into the monopoly (neither a group without its own internal and intense differences) – and nothing so far enables us to say that in these political realities the future revolution was being prepared.

Thus, this attempt to explain the situation of 1640–2 by means of a comprehensive generalization fails, like its predecessors. Since Court and Country are proper terms to use, though not necessarily quite in the sense used here, Zagorin's account is superior to those which use the improper categories of class or of precise religious parties. But it remains true that the struggle of Court and Country led really not to what actually happened – the overwhelming of the king's government, rebellion, civil war – but to the sort of political melée which is commonplace in any political system. If we are to break out of this impasse, we must attend to two ingredients in this particular story which Zagorin's preoccupation with his parties has caused him to ignore too much: the existence of 'real' issues transcending the struggle for power, and the changes brought by time. Revolutionary inklings occur among the fringe elements of the Country and in some speeches and sermons, as Michael Walzer has sufficiently proved; though these were far from prominent before the war, they should have been mentioned here because they may help to explain how solid gentlemen could move from exasperation to rebellion. More important, if the nature of opposition is to be properly grasped, the dark spectre of Protestantism's fate in Europe needs to be constantly kept in mind – but I do not remember it being mentioned at all. The Palatinate does not make the index, and the one mention of the Thirty Years' War (p. 4) fails to see the point which is not that revolution in England should be explained by the direct effects of the war. In fact, the English situation alone explains nothing: let us not forget the tears of Germany.[1] And lastly, the one thing strikingly missing here is a full account of the Eleven Years' Tyranny. The 'Country' which stood forth in 1640 was the product of the 1630s; the book obscures the quite fundamental difference between the age of Buckingham and the age of Laud. Like so much else lately written on this period, even this work, which includes some excellent narrative and much splendid reality, still suffers from attending too much on social analysis and too little on history.

If we are ever to get further with what is after all an important problem, we need (it seems to me) to start again. We need to reconsider our preconceived notions about this age of upheaval and especially to ask ourselves whether a situation in which highly intelligent and ingenious answers, offered by historians of manifest worth, so regularly fail to satisfy does not arise from the causes usual in such cases: namely, that the question is wrongly put. It seems to me that the usual posing of the question contains at least two misleading essentials. In the first place, we still have no history of those times which remembers that no one knew of the ultimate outcome. The whole search for 'the beginning of the English Revolution' in the previous forty years' history rests on the supposition that 1640 was implied in 1628 and 1621 – and further back still. But was it? So far, at least, we do not seem to do very well on the assumption that it was. We need now to understand these events – these disputes and crises – in their own right, because only in that way shall we succeed in discovering how and why the normal, if agitated, life of affairs, with its successes and failures, its satisfactions and exasperations, came in the end to a point where

---

[1] *Lacrimae Germaniae*, a German sermon of 1638 which was at once translated as a shot in the campaign against England's failure to intervene in the war.

normal gave way to exceptional and unpredictable. I do not call for a shutting of eyes to the ultimate crisis, but for an investigation which is not blindly fixated on that last explosion. And secondly, a more radical suggestion still may be made. Have we perhaps, in a way, misconceived the exceptional character of the events to be explained? We take it for granted that the rebellion and Civil War prove things to have been drastically amiss. But was this so? Was political conflict even of a drastic kind so unusual? Was war among Englishmen – and we might remember that it would have been a very different war if Scotsmen and Irishmen had not also been involved – so totally out of the reckoning?

These are questions, but so far there are no answers. I do not doubt that the Civil War was a national disaster, or that people were in measure surprised by it. But the common view makes it a monstrosity in creation, and it does so because we labour under another conventional notion, that of the Tudor peace. One hundred and fifty years before Edgehill, rival armies were moving about the English countryside – and they were far from new then. Since those days, several major and many minor risings had occurred; real war had on occasion been barely averted. No Tudor ever made the mistake of supposing that physical violence between factions of Englishmen had ended for ever. The country carried arms and was trained to them. Certainly, no one, in 1640, wanted civil war, and not many positively hoped for it even in 1642. That in fact it came is something that needs explaining from the sequence of events and the clash of men in affairs. But it seems to me that the resort to arms and the lapse into revolution were easier for that generation than historians since that day, aware of what the war was to be like and how futile its outcome, have been willing to recognize.

IV

POLITICAL THOUGHT

30

THE DIVINE RIGHT OF KINGS*

John Neville Figgis was born on 2 February 1866, at Brighton in Sussex, even then something of a place of resort and retirement for the upper middle classes. His father, the Reverend John Benjamin Figgis, was a minister in the sect known as the Countess of Huntingdon's Connexion, a narrowly Calvinist by-product of the eighteenth-century Methodist movement. In 1886 he went to St Catharine's College, Cambridge, to read mathematics; moderate success in that Tripos (1888) was followed next year by a brilliant performance in the Historical Tripos. In reaction against his upbringing, he turned agnostic, in the undergraduate fashion of his day, but his father's powerful personality never let him be himself, and he looked for father-substitutes for the rest of his life. In his early twenties he attached himself to Mandell Creighton, Regius professor of history at Cambridge[1] and later bishop of London; there followed a move into the Anglican Church, ordination in 1894, and an unsatisfactory year as curate in the market town of Kettering (Northamptonshire). From 1896 to 1902 he was very busy indeed, combining a teaching post in history at St Catharine's with the chaplaincy of Pembroke College and a curacy at the University church. Singlehanded he gave to his old College, notorious even in the Cambridge of its day for its low standards and philistinism, a respectable position in the University. But in 1902 preferment called him to the rectory of Marnhull (Dorset) where he spent five rather frustrating years, an intellectual parson in a backward village which respected but hardly understood or used him. Then, in 1907, he took the decisive and in many ways disastrous step of moving to the wing of his Church right opposite that with which by upbringing he should have had most sympathy. Strongly influenced by the relentless and magisterial figure of W. H. Frere, he joined the Anglican monastic community at Mirfield in Yorkshire. A busy but, to him, barely tolerable life of austerity was spent in the religious duties of the house, in preaching and writing, and in American

---

* [Introduction to J. N. Figgis, *The Divine Right of Kings*, Harper Torchbook ed., 1965.]
[1] [A ridiculous howler: Creighton was Dixie professor of ecclesiastical history.]

lecture tours. On his third trip, he was torpedoed in January 1918; and though he survived, his health suffered permanent damage. Early in 1919 his mind gave way, and he died in a mental home on 13 April 1919.[1]

Figgis was fundamentally an unhappy man with a sad history. By nature large, greedy, desperately untidy, kind, lively, gregarious, spontaneous, he suffered through life from a heavy sense of sin and inadequacy. He was manifestly an unconscious homosexual, surrounded by young friends and pupils, uneasy with women unless they were much older and could be met on the intellectual level only. He entered the communal life in a search for the discipline which he believed he needed and could not find within himself. Like many a good College man before and since, he was shamelessly overworked and exploited by colleagues who were only too willing to leave the hard work to the willing horse.[2] The stringent regime of Mirfield helped to undermine his health and – possibly worse – forced him to devote his intellect to the ephemera of ecclesiastical and theological argument at the low level suitable to the aspirant cleric. Though in his circle he had a high reputation as a preacher, he displayed in his sermons and correspondence much of that distance from the world of men characteristic of his age, class and calling. In particular, he bore the two unmistakable hallmarks of this remoteness: he (as he himself might have put it) commonly larded his discourse with misapplied slang and excruciatingly bad jokes, so that the luminous and lucid style usually at his command suffered lapses into mental stuttering which are painful to read. The collapse of his mind did not come out of nowhere. Though no doubt assisted by the severe strains within himself, it was in the main brought on by the labours of his acquaintances, well-wishers as well as indifferents, who would not let him be himself. From his father to his superior, he was always attaching himself to simpler, stronger men who knew what was good for him; unco-ordinated and diffuse in himself, he humbly accepted their guidance, and between them they destroyed him.

All this must be said in order to bring out more clearly Figgis's positive and very remarkable achievement. Contrary to what he him-

---

[1] For Figgis's life and person I have relied on W. H. Frere's curiously unsympathetic account in *DNB*; Maurice G. Tucker's *John Neville Figgis* (1950), a simple piece of hero-worship; and on memories still current at Cambridge. Tucker's book makes reading between the lines both easy and necessary.

[2] [Since this passage has given rise to misunderstandings I want to make it plain that I have St Catharine's, Cambridge in mind, not Mirfield.]

self was led to believe, this lay in the work of a university teacher and a student of history. As a historian, too, he over-eagerly sought guides and heroes, and here too he displayed less than perfect judgment. After Creighton, the two men he most admired were F. W. Maitland, the great legal historian, and Lord Acton, Creighton's successor as Regius professor.[1] But while he always acknowledged the superb quality of Maitland, he followed more readily the inspiration of Acton, away from institutions and laws to the history of ideas. When Maitland discussed ideas (as he often did) he never forgot that they are only meaningful with reference to the people who hold or denounce them. He never fell victim to the fallacy which sees the past solely through the books written in the past, for he had the discipline of the record to steady his passionate interest in the world of thought and speculation. This Acton lacked, despite all his notable gifts and his wide involvement with men of affairs. Acton may have been a wise man, but he was an indifferent historian, often surprised by the discovery of intrigue or double-dealing behind an official façade into a somewhat amateurish reaction: astonishment at the commonplace, overemphasis on the insignificant, heavily moral attitudes. But his powerful presence and public figure, together with the influence, just beginning to be felt, of Ranke's school, set an imprint on the incipient Cambridge school of history. International relations and the history of ideas, both unusually selfcontained forms of historical enquiry and both capable of being studied in printed books, were to form its staple for a long time. Maitland left a glowing memory, much admiration, and no disciples.

In one respect Figgis did better than his mentor: he wrote books, serious and good works of history in his chosen field. If today he is himself worthy of memory, as he is, he owes this entirely to his two studies in the history of political thought, *The Divine Right of Kings* (first ed., 1896), and *From Gerson to Grotius* (1907). The second book in many ways follows up the suggestions of the first, fills in some gaps and corrects some errors of interpretation. Most competent critics would probably agree that it represents not only wider knowledge but also more adequate views. Nevertheless, it is with his first book, a prize essay written before he was thirty, that Figgis's name is commonly linked; and this is just. *From Gerson to Grotius* was based on lectures; *The Divine Right of Kings* is much more of a book. It rests on astonishingly wide reading, carried out, before the days of modern editions, in

---

[1] [Acton's predecessor was Sir John Seeley.]

clumsy sixteenth and seventeenth century versions. Unlike his later work, it is unaffected by his conversion and the religious preoccupations which increasingly interfered with a clear view of the past. And it is more truly original in that it discusses not this writer or that but one particular idea. Most of the vast work done in English in what one may call pure political theory – before sociology, psychology and social anthropology complicated the situation by introducing important but indigestible dimensions – follows in some measure from the great impression made by Figgis's youthful work. He established the method: to study the writers from the point of view of a particular problem, collect and collate their views, establish lines of influence and descent. He stressed the importance of the historical setting, a sufficiently new notion then, now the merest tired commonplace. He directed attention to the leaders of thought and the purer intellectuals, where (unfortunately) it has in the main stayed since. If Figgis's book does not today read like a work seventy years old, this is because in method and approach writers on the history of political thought have added remarkably little to his, though they have thickened the texture, enlarged the catchment area, and rendered the argument more sophisticated. In the process, it may be added, too many of them have also lost his skill in conveying complex problems in simple and attractive language. There is no jargon in Figgis, and he would be worth re-reading for that fact alone.

Since his book has retained its life for such a long time – long in the academic context – he has naturally exerted even more influence in his chosen field than in the whole genre. When Figgis started work on the divine right of kings, no one took that theory seriously. John Locke had effectively destroyed it in the seventeenth century; all men with ambitions to be thought well-informed knew that it was laughable – a huge joke. Figgis soon discovered its logical coherence and its ancient ancestry; he realized that, given a point of view which saw in politics the hand of God, the doctrine was both more obvious and more convincing than the utilitarian liberalism which dominated English thinking in his own time. He therefore spent much labour in defending his choice of subject and explaining the link which, in the seventeenth century and earlier, had connected theology and political thought. All this is now so familiar that the reader may be bored by Figgis's insistence; but there is historical value in these constant affirmations. If at times Figgis seems excessively aware of his potential readers' preconceptions, it is worth remembering, once again, that he was a pioneer, addressing an audience particularly ill-qualified to grasp the religion-dominated and king-oriented thought of a lost past, a past before Enlightenment and Bentham and John Stuart Mill and Darwin and Mr Gladstone had been. Since Figgis's day, on the other hand, it has been difficult to free the sixteenth and seventeenth centuries from an air of being exclusively peopled by divinely entitled and therefore absolutist kings. Theories of kingship which stressed the rights of subjects and the dominance of law have tended to be overlooked in the dazzling light of God-granted authority. Figgis himself redressed the balance a little in *From Gerson to Grotius*, and constitutional historians have long been pointing to the institutional and practical limitations upon divine-right kingship; but the serious analysis of doctrines opposed to the absolute assertion of divine right – doctrines inevitably less straightforward or logically conclusive within their own terms – has only recently been making progress and has not yet achieved the coherence of statement which Figgis gave to the other side.[1] Figgis's book was almost too successful in displacing the contempt and neglect which he disputed.

Naturally enough, a book so many decades old – decades filled with an ever-widening stream of historical research, analysis and description – can be corrected in a good many details. Figgis saw the English middle ages through the eyes of Stubbs, and few today would interpret the fourteenth and fifteenth centuries so simply as times of constitutional conflict between prerogative and feudal or popular rights of consent.[2] Widely read as he was, he could not anticipate future labours: the important medieval canonists and civilians, especially, were less well known to him than they have since become.[3] He did not grasp how traditional and even commonplace – how unrevolutionary – the

---

[1] See esp. William F. Church, *Constitutional Thought in Sixteenth-Century France* (Cambridge, Mass., 1941); John G. A. Pocock, *The Ancient Constitution and the Feudal Law* (Cambridge, 1957); J. W. Gough, *Fundamental Law in English Constitutional History* (Oxford, 1955); Franklin L. Baumer, *The Early Tudor Theory of Kingship* (Cambridge, Mass., 1938).

[2] E.g. Figgis, 28, 73 ff., 81. For more recent interpretations, see May McKisack, *The Fourteenth Century* (Oxford, 1959), and E. F. Jacob, *The Fifteenth Century* (Oxford, 1961), with good bibliographies; and particularly, Stanley B. Chrimes, *English Constitutional Ideas in the Fifteenth Century* (Cambridge, 1936), and his edition of Sir John Fortescue's *De Laudibus Legum Anglie* (Cambridge, 1942).

[3] E.g. Cecil N. S. Woolf, *Bartolus of Sassoferrato* (Cambridge, 1913); Walter Ullmann, *The Medieval Idea of Law as represented by Lucas da Penna* (1946), and *Medieval Papalism* (1949); Brian Tierney, *Foundations of Conciliar Theory* (Cambridge, 1955); and the works mentioned below, p. 199, n. 1, and p. 207, n. 1. There are useful bibliographies in Kantorowicz (below, p. 199, n. 1) and Lewis (next note).

political thinking of leading reformers like Luther and Calvin really was. But what strikes the mind forcibly is the degree to which some of his suggestions proved seminal, to be traced further by others, even if some of these developments do not now command general acceptance. He introduced writers in English to the notion that the middle ages, holding to a Platonic and Thomist concept of human law as reflecting the eternal law of God (the order of the universe), could not strictly conceive of the possibility that man might *make* law: this view was to underlie all C. H. McIlwain's massive work, though we have come to realize that it both underestimates medieval realism in such matters and overestimates the exclusive hold of Thomist thought on the fourteenth and fifteenth centuries.[1] Earlier than anyone else, Figgis realized how much the political thought of sixteenth-century France influenced the arguments of seventeenth-century England; this has been followed up only to a limited extent.[2] Figgis treated the political thought of Elizabethan puritanism with more respect than was usual in his day, and his view that Thomas Cartwright, for instance, believed in the existence of 'two kingdoms' (a clear separation of Church and State) formed the basis of A. F. Scott Pearson's work on that writer.[3] The insight and rapid association of ideas which mark Figgis's mind are characteristic of the best work done in the history of political theories; are indeed required for it. They are certainly more noteworthy than the inevitable errors and insufficiencies of the pioneer. Figgis's is a mind worth meeting, and his book must still be read by anyone interested in the subject. After seventy years, that is a considerable achievement.

[1] Charles H. McIlwain, *The High Court of Parliament* (New Haven, 1910); *The Growth of Political Thought in the West* (New York, 1932), esp. 323 ff.; *Constitutionalism Ancient and Modern* (Ithaca, N.Y., 1947). Attacks on his views are widely scattered, e.g. through the works of Gaines Post and Brian Tierney cited below, pp. 206–7; for a useful summary of the problem see Ewart Lewis, *Medieval Political Ideas* (1954), ch. 1, esp. 18 ff.

[2] G. P. Gooch, *English Democratic Ideas in the Seventeenth Century* (Cambridge, 2nd ed. 1927), ch. 1; J. H. M. Salmon, *The French Religious Wars in English Political Thought* (Oxford, 1959).

[3] *Thomas Cartwright and Elizabethan Puritanism* (Cambridge, 1925); *Church and State: Political aspects of sixteenth-century Puritanism* (Cambridge, 1928). I cannot agree with this view which ignores the essential Puritan belief in theocracy – government on earth by God's ministers – and forgets the degree to which pamphleteers adapted their tenets to the pressures of political circumstance. Figgis himself says (p. 190) that in Cartwright's teaching the Church was to dictate the use of the sword held by the State; where, then, are the two independent kingdoms? The vast literature of puritanism is outside our present concern; see, e.g., M. M. Knappen, *Tudor Puritanism* (Chicago, 1939), and C. H. and K. George, *The Protestant Mind of the English Reformation* (Princeton, 1961), for useful bibliographies. [Add now esp. P. Collinson, *Elizabethan Puritanism* (1967) and M. Walzer, *The Revolution of the Saints* (Cambridge, Mass., 1965).]

A good many threads run through this book, but some may be isolated as particularly important to Figgis himself. He believed that the seventeenth-century doctrine of the divine right of kings, as he found it in the teaching of Stuart apologists and French absolutists, was peculiar and in essence distinguishable from earlier views which linked monarchy with delegation of power from God. He held that the doctrine grew out of the necessity to find a positive theoretical support for the rejection of papal claims to spiritual, and sometimes temporal, overlordship, that the political thought of the Reformation (in particular, Luther's) formed one major pillar for it, and that the concept of sovereignty (resulting in the separation of Church and State, the emancipation of the State from clerical control) could never have been developed except by way of the divine right of kings. That is to say, he regarded medieval thought on society and political authority as essentially different from modern: the first stage of the modern situation was embodied in the emergence of national states ruled by absolutist princes claiming God-granted authority. Both in general and in particular, these points have been much debated, further developed, and often attacked.

Since 1896 a great deal has been written on medieval kingship.[1] Study has in the main concentrated on theories in justification of royal power and on the symbolism with which monarchy surrounded itself; the result – perhaps predictably – has been to bring out the mystic, semi-priestly, and potentially autocratic elements, to the relative neglect of such limitations, theoretical and practical, as undoubtedly existed. Through most of the middle ages, those who wrote on such topics were necessarily clerics, which helped to direct attention to this more religious side of kingship. Royal coronations partook of the character of episcopal ordinations; the anointing replaced the old Germanic 'election' or acclamation as the chief element in the making of a king; some kings even used a holier oil than the bishop's chrism, while the papacy would permit only an inferior grade to the emperor. (The king of France was *rex Christianissimus*, the Most Christian king,

---

[1] A small selection: Frederick W. Maitland, 'The Crown as Corporation,' *Select Essays*, ed. Hazeltine, Lapsley and Winfield (Cambridge, 1936), 104 ff.; Marc Bloch, *Les Rois Thaumaturges* (Strasbourg, 1924); Percy E. Schramm, *A History of the English Coronation* (Eng. trans., Oxford, 1937); *Der König von Frankreich* (Weimar, 1939); *Herrschaftszeichen und Staatssymbolik* (Stuttgart, 1952–4); F. Schulz, 'Bracton on Kingship,' *EHR* 60 (1945), 136 ff.; Jean de Page, *Le Roi Très Chrétien* (Paris, 1949); E. Kantorowicz, *The King's Two Bodies* (Princeton, 1957); Walter Ullmann, *Principles of Government and Politics in the Middle Ages* (1961), Part II.

because the oil used in his coronation had come direct from heaven, the unlikely recipient being that barbarian of genius, the Merovingian Clovis.) Comparisons with Christ, claims to Christ's vicariate on earth, were freely made. All this royal semi-divinity was worked out and stressed at the very beginning of medieval kingship, from the eighth to the tenth centuries. It was then that divine-right (theocratic) kingship was at its height, summed up in the phrase which, from Charlemagne onwards, kings came generally to use: the phrase *dei gratia*. They were kings by the grace of God, by God's gift and permission; and this was elaborated to mean that they could be held responsible only to God, that the governed people were by God committed to their charge (*populus mihi commissus*), even that the body of subjects were in the position of a minor, in tutelage to the guardian instituted by God. There is very little in seventeenth-century views of divine right that may not be traced in the claims put forward by the Carolingian, Saxon or Salian kings of Germany, in the practice of Anglo-Saxon kings calling themselves emperors, in the writings of an extreme defender of the rights of kings like the eleventh-century Norman Anonymous. The systematic study of Roman law renewed in the twelfth century, added to the armoury of royal pretensions with such famous texts as that 'what has pleased the prince has the force of law' or that the prince is 'free of the laws' (*legibus solutus*), and the fourteenth-century definition, *rex est imperator in regno suo*, ascribed to kings the attributes to be found in the Roman emperor. But none of this could raise royal claims above those of a Charlemagne, a William the Conqueror, or of a man like the emperor Henry III who appointed popes at his pleasure.

In fact, so far from the divine right of kings being developed against the papacy, it would to some extent be truer to turn the notion round. The divinity of early-medieval kingship arose not only from the *dei gratia* concept and the example of Constantine; it owed a great deal also to the practical facts which left kings alone capable of acting as God's agents on earth in the protection of men's bodies and souls. Before the eleventh century at least, the Church could not help but look to kings for the preservation of order, the safeguarding of its property, and the advance of God's cause. 'Proprietary churches', whether the individual benefice controlled by a local lord or the body of a regional (national) Church controlled by a king, were the necessary order of the day. Where else should authority lie? True, the papacy had from an early date put forward claims which could extend to a universal monarchy. The superiority of the spiritual to the temporal was generally acknowledged, but kings were granted possession of spiritual authority, too. Melchisedek, king and priest, was to the monarchists of the middle ages the prototype of kingship. The collapse of the papacy in the tenth century left the field to kings. Thereafter the great papal revival, culminating in the world monarchy of Innocent III and the unrealistic assertions of Boniface VIII, altered the position: in theory, at least, kings were deprived of their spiritual authority, quarrels developed over rival jurisdictions and powers, popes asserted a superiority which might include a claim to make and unmake kings. The outward attributes of divine right remained (kings were the Lord's anointed, *divi* and *sacri*), but no late-medieval king was so manifestly God's deputy in matters both spiritual and temporal as had been his tenth-century ancestor. In truth, as a developed doctrine, the king's divine right to rule preceded the pope's divine right to oversee all rule. When one remembers that the papacy had a long struggle before it was accepted as leader even of the estate of the clergy, whereas kings could look to Constantine and Charlemagne as models, this may seem less surprising. It was indeed the peculiar strength of medieval kingship that it never abandoned the notion of a God-given authority not mediated by the pope; the supposedly grander medieval emperor always suffered from being linked in a notional world monarchy with a partner who, by crowning him, symbolized his own primacy.

Of course, once the reformed papacy got down to business, its spiritual eminence, its universal reach and claim, its exceptional organization, and its mass of agents and propagandists enabled it to proclaim the full logic of its position in a way that neither kings nor emperors could ever emulate. The divine right of a priest like the pope was more probable and manifest than the divine right of kings. Figgis was therefore quite right to interpret the doctrines of the sixteenth and seventeenth centuries against the background of the break with the papacy. When Henry VIII of England adopted the title of supreme head of the Church, his position owed a great deal to the supremacy, resting on right divine, which papal doctrine had erected upon the *successio Petri*. While divine right is a term which one would readily apply to tenth-century kingship, *plenitudo potestatis*, the pope's special preserve, is not. The divine right of Henry VIII and Elizabeth inherited at least elements of this papal fullness of power which had not been present in the 'thaumaturgical' kingship of the Anglo-Saxons or the practical divine right of that protector of the Church, William the Conqueror. But when Henry claimed, as he did, that he was merely restoring the true preeminence of kings, long disturbed by papal interference and usurpation, he was neither so wrong nor so hypocritical as is usually alleged. There were real links between the divine-right monarchy of the Tudors and the *dei gratia* monarchy of the Carolingians; and both quite properly looked back to Constantine the Great.

Certainly they were not the same in every essential. Tudor divine right, and even up to a point the Bourbon monarchy of the seventeenth century, contained far less of that magic or mystic element that distinguished the newly Christianized barbarian kings. Mysticism there was, but attenuated; religion formed the ceremonial dress rather than the passionate essence of post-medieval kings by right divine. On the other hand, their actual power over both State and Church was as a rule markedly greater; the machinery, the economy of their realms saw to that. More significantly, a different aspect of the complex doctrine came to receive chief attention, and it did so (as Figgis divined) because the doctrine was reconsidered under the stress of the attack on Rome and of the Reformation of which this attack formed a part. The aspect now stressed was not so much the will of God in making the king, or the king's duty to govern his people on God's behalf (though no one doubted these points), as the subject's duty towards his king. The theory of the divine right of kings resolved itself into a discussion of obedience and resistance. And it did so, to be brief, because the Reformation everywhere introduced revolutionary situations in which men's loyalties could easily divide.

Luther himself has often enough been credited with an excessive worship for princes; it is even supposed that he really transformed political thought by demanding obedience at all costs. This is going far too far, though there is some truth in it. The Reformation in a sense revived the situation of the tenth century when order and the struggle against anarchy depended exclusively on the power of secular princes; the end of the papal monarchy, however purely theoretical it had already become, left kings again as the necessary residuary legatees, and the theory of divine right stood ready to exalt them into sole occupation of the saddle. Luther, a true conservative, was extremely sensitive to the danger that what he regarded as a necessary return to an uncorrupted condition in the Church could lead to the dissolution of all secular ties and therefore to disastrous anarchy in God's natural creation. The government of this creation, he believed to be the consequence of the Fall; God's order for the fallen universe involved obedience to constituted authority. St Paul's few words in Romans 13 run right through all post-Reformation writing on authority and obedience. To Luther, the only liberty worth thinking about was Christian liberty, by which he meant salvation – nothing to do with men's temporal state. It did, however, lead him to make an important reservation to his general injunction of obedience: if the ruler ordains anything contrary to the truth of God, as revealed in Scripture, obedience is unlawful. So, however, is resistance: the Christian must confine himself to non-obedience, taking the consequences in this life and bliss in the next.

Calvin's teaching was in essentials the same, though he hinted at the possibility that there might exist inferior magistrates (like the Spartan ephors or modern Parliaments) who, having their power also from God, might in given circumstances be entitled to preserve God's good order against a tyrant. Here lay the germ of a useful idea, to be tended and developed by later generations of Calvinists when they came into conflict with their princes. In general, however, all the leading reformers preached non-resistance because kings were kings by right divine, responsible to God and punishable by Him alone, and because resistance meant the dissolution of God's decree for the fallen creation. Just because they saw the kingdoms of this world in so much worse a light, by comparison with the kingdom of God, than had the theorists of the later middle ages, they would not consider the questions of political liberty or limitations upon the powers of the magistrate. But that is only to say that they were good Augustinians, not Thomists, stressing the logical implications of ancient tradition.

Naturally this suited princes. The *Homily of Obedience* of 1547 expressed the whole doctrine of obedience and non-resistance in terms which no devotee of divine right in Louis XIV's France or Charles II's England could have bettered. 'We may not resist, nor in any wise hurt, an anointed king, which is God's lieutenant, vicegerent and highest minister in the country where he is king.' The whole history of the divine right of kings, both its ancient belief in the sole source of royal power and its more recent preoccupation with obedience, is here neatly summed up. What, then, could the Stuarts add to it – to a doctrine not only, as Figgis thought, as old as the Reformation but in fact as old as Christian kingship? Yet there was an element missing, or at least not firmly stated, and here James I put in his pennyworth.[1] He added indefeasibility – or rather, since the notion of royal power as inalienable and, once created, irremovable also had a long history, the identification of indefeasibility with hereditary succession by primogeniture in the legitimate line. The one question left open in Tudor divine right teaching was this: who is the king appointed by God? The Tudor answer was pragmatic: whoever happens to be recognized as king. Anything more philosophical would have been awkward for a dynasty whose original claim was very weak and which encountered a series of succession problems. But the Stuarts, safer in their descent and happier in their production of progeny, felt able to claim that God's choice was announced by birth: at any given moment, there was always only one true king, whether or not he in fact ever managed to sit on a throne, and he was his predecessor's legitimate heir. Thus the doctrine received its final logical elaboration, and also (characteristically) the one touch of true absurdity to be found in it.

Figgis thus underestimated the antiquity and foundations of the doctrine and overestimated the contribution made by the Reformation. Yet he was right to see the particular form it took in the seventeenth century as the product of the situation, political as well as doctrinal, which grew from the rejection of the papacy and the breakup of Christendom. Next, he argued that this development led to the formulation of a true theory of sovereignty, and that nothing else could have done. When he talked of sovereignty he was thinking of the definition given by John Austin in lectures published in 1832: that sovereignty resides in the individual or aggregate body to whom a given society is in the habit of rendering obedience or submission, but who himself is not in the habit of obeying any determinate human superior. Austin's sovereign is principally a law-maker whose edicts command habitual obedience (or punishment for disobedience) and are the emanation of his sole will. It is generally agreed, with Figgis, that in this special sense sovereignty cannot be said to exist in a society which acknowledges a variety of intermediate or sectional superiors, or one whose laws are treated as the reflection of transcendental law, to be judged good or bad, valid or invalid, according to their consonance with it. However, many would now doubt whether 'Austinian' sovereignty is to be found even in the seventeenth century: some argue that it has

[1] For James I see *The Political Works of James I*, ed. with a valuable introduction by C. H. McIlwain (Cambridge, Mass., 1918). A remarkable variant of the doctrine, deriving royal power from biblical and sociological patriarchalism, was put forward by Sir Robert Filmer in his *Patriarcha*: see the edition by T. P. R. Laslett (Oxford, 1949).

never really existed anywhere, while others hold that even if it ever
had reality it is too narrow to be treated as universally valid. There is
therefore now a tendency to trace such sovereignty as is supposed to
have existed in the seventeenth century further and further back into
the middle ages.[1]

The conventional notion, propounded by Figgis, was that sovereignty
could not exist before the political developments of the sixteenth
century (the growth of selfcontained nation states) which were first
clearly summed in Jean Bodin's definition of the 'modern' notion of
sovereignty (*Six Books of the Republic*, 1567). As against this, we are
now commonly told two things: one, that late medieval states were
quite as selfcontained and 'sovereign' as their post-Reformation successors, and two, that the limitations upon sovereignty which operated
in the seventeenth century (respect for natural law, respect for customary rights and restraints) made the sovereignty of Stuart kings and
Bourbon monarchs more like that of their Yorkist and Valois predecessors than that of the nineteenth century. Both points have force;
neither is entirely true. The political situation in the later middle ages
is not really relevant if it remains true that those societies regarded
themselves as seriously constrained by abstract laws (which to some
extent they did) or as sharing power among a variety of authorities
(which they certainly did). And the second point is less important than
it might seem, because the real question is whether at any given moment
a single authority exists on the earthly plane, rather than whether respect remains for superhuman authority. However attenuated, some
such respect nearly always remains, which means that the discussion
would have to turn upon degrees of approximation to an ideal definition rather than upon the realities of political thinking. In some very
important respects the State of the sixteenth and seventeenth centuries
could entertain an opinion of itself which gave it selfsufficiency and
selfcontrol; its predecessor could sometimes demonstrate these qualities
but did not consciously believe in their existence. In practice this
meant that sovereign activity increased quite as much as doctrines of
sovereignty, which makes the distinction important.

Nevertheless, Figgis's outright denial of the possibility of sovereignty
in the middle ages will not do. Some scholars have found in the
claims of the papacy the full equivalent even of Austinian sovereignty:

[1] For Austin see H. L. A. Hart's edition of his *The Province of Jurisprudence Determined*
(1954), esp. 193 ff.; for an attack on his views, see Hans Kelsen, *General Theory of Law
and State* (Eng. trans., Cambridge, Mass., 1949).

not only did the *plenitudo potestatis* include all power to govern, not only was the pope thought free of all earthly superiors, but when in the later middle ages it came to be more widely held that law depended for its validity solely on the ruler's will papal legislation, claimed to be universally applicable, achieved true sovereignty.[1] Papalism could assuredly lead to this view. Some writers came to eliminate the division between secular and ecclesiastical power, drew the logical conclusion from the God-given and monopolistic power of the Church's ruler, and subordinated all other authority, ecclesiastical or lay, to the papal monarchy which was thus invested with all the attributes of a genuine sovereignty – that is, with total irresponsibility. It may be objected that this was only one strand, and that the constitutionalist doctrines of those who in the fifteenth century advocated conciliar rule in the Church prove the existence of quite different views among the defenders of ecclesiastical pre-eminence:[2] but the brief importance of such teaching resulted simply from the accident of the papal schism, and the rapid restoration of papal despotism proved where the main-stream ran.

A more weighty objection to this identification of papalist doctrine with true sovereignty lies in the reminder that in practice late-medieval popes exercised no such powers. Secular states, at least closely resembling those found in modern Europe, are easily found in the fourteenth and fifteenth centuries, and their rulers, asserting a form of divine-right monarchy, may be credited with an equal claim to the possession of sovereignty. After all, they were usually called sovereigns. But this is where the term has proved too protean. By redefining it, scholars have found sovereignty in the thirteenth-century lawyer Accursius, allegedly nearer to present-day teaching on the subject than to Austin;[3] both canonists and civilians from that time on have been interpreted as expounding doctrines according to which 'the state itself, being superior to all private rights, was by the mid-thirteenth century becoming sovereign', such sovereignty being in practice vested in its

[1] Michael J. Wilks, *The Problem of Sovereignty in the Later Middle Ages* (Cambridge, 1963), esp. 151–83. For papal doctrine see also Walter Ullmann, *The Growth of Papal Government in the Middle Ages* (2nd ed., 1962), and *Principles*, Part I.

[2] E.g. Brian Tierney, 'Some recent works on the political theories of the medieval canonists,' *Traditio*, 10 (1954), 594 ff.

[3] Brian Tierney, '"The Prince is not bound by the laws": Accursius and the origins of the modern state,' *Comparative Studies in Society and History*, 5 (1963), 378 ff. His argument does not convince me: he creates modernity in Accursius by smudging all proper distinctions and never comes to grips with the problem of the *making* of law as distinct from living with that which exists.

head, the prince, with his power 'of legislating, judging and administering, of doing all that was necessary for the common and public welfare'.[1] That such unequivocal assertions are immediately followed by very large exceptions and reservations, from the law of God to the rights of subjects, sounds a warning to those who would like to wipe out the distinction between medieval and modern. However, late-medieval kings could do most of these things most of the time, and could do them with only intermittent interference from elsewhere, or from inferiors: Figgis's 'radical discontinuity' between these ages does not convince either. We no longer believe in a 'new monarchy' in the sixteenth century. In both England and France clear-cut concepts of sovereignty remained difficult to develop as long as theorists acknowledged the presence of such limitations as *leges imperii* (fundamental laws which no human agency could alter) or the supposed ability of the existing law to control the validity of new law:[2] McIlwain refused to see any recognition of real sovereignty as late as the age of Louis XIV.[3] Figgis's clear distinction has become blurred by medievalists looking to the practical effects of kingship and by modernists paying heed to conventional limitations on freedom of action. The fact that, with reservations, Figgis was probably nearer the truth is worth restating.

For one thing, the attack on Austin has gone too far. His definition fits best the sort of unitary, centrally controlled and all-powerful state which he had before him in nineteenth-century England; and the excesses practised by such states in conditions of twentieth-century totalitarianism have done much to discredit his somewhat rigorous opinion. A country like the United States, with its fundamental constitution and its devolution of powers upon constituent states, may be said to practise a system in which there is no room for Austin's sovereign. The British Commonwealth of Nations, resting (in law) upon the Statute of Westminster (1931) in which the sovereign law-maker renounced the power of sovereign law-making, forms an even more

---

[1] See the writings of Gaines Post in *Traditio*, 1 (1943), 355 ff., and 10 (1953), 281 ff.; *Speculum*, 29 (1954), 417 ff.; *Welt als Geschichte* (1961), 8 ff., 71 ff. The above quotations come from Mr Post's summary of his own views in his review of Wilks's book in *Speculum*, 39 (1964), 365 ff.

[2] Bodin believed in fundamental laws; it has even been possible to treat him simply as a constitutionalist (which he was not): Beatrice Reynolds, *Proponents of Limited Monarchy in Sixteenth-Century France* (New York, 1931). For common law and statute law in England see the summary in *Tudor Constitution*, 233 f.

[3] But see George L. Mosse, *The Struggle for Sovereignty in England* (East Lansing, 1950), for a strong dissenting view.

striking argument against it.[1] But these are superficial views. The excesses of Hitler or Stalin do not prove that the essence of the State is not found in its right to demand obedience to its laws. The United States has several times shown itself possessed of the power to amend its constitution or coerce its component parts: there is an ultimate, if rarely used, sovereign authority there somewhere. And the Commonwealth is only in the process of proving that it has ceased to be relevant to the discussion: it no longer is, in Austin's phrase, 'a society political and independent' but a loose collection of sovereign states. Austin did seize on the crucial point, whereas his critics drift around the edges. Kelsen's definition of law as 'norm', as a rule of conduct generally accepted by a given society, may be wider and jurisprudentially more useful than Austin's law as command. But we are concerned with sovereignty, which is a dynamic quality: the power and right to make new law, the ability to order the doing or abstaining from something not hitherto enjoined or forbidden. And every non-Austinian definition of law sooner or later grounds upon this rock: whence does new law derive its authority and effect?

If legislation, then, is the criterion which must define the nature of the power structure within a state, the late-medieval concept of sovereignty will be seen to differ significantly from the modern. The pope was then the only possible medieval sovereign (in the modern sense) because he claimed superiority to all other laws for his edicts. So far Mr Wilks's theorists are right. But because the pope's 'sovereignty' was so universal – because his 'state' embraced all Christendom – his sovereignty had no reality. Everywhere, the law of the secular community, the prince's law, rivalled the pope's, either co-existing with it or occasionally superseding it. But the prince's law was no more sovereign because everywhere the validity of the papal law in certain defined spheres of life was fully admitted. All this is quite apart from the view still firmly current that law, to be good, must please God, that there existed a superior standard of validity in the non-human law of nature. In practice, medieval legislators may not have been more notably bound by purely moral or religious scruple, though in fact it seems clear to me that the force of these beliefs declined in the course of the sixteenth century. The point is not important, any more than is the real meaning of natural law in the seventeenth century. As has already been said, men at all times make reservations to their total freedom to act as they please. What really limited medieval sovereignty

[1] These are the instances used by Tierney.

was the existence of the papacy and its at least theoretically over-whelming claims. In the later middle ages, sovereignty meant no more than supremacy, chief magistracy, the right to govern within the agreed and limiting confusion of laws and legislative authorities. The Reformation was required to release sovereignty from its limitations and turn it into the power to make law superior to any other within a given society. This was most easily seen in such countries as England or Sweden where the medieval sovereign (the prince regnant) absorbed his rival's powers and so became sovereign in quite a different sense.[1] But in due course it became manifest also in states in which the papacy continued to exercise a theoretical influence. Figgis was right when he pointed to the separation of Church and State as the hallmark of sove-reignty, though the story and the problems were much more com-plicated than he realized and the last word has certainly not yet been said. The middle ages did have a concept and practice of sovereignty, but these differed from what, quite slowly in most places and more slowly in most minds, developed from it after the Reformation. As for divine right, Figgis correctly supposed that it was closely involved in the emergence of clearer thinking about sovereignty and the state, but he mistook an accident for a causal relationship. Though quite often sovereignty and divine right went hand in hand, they did not have to do so; other concepts of monarchy and society existed which were equally capable of reconciling themselves to the notion of sove-reignty.

This raises the whole question of the dilemma of medieval and early modern kingship. Figgis, concerned with the divine right of kings, ignored other strands in the history of monarchy. If I now briefly go outside the confines he set himself, that is because a wider view will throw light on the divine right itself and help to explain the collapse of a doctrine which had so much logic and so much age to recommend it. The truth is that the medieval king combined within himself several dualities. There were the 'two bodies' studied by Kantorowicz, the mystical entity which never died and the physical being which under-went the normal human vicissitudes. *Rex et sacerdos*: at least until the eleventh century, kings commonly claimed to be both. Reservoir of justice, reservoir of mercy: he was both. But these dualisms presented no difficulty to the single human being. It was otherwise with the double

---

[1] For England and its mixed sovereignty, see my *England under the Tudors* (1955), 160 f.; *Tudor Constitution*, 230 ff.

source of his power. To the fundamental questions – what made a man king, and by what right could he claim obedience – there were two discordant, even irreconcilable, answers. He was king by right divine, *dei gratia*, enjoying (to borrow Ullmann's graphic distinction) a power descending upon him from above. But he was also a king chosen by his people, bound in a relationship of mutual duty, enjoying a power ascending to him from below. From the ninth century onwards, the practical facts of a fragmented authority (feudalism) reinvigorated this second character of kingship by giving a political reality to his obligation to the governed. The people were subjects, committed to him and in his care. They were also vassals and counsellors whom he was bound to consult in what touched all: *quod omnes tangit ab omnibus approbetur* was no less serious a concept for being a tag. In the one capacity he is solely responsible to God, free of both control and punishment by any human agency, incapable of being sued for breaches of the law – strictly even incapable of being charged with any. In the other, he must observe the order acceptable to his subjects; he cannot touch their lives or property outside the established processes of the law, he must seek their advice, he cannot revoke grants and concessions once made, he can even be resisted and deposed. The dualism crops up in unexpected places. The very legists who read virtual absolutism into theocratic kingship and the dicta that the prince's pleasure is law and he is *legibus solutus*, also came to treat the supposed *lex regia*, by which the people had allegedly bestowed upon their ruler a power originally theirs, as grounds for the ruler's responsibility to the ruled.

This dualism is well exemplified, in English terms, by the meaning given to the royal prerogative. At heart this is nothing but those special rights, over and above those available to everybody, which the king enjoys by virtue of his office: they enable him to carry out his unique task in the State. Commonly they were divided into the two categories familiar from Chief Baron Fleming's famous judgment in Bate's Case in 1606: the ordinary and absolute prerogative. When one traces the terms back one finds the ordinary on occasion described as ordained (*potestas ordinata* instead of *ordinaria*),[1] and here lies the necessary clue. The ordinary power of kings is that which is laid down in the law – entitlement to certain revenues, powers of patronage, and so forth. His absolute power (*legibus soluta*) is that to which the law does not apply

---

[1] See J. Holub, 'Ordinaria potentia – absoluta potentia,' *Revue Historique de Droit Français et Etranger* (1950), 92 ff.

because it cannot: these are the rights of free action, unknowable until the occasion arises, which any ruler must possess if he is to deal with the crises of the body politic. His ordinary power he enjoys by agreement, by contract, with his people, a contract embodied in the binding details of the law accepted by both parties; his absolute because he is God's chosen instrument for the governance of His people. The problems which arise in defining the borderline between the two, or in discovering whether the king is exercising a proper or improper 'absolute' power, are a special case of the general dilemma which arises from the dual basis of royal authority.[1]

For in the last resort there could be no theoretical resolution of this particular dualism. The king either held a descending power, in which case he looked only upwards for control over his actions and judgment on his misdeeds; or he held an ascending power, in which case he was at least in considerable measure responsible to his people. One medieval attempt to dispose of the problem has already been hinted at in what was said of the prerogative. There was always the law, the *tertium quid* between king and people, possibly even between king and God but at least the expression of God's order equally binding upon king and people. Bracton's famous assertion that the king, though under no man, is under God and the law tackled the dilemma in a way which proved satisfactory to many, though his inference that a king who fails to do justice thereby ceases to be king cannot be reconciled with any form of divine-right doctrine. But Bracton's answer really evades the problem by the characteristic device of supposing that the law somehow exists apart from men. Once again we are up against the question of legislation: the king may be under the law as it stands and is known, but what happens when the law requires addition, subtraction or modification?

It therefore remains true that the double authority of kings could not be brought into theoretical accord as long as sovereignty or supreme power was seen as vested in one being. This did not, needless to say, prevent kingship from working: graver problems of logic have not affected practical efficacy in institutions. But it did mean that there was a flaw in the system which only political competence – ability to operate an essentially double-ended position – could over-

---

[1] The Tudors regarded the two kinds of prerogative as co-ordinate, each competent within its own sphere; the Stuarts held the absolute to be in control of the ordinary. A fine case study of the difficulties raised by divine right and the absolute prerogative in practice is provided by the Angevin monarchy of the twelfth century: J. E. A. Joliffe, *Angevin Kingship* (1955).

come, and this meant that crisis was built into medieval kingship. After a series of lesser crises, both French and English kingship met the conflict head on, as a consequence of the Reformation and the strains on loyalty which it introduced. In France the crisis came in the second half of the sixteenth century, in England in the first half of the seventeenth, as political and social stresses amalgamated with bewildered men's passionate doubts whether their God in heaven or His human deputy should receive their obedience.

Political theory really comes into its own only in a crisis, when the conventional beliefs and unargued assumptions of men are suddenly called in question. This accounts for the enormous output of relevant literature, running round and round the same issues, in both countries at those times. In both we find newly sharpened statements of divine right, clearer approaches to notions of sovereignty, fully worked out constitutionalist doctrines and even expressions of populist and democratic views. Medieval kingship was dissected into its component parts; if some of the tools were old (which accounts for the discovery of 'predecessors' among medieval writers), some were newly provided by Protestantism and reformed Catholicism. This is particularly true of explicit doctrines of tyrannicide. The opening up of the question naturally revealed the flaw at the heart of kingship and worried away at it to the point where neither repair nor disguise was any longer possible. The results differed in the two countries. In France, divine right triumphed and the contractual side of the old kingship in effect vanished. In England, by 1688, the king was forced to abandon all claims *dei gratia* and to become his people's first official. The fact that both types of monarchy preserved some ceremonial vestiges of the attributes which they had lost is neither here nor there. This divergent outcome owed a good deal to the way in which the actual battle went, with the king emerging as saviour from a civil war in France, while the English monarchy experienced execution and abolition. It is, however, easy to see that past development had much to do with it – so easy that in England, at least, profound differences between French absolutism and English constitutionalism have commonly been backdated far beyond the truth.

The French triumph of divine-right kingship may have been unavoidable; the English crisis was much more unnecessary because a workable and intellectually possible solution to the dilemma had been provided by the Tudor monarchy. A better understanding of it might at least have saved the changes necessitated by time from involving civil war and revolution. The Tudor system rested on the concept of a unitary body politic, both State and Church, governed respectively by a king and supreme head, one person executing two distinct functions definable as the rule of men's bodies and the protection of their souls. So far it was pure divine-right monarchy. But it had managed to accommodate the contractual aspect of monarchy by recognizing in Parliament (the assembly of king, Lords and Commons) a replica of the body politic. It was a Tudor commonplace that the edicts of Parliament were binding on all because all were there present, in person or by deputy. The law there made was valid because it carried both common consent and executive sanction – was both 'norm' and 'command'. By anybody's standard, the Tudor king-in-Parliament was a true sovereign. Unfortunately it was also a mixed sovereign, a difficult thing to conceive of in theory and even more difficult to operate in practice. The whole weight of past and present opinion, and especially the hitherto clearest claim to true supremacy (the pope's), all seemed to demand a single person for sovereign. Bodin, summing up the tradition in a new situation, specifically denied the possibility of a collective sovereign power. When the crisis came it naturally took the form of a struggle within the political machine, within what was really the sovereign body, and those who by stages realized that sovereignty was in issue were thus induced to locate it in a single person, which meant that they asserted an unqualified doctrine of divine right. However, ancient its basis, Stuart divine right was revolutionary because it dispensed with the contract and attacked an existing mixed sovereignty. In due course, its opponents produced equally revolutionary ideas of popular sovereignty, or even of the sovereignty of the abstract State (Hobbes). The truer tradition was not forgotten, but the few writers who in the midst of civil war defended a mixed sovereign body met nothing but abuse.[1] On its return in 1660 the tradition was a little modified; at the end of the struggle, in 1689, it overbalanced against divine right. Divine right died in England because the kings of the house of Stuart failed to accept the dual nature of their authority and to use the political weapons of persuasion and management upon which the Tudor reconciliation of the irreconcilable had so successfully rested.

[1] See Charles H. McIlwain, 'A Forgotten Worthy, Philip Hunton,' *Constitutionalism and the Modern World* (Cambridge, 1939), 196 ff.; Margaret A. Judson, *The Crisis of the Constitution* (New Brunswick, N.J., 1949), index-entries under 'Hunton, Philip' and 'Parker, Henry'.

Figgis understandably studied the divine right of kings when he could see it clearly defined in the floodlight thrown by crisis. He therefore studied it on its deathbed, and though he realized something of its ancient history he did not fully grasp how permanent an attribute of European kingship it had been. It was the contribution made by Christianity to a form of government which also derived from Roman imperialism (incorporating at least a trace of Hellenistic kingship) and tribal barbarism. All things considered, it had a long history, and it may well be doubted whether it was in any way less defensible than the divine right of peoples.

31

THE POLITICAL CREED OF
THOMAS CROMWELL*

Two views are current concerning the political views of Thomas Cromwell. One – the more common – holds that he believed in absolute monarchy and desired to establish it in England. The Abbé Constant, summarizing (as was his wont) other people's views in language free from other people's reservations, stated it most starkly: he thought that Cromwell aimed at making Henry 'tout-puissant' and that his ministry was the golden age of Tudor despotism.[1] Quite recently, an ingenious theory, buttressed with a misunderstood document, based itself on this general conviction.[2] This view has suffered curiously little from the growing realization that the Henrician Reformation rested on conscious co-operation with Parliament and that the propagandists of the time never produced a theory of absolute monarchy.[3] Pollard, the defender of Henry VIII's constitutionalism, seems to have held that, though the king had no ambitions for a genuine despotism, Cromwell certainly harboured such ideas.[4] The other view, recently given support for Dr Parker,[5] holds that Cromwell did not bother at all about theoretical issues, that his 'resolutely Philistine type of mind' despised political theory, and that he never thought beyond the establishment of a sovereign monarchy. Thus, too, Mr Baumer thought that Cromwell saw in Parliament 'only a means of executing the royal will', but also that he 'had no theoretical views whatever about the relation of the king to the law' – passages hard to reconcile but suggestive of Dr Parker's views rather than M. Constant's.[6]

In opposition to these views I should like to put forward an inter-

---

* [TRHS (1956), 69–92.]

[1] G. Constant, La Réforme en Angleterre: Henri VIII (1930), 179 f. Cf. Merriman, i. 112; K. Pickthorn, Early Tudor Government, i. 203, and J. B. Mackie, The Early Tudors (1952, Oxford), 417 (with reservations); P. Hughes, The Reformation in England: The King's Proceedings (1950), 225.

[2] L. Stone, 'Thomas Cromwell's Political Programme,' BIHR 24 (1951), 1 ff.; and cf. my reply, above, pp. 72–7.

[3] Baumer, Early Tudor Theory of Kingship; Zeeveld, Foundations of Tudor Policy.

[4] Pollard, Henry VIII, 323.

[5] T. M. Parker, 'Was Thomas Cromwell a Machiavellian?,' Journal of Eccl. Hist. I (1950), 63 ff.   [6] Baumer, Kingship, 152, 169.

pretation which, starting from the supposition that Cromwell was greatly interested in theories of the state and of law, arrives at the conclusion that his political creed centred on the legal supremacy of the king in Parliament and included no ambitions for a purely royal despotism. Admittedly, the attempt will encounter formidable difficulties. Interested in theory or not, Cromwell was certainly no writer of theory, and the only direct testimony to his political views is that on which rests the opinion that he favoured despotism. He is that bane of the historian – a man whose awareness of theory and capacity for real thought cannot be doubted, but whose tenets have to be laboriously extracted from his deeds. Yet, as Dr Parker has recognized, Cromwell's mind matters because it was he who directed the Henrician Reformation and in all probability determined its 'unique and peculiar course'. I have offered proof of this elsewhere,[1] here I must content myself with asserting that the ideas underlying the Reformation emanated from Cromwell rather than the king, and that the Reformation legislation embodies his views of Church and State. Furthermore, difficult though it is to maintain the distinction, I have time on this occasion only to discuss Cromwell's theory of the State; his attitude to Church and religion must on the whole be left out. In any case, he was notoriously secular in his thought, and an understanding of what he held about the nature of the State he was reconstructing is the first essential for an understanding of the man.

I

It is first necessary to dispose of the two established views just outlined. The notion that Cromwell had no time for theories is easily disproved. Whatever the value of Reginald Pole's famous account of his conversation with Cromwell on the State and the duty of a councillor (and it must engage our attention in a moment), it shows plainly that Cromwell, though he thought little of Plato, was well acquainted with writings on the State.[2] There are traces of a lively concern with ideas in his letters. An interest in theology appears in such remarks as his refutation of Fisher's citation of Amos or his reproof to Shaxton, whose scriptural quotations he confidently asserted were out of context.[3] A real acquaintance with legal theory is argued by his bold

---

[1] Above, no. 9.
[2] Reginald Pole, 'Apologia ad Carolum Quintum Caesarem,' *Epistolarum etc. Pars Prima*, ed. Quirini (Brescia, 1744), 133 ff.
[3] Merriman, i. 376; ii. 128 f.

claim that the law divine is irrelevant to affairs in England.[1] Most conclusively, there is the testimony of Thomas Starkey, himself an undoubted theorist. He had, says he, many a talk with Cromwell 'of god, of nature & of other polytyke & wordly thyngys' from which he had 'geddryd more frute of truth then I haue downe of any other man lyuyng syth I cam here to my cuntrey'.[2] The praise may mean little, but the fact of those discourses cannot be ignored. On one such occasion Cromwell asked Starkey 'what thyng hyt ys aftur the sentence of aristotyl & the ancyent perypatetykys that commynly among them ys callyd pollycy', to be answered with a little pamphlet on the subject.[3] Clearly, Cromwell devoted time to enquiry about fundamentals; the assumption that he was capable, even avid, of genuine political speculation needs no further proof.

The other view, that Cromwell wished to establish a 'Machiavellian' despotism, is much more firmly entrenched and harder to shake. Its strength derives from its being based on the only detailed account of Cromwell's views which has survived. This is Reginald Pole's description, written a few months after Cromwell had assisted in wiping out Pole's family. The general unreliability of his *Apologia*, with its delineation of the satanic disciple of Machiavelli fouling the pure spring of Catholic doctrine, was exposed a half-century ago by Van Dyke;[4] nevertheless his picture, etched with the acid of personal hatred, continues to be accepted. For while Van Dyke showed that Pole's general story will not stand up to examination, he failed to shake Pole's account of Cromwell's credo, and it is this that matters.

In the speech which Pole puts into Cromwell's mouth at his alleged (and mythical)[5] first interview with the king, he elaborated these arguments: a prince, being above the law, can alter the laws and give them to others; the distinction between right and wrong is relative and does not apply to kings in the same way as to lesser mortals – that is, political morality differs from abstract ethics; no realm can have

---

[1] Ibid. i. 376: anticipating Fisher's argument that one line of thought agreed with the law of God and another did not, Cromwell supposed that 'this had been no greate cause more to reject the one than thother, for ye know by histories of the bible that god may by his reuelation dispense with his owne Law'. Dr Parker's comment on this passage (op. cit. 73 f.) seems to me entirely tendentious. Cromwell here came as near to denying the place of the law divine in matters affected by the positive law of the realm as a man could who wishes to avoid a charge of heresy.

[2] P RO, SP 1/89, fo. 138; *England in the Reign of King Henry the Eighth*, ed. S. J. Herrtage and J. M. Cowper (E.E.T.S., 1878; hereafter cited as *Starkey's England*), p. lxxi.

[3] Zeeveld, *Foundations*, 143. [Cf. on all this *Reform and Renewal*, 49–52.]

[4] P. Van Dyke, *Renascence Portraits* (New York, 1906), App., 377 ff.

[5] *Tudor Revolution*, 73 f.

two masters and the king must not be deprived of 'maximum aucto-
ritatis nomen . . . Caput Ecclesiae'.[1] To this may be added the points
which Pole says Cromwell made in conversation when they discussed
the proper duty of a councillor.[2] In reply to Pole's view that a councillor's first concern was to serve the honour and advantage of his
prince and to his academic citation of authorities, Cromwell replied
that that was all very well for the schools and for popular consumption
but of little use in practice. Advice must be suited to the time, the place,
and the audience. A minister must study 'quo tendit voluntas principis',
taking into account even unspoken desires. If he does his work well he
will achieve the prince's ambitions without any appearance of disaffection or religious schism.[3] A show of moral virtue must be maintained. He rallied Pole on his inexperience of public life which made
him feel shocked by these sentiments, and finished by recommending
a book which Pole says he later found to be Machiavelli's *Prince*.

This description of a worldly-wise politician, concerned only with
serving the powers that be and with saving face, is superficially credible
enough. Whether it represents anything like Cromwell's true opinion,
or more than the passing mood of an argument in which Cromwell
grew more cynical as Pole grew more priggish, is quite another matter.
It is important to know whether Pole had good warrant for ascribing
such views to Cromwell. He himself admitted that he could not report
accurately a speech whose delivery he had not attended, and that he
had never heard Cromwell make public statements of this kind.[4] But,
he claimed, he had put nothing into Cromwell's mouth 'quod non
vel ab eodem . . . eo narrante intellexi, vel ab illis qui eius consilii
fuerunt participes'. The sayings which he had collected into one speech
he had not spun out of his own mind but in effect had taken from
Cromwell's own lips.[5] This seems an impressive voucher, until one
looks at the facts. By his own admission, Pole had met Cromwell only
once in his life;[6] in 1535, Starkey, who knew them both well, said they
were 'almost vnacquaynte & of smal famylyaryte'.[7] Pole also
admitted that he was never sufficiently familiar with Cromwell's circle

---

[1] Pole, 'Apologia', 118 ff.   [2] Ibid. 133 ff.

[3] '. . . ut et Princeps sua desideria consequatur nec tamen defectio ulla vel schisma in
religione appareat.'

[4] Pole, 'Apologia', 123, 127.   [5] Ibid. 123 f.

[6] Ibid. 132: 'semel et iterum, numquam amplius', which means twice. As Van Dyke
has pointed out (*Portraits*, 393 n.), this conflicts with Pole's repeated mention of one conversation; it can only be reconciled on the likely supposition that the editor's comma
ought to be shifted to after 'semel'.   [7] *Starkey's England*, p. xv.

to have been made privy to their inmost thoughts, a reservation which must be taken in conjunction with his statement that Cromwell never put forward his blasphemous ideas in public where he always appeared as a good Christian.[1] Nor will Pole deny that a man's actions may be variously interpreted and cannot afford an absolute insight into his mind; only God will see there. What then is left as the source of Pole's account of Cromwell's opinions? After all these concessions it is certainly surprising to find him offer these foundations: the single conversation about a councillor's duty, and those very actions whose utility for this purpose he had just queried.[2] Since his own report of his talk with Cromwell shows that they spoke of nothing except the office of a councillor and did not stray into such large fields as the king's relation to the law or the impossibility of two rulers in one realm, it follows that Pole had nothing to show for all his argument except his own prejudiced interpretation of events, which he had himself agreed to be an unsafe guide.[3]

Pole is thus not to be relied on, but it is of course possible that, blinded by personal hatred though he was, he may yet have hit upon the truth. His accusation that Cromwell wished to elevate the king above the law has found the readier credence because there appears to be confirmatory evidence. In 1547 Stephen Gardiner wrote to the Protector Somerset a letter of self-defence in which he told how Cromwell had once, in Henry's presence, challenged him with the words: 'Come on, my Lord of Winchester . . . is not that that pleaseth the King, a lawe? Have ye not ther in the Civill Lawe . . . *quod principi placuit*, and so fourth? . . . I have somwhat forgotten it now.'[4] Gardiner, of course, gave the king much better and more constitutional advice. Once again, a leading enemy's word is taken without question. Gardiner himself admits that Cromwell 'turned the cat in the panne afore company' and pretended their parts had been reversed. Can we

---

[1] Pole, 'Apologia', 131 f. [2] Ibid. 132.

[3] Having found Pole out in so much question-begging and feeble argument, one might be tempted to doubt the whole story of the conversation. Pole certainly did not think Cromwell so satanic as early as Wolsey's last year of office, for he later corresponded with him and had proof of potential favour (Van Dyke, *Portraits*, 406 ff.). Moreover, the whole argument about the schools and life – academic and political employment – sounds suspiciously like the points which in 1535 Cromwell told Starkey to put to Pole in an effort to win his services for the king's cause (*Starkey's England*, pp. xxii–xxiii). But we may let the interview stand, so graphically described by Pole, who did not seem to realize what a poor figure he cut in his own account – priggish, narrow-minded, inexperienced, and humourless.

[4] *Letters of Stephen Gardiner*, ed. J. A. Muller (Cambridge, 1933), 399.

be sure that 'Wily Winchester' was telling the story the right way round? And even if he was, have we here more than an example of Cromwell's well-known lively conversation and sharp wit?[1] He had 'somwhat forgotten'. Indeed, he might easily have done so, for unlike Gardiner (who prided himself on his knowledge and – in Dr Parker's words[2] – showed a 'donnish contempt for the unlearned Cromwell') he had never studied the civil law. Such casual talk should no more form the basis for an estimate of Cromwell's views than should another oft-quoted remark reported by Chapuys: Cromwell allegedly said that the Turk might well be called king and prince 'for the absolute authority he exercises over his subjects'.[3] To read into this more than the momentary exasperation of a minister overwhelmed with the labour of governing a litigious and recalcitrant people is to use evidence by quantity instead of quality.

Cromwell's supposed liking for a true despotism – as distinct from strong and energetic rule – thus rests on quite insufficient foundations. What, then, can be made of the Machiavellian label stuck on him by Pole? Van Dyke argued that in 1528 Cromwell could not have recommended the *Prince*, not printed until 1532, and suggested that he was thinking of Castiglione's *Courtier*.[4] This idea found favour with L. A. Weisberger, who held that no Tudor statesman can be shown to have been a disciple of Machiavelli even if his actions agreed with the precepts of the *Prince*.[5] Of course, since Machiavelli did not so much teach new maxims of statecraft as summarize recognized and necessary practice, a touch of 'Machiavellianism' will be noticeable in every competent politician's actions as long as circumstances are as they are. Nevertheless, it would be interesting to know whether Cromwell did or did not read the book. Independently, Mr Zeeveld and Dr Parker have rejected Van Dyke's attempt to substitute the *Courtier* for the *Prince*;[6] the sentiments expressed by Castiglione certainly bear no relation to the points which Cromwell apparently made in his conversation with Pole.[7] On the other hand, Machiavelli's treatise also contains nothing about the duties of a councillor. Cromwell cannot be saved for Machiavelli's school by Mr Zeeveld's argument that his

[1] Van Dyke (*Portraits*, 144) rightly speaks of Cromwell's 'habit of not taking himself too seriously'. [2] Parker, op. cit. 73.

[3] *LP* vii. 1554. [4] *Portraits*, 400 ff.

[5] 'Machiavelli and Tudor England,' *Political Science Quart.* 42 (1927), 589 ff.

[6] Zeeveld, *Foundations*, 184 ff.; Parker, op. cit. 67 ff.

[7] The *Cortegiano* (trs. Thomas Hoby, 1561; L. E. Opdycke, 1902) does not deal with ministerial duties, but only with the ceremonial, athletic, and artistic performances of the courtier.

mouthpiece Richard Morison knew the Florentine's works in 1535, immediately after his return from Italy;[1] 'the question is whether Cromwell knew the *Prince* much earlier. One must in general agree with Dr Parker that it cannot be shown whether Cromwell ever studied Machiavelli, while reserving judgment on his unsupported conclusion that Cromwell was in any case 'Machiavellian' in the sense that he shared his 'drab outlook upon the world'.[2]

II

So much for the received notions; now to turn to Cromwell himself. His letters are those of a practical man; they stick to the point and rarely indulge in those generalizations which give an insight into a man's mind and of which even the few examples extant show him to have been perfectly capable. 'My prayer is,' he wrote in March 1538, 'that God gyue me no longer lyfe than I shall be gladde to vse myn office in edificatione, and not in destruction.'[3] As it turned out, he was to be cut off in the middle of vigorous activity and yet full of plans for the better organizing of the realm.[4] It is usual to speak of him as a radical, and inasmuch as his work involved much sweeping away of men and institutions, and a cold-blooded disregard of obstacles, he deserves that name. But his positive notions seem to have been less radical than is supposed: he preached moderation, especially in innovation, though admittedly for a good practical reason. The bishops were warned to avoid extremes in enforcing the new teaching, so as not to 'brede contention Deuision and contrariety in opinion in the vnlerned multitude'.[5] He made much the same point in the debates preceding the publication, in 1537, of the *Institution of a Christian Man*, when he demanded unity on a basis of moderation, avoiding both popery and sacramentarianism.[6] Very nearly the same words recur in

[1] [Morison returned from Italy in early 1536 (*Reform and Renewal*, 58).]
[2] Op. cit. 74 f.   [3] Merriman, ii. 129.
[4] *Tudor Revolution*, 416 f., and above, no. 10.
[5] Merriman, ii. 112.
[6] A. Alesius, *Of the auctorite of the word of god agaynst the bisshop of London* (?1540; cf. *LP* xii. I. 790). The occasion and date of the speech there reported are conjectural. Since the number of sacraments was the main topic of debate, 1536–7 is presumably right, though I had a passing thought of identifying this speech with that made in 1540 (next note). The difficulty is that Alesius speaks very definitely of the Parliament House as the stage of the disputation. The Parliament of 1536 cannot be meant because Cromwell did not attend the Upper House until the last day of that session (*Lords' Journals*, i. 101); the next Parliament met in 1539. Nor did Convocation meet in the interval. Perhaps one may guess at an informal meeting of the bishops, early in 1537, which happened to be held

his address to the House of Lords in 1540 when once more he insisted on the need for moderation and unity in religion.[1] In 1539 he wished to treat the Calais sacramentarians with 'charyte and myld handeling ... without Rigour or extreame dealing',[2] and this should not be put down to his reformed sympathies which stopped well short of sacramentarianism and nonconformity. Though pressure from the king induced him to think them more dangerous than he had at first believed, he adhered to a preference for relative gentleness, if only because public and extreme measures would advertise disunion in the realm.[3]

Another important strand in his thought must be looked for in the idea of law. Like all Tudor councillors, Cromwell devoted much time to sifting petitions and adjudicating upon claims, though he showed no liking for the formal duties of a judge.[4] But if, unlike Wolsey, he did not wish to preside in a court, he seems nevertheless to have cultivated a reputation for strict 'indifference' or judicial fairness.[5] Several times he expressed specific respect for the law, telling Fisher that 'your thinking shal not be your triall, but the Law must diffine' his guilt,[6] or admitting even in his extremity that he was 'A Subiect and boorn to obbey lawse'.[7] 'The tryall of all lawse', he wrote in the same letter, 'only consystethe in honest and probable wytnes' – an interesting comment in itself as showing him capable of philosophizing about the law, but particularly interesting from one who is commonly charged with condemning men on slender grounds and even unheard. Whether, in fact, Cromwell was as black in these respects as he is painted it is outside the scope of this paper to enquire; in passing we may note that the point has never been proved, being merely repeated by one writer after another.[8]

in the 'Parliament House'; this is supported by Cromwell's reported thanks to the prelates for turning up and by the informality of his introducing Alesius, whom he happened to run across on his way to the discussion, into the meeting.

[1] *LJ* i. 128 f.   [2] Merriman, ii. 223 f.
[3] Ibid. 139 f., 142, 148 f., 226 ff.   [4] *Tudor Revolution*, 132 f., 139.
[5] Cf. Van Dyke, *Portraits*, 163 f. There are many references to this 'indifference' in his correspondence, and not all of them can be put down to an interested party's attempt to flatter him.
[6] Merriman, i. 377.   [7] Ibid. ii. 273.
[8] The whole notion of Cromwell's 'terror', spy-system, and extra-legal practices rests, so it seems to me, partly on ancient misunderstandings (first created by Henry VIII's desire to throw all the blame for his vengeful deeds on others) and partly on Merriman's astonishing readiness to blow up every stray suspicion into fact. The strength of his argument may be gauged from one quotation: 'The punishments in these cases were very severe: there are almost no records of penalties inflicted on those against whom the

Cromwell, then, regarded the law with theoretical respect, and the respect was that of the common lawyer. Maitland's thesis that in the 1530s the fate of the common law hung in the balance – that England nearly had a 'Reception' of Roman law – has been laboriously and successfully overthrown by Holdsworth.[1] At most we can speak of danger to the old courts of the common law, which were being rivalled by new courts where the common law, augmented by statutes, was enforced more efficiently. The law itself never budged before the civil law, confined from the first to those spheres which the common law did not touch. It is, however, still supposed that it triumphed despite the intentions of the government. But was it the government who favoured a 'Reception'? Wolsey may have been influenced by civil-law principles, and in the 1530s many of Henry VIII's lesser servants were civilians. So were some bishops of the conservative party – Gardiner, Tunstall, Sampson, Clerk. If Starkey may be believed, Pole strongly favoured the sweeping away of the barbaric common law and its replacement by the enlightenment of Rome.[2] But all these supporters of the civil law were either subordinates, or in exile like Pole, or virtually excluded from a share in shaping policy.

Cromwell dominated the king's counsels, and his party included no civilians of note. The more or less radical bishops who looked to him – Cranmer, Foxe, Latimer, Shaxton – were theologians, not lawyers, and his leading professional assistants – Audley, the lord chancellor, or Riche, the chancellor of Augmentations – were common lawyers tried and trained. It was during his tenure of office that the Court of Requests, a stronghold of civilians, acquired a common lawyer as a member of its permanent staff.[3] And he himself had long practised in the common law. His earlier correspondence abounds with notes of such work; he held powers of attorney, represented in suits, acted in cases of debt.[4] Even after he had entered the king's service he did not surrender his private practice;[5] later, legal work on the king's behalf occupied much of his time. He was a member of Gray's Inn.[6]

depositions were brought, but there is reason to believe that comparatively slight misdemeanours were not seldom rewarded with death' (i. 118). Comment is superfluous on this cavalier treatment of one of the most difficult sixteenth-century problems: what happened when a man was denounced, and how far were laws effective? [Cf. now *Policy and Police*.]

[1] F. W. Maitland, *English Law and the Renaissance* (Cambridge, 1901); W. S. Holdsworth, *History of English Law*, iv. 217 ff.

[2] *Starkey's England*, 192 ff. [3] *Tudor Revolution*, 136, n. 11.

[4] E.g. *LP* iii. 2441, 2445, 2557, 2754, 3530.

[5] *Tudor Revolution*, 87. [6] *DNB*.

The man who knew his Bracton well enough to recommend him to others for giving the king the title of *vicarius Christi* is at least as likely to have remembered that 'rex debet esse sub lege' as the civilian principle to which Gardiner (as we have seen) said he appealed.[1] All we have heard about the 'toughness' of the common law and the unshakable devotion of its devotees applies also to Thomas Cromwell. Small wonder that the common law regained much ground during his ministry.

But Cromwell was more than just another common lawyer, and nowhere is this seen more clearly than in his attitude to Parliament. He took an early opportunity to familiarize himself with its workings, sitting in the tumultuous assembly of 1523 which Wolsey found so intractable. Cromwell himself described in a letter how in that Parliament members had talked for sixteen weeks of

warre pease Stryffe contencyon debate murmure grudge Riches pouerte penurye trowth falshode Iustyce equyte discayte opprescyon Magnanymyte actyuyte force attempraunce Treason murder Felonye consyli[ation] and also how a commune welth myght be ediffyed,

and how in the end they had done as their predecessors, 'that ys to say, as well as we myght and lefte wher we begann'.[2] It is a little difficult to understand why writer after writer has taken this amusing note to show contempt for Parliament. Since one cannot wish to accuse so many acute historians of collectively failing in humour,[3] one must suppose that they found in the letter something which they sought. But the long recital of absurdities should have put them on their guard: this is no weighty and pompous judgment, but a man of affairs laughing at himself and his fellows. We might suspect even from this letter that Cromwell was fascinated by the work and potentialities of Parliament.

Six years later, in 1529, he found himself at a crisis in his career and perhaps even in danger of his life. Significantly enough he solved the problem by entering Parliament. That he meant to get in by hook or by crook is plain from the letter in which Ralph Sadler reported the negotiations to him.[4] He may have hoped to hide from his enemies

---

[1] *LP* xiii. I. 120. Cf. F. Schulz, 'Bracton on Kingship', *EHR* 60 (1945), 136 ff., for a citation of the relevant passages in Bracton. [2] Merriman, i. 313.

[3] E.g. Merriman, i. 27; H. A. L. Fisher, *Political History of England 1485–1547*, 247 ('cynical view'); H. Maynard Smith, *Henry VIII and the Reformation*, 49 ('Cromwell no doubt continued to despise parliaments'); A. D. Innes, *Ten Tudor Statesmen* (1906), 119; Parker, op. cit. 70 f. (though he qualified his statement).

[4] *LP* iv. App. 238. For Cromwell's entry into the 1529 Parliament, cf. *Tudor Revolution*, 77 ff., where the whole question is discussed at length.

under the cloak of parliamentary immunity, but there is fortunately quite conclusive evidence that he meant to do more. Parliament was to be the means to make him great – the scene and agent of his career. When he was in very low spirits, in October 1529, he wondered what to do; then, shaking off this uncharacteristic mood of indecision, he determined to ride to Court and either 'make or mar'. On his return he told Cavendish 'that he once adventured to put in his foot, where he trusted shortly to be better regarded or [before] all was done': he had got into Parliament.[1] How well he succeeded in his aim it is both unnecessary and here irrelevant to elaborate. By the middle of 1531 rumours of his activity in the House were spreading far and wide,[2] and the lists of matters to be done, letters of contemporaries, many corrected drafts, and entries in the *Lords' Journals* of bills brought by him from the lower house all indicate the hard work put in and the great influence gained. Entering Parliament to make a career, unprecedently active in it, using it to a degree which was novel and remained unrivalled for a long time, he well deserves the name of England's first parliamentary statesman.

His belief in Parliament appears most clearly in a striking devotion to statute. His papers are full of draft acts, and his memoranda suggest others.[3] The numbers of statutes passed during his ascendancy were prodigious.[4] The first nine sessions of Henry VIII's reign, spread over 22 years,[5] produced 203 acts of which 148 can be called public. Cromwell's eight sessions in eight years resulted in a total of 333, or at least 200 of general importance on which he exercised the influence of a chief minister. This average of about 25 public acts per session was maintained in Henry VIII's last years and under Edward VI, but declined under Mary and Elizabeth to about 20. In the 45 years of Elizabeth's reign only 79 more public acts were passed than in the eight years of Cromwell's ministry. More significant still is the space taken up by the acts, for this reflects the relative importance of legislation. From 1509 to 1531, 416 pages (in the *Statutes of the Realm*) were filled, and of these 135 resulted from the first two sessions of the Reformation Parliament. Cromwell's eight years produced 409 pages, and the consolidation of his work in 1540–7 another 207. Edward's six years can show only 196 pages, Mary's five 152, and the 45 years, 13

---

[1] G. Cavendish, *Life of Cardinal Wolsey* (Singer's ed., repr. in Morley's Universal Library, 1887), 149 f., 156, 159 f.   [2] *LP* v. 628.

[3] E.g. *LP* vi. 299 (ix. D, xi), 1381 (1); ix. 725 (ii).

[4] All the following facts and figures are derived from *Statutes of the Realm*, vols. iii and iv.

[5] 1510, Feb. 1512, Nov. 1512, 1513, Feb. 1515, Nov. 1515, 1523, 1529, 1531.

sessions, and 444 acts of Elizabeth's reign only 666. The figures demonstrate how much weighty legislation was crowded into Cromwell's years of power. There are obvious reasons for these differences – the demands of the break with Rome, Mary's lengthy repeals, Elizabeth's difficulties with her Parliaments – but they do not detract from the evident liking for statute and the amazing productivity displayed by Cromwell.

There are sufficient signs that Cromwell preferred statute to any other form of law-making, distrusting both the slow operation of judge-made law and the dubious authority of proclamations. He deliberately saw to the inclusion of treason by words in the 1534 Treason Act, although the principle had already earned recognition at common law in the 'constructive' treasons created by judges in the preceding century.[1] In 1535, the Council debated whether the new ordinances for Calais should be enacted by Parliament or by proclamation;[2] Parliament won, and we cannot doubt that in that year, when his power in the Council was at its highest, Cromwell must have spoken a decisive word. The best example of all is provided by the Act of Proclamations, still wrongly regarded as an attempt to supersede statute. The act's chief practical purpose was undoubtedly to create machinery to enforce proclamations.[3] But further, it placed the powers of proclamations on the authority of statute by stating that the king with his Council 'may set forthe at all tymes by auctoritie of this Acte his proclamacions'.[4] The point assumes its full significance when it is compared with Cromwell's known attitude to proclamations. In July 1535, at a time when Parliament was not sitting, it became necessary to prohibit the export of coin, a common administrative measure and the sort of thing for which proclamations were specifically designed. Nevertheless, Cromwell thought it desirable to consult the judges, and a search of the statutes discovered an act of Richard II on which the relevant proclamation could be grounded. In the discussion Cromwell asked what the king could do if 'there wer no law nor statute made alreadye for any suche purpose'. The lord chief justice replied, quite correctly, that this would not prevent the issue of a proclamation 'of as good effecte as Any law made by parlyament', an opinion which

---

[1] Cf. I. D. Thornley, 'The Treason Legislation of Henry VIII,' *TRHS* (1917), 87 ff., esp. 111.

[2] *LP* ix. 766.

[3] Cf. E. R. Adair, 'The Statute of Proclamations,' *EHR* 32 (1917), 34 ff., and *Tudor Revolution*, 343 f.

[4] 31 Henry VIII, c. 8 (*Stat. of the Realm*, iii. 726).

Cromwell was 'veray gladde to here'.[1] It appears then, that Cromwell – far from wishing to supersede statute – did not feel sure whether proclamations were ever effective unless specifically based upon it, and though he was delighted to have his doubts resolved it appears more than probable that the act of 1539 was designed to put the matter beyond question by securing the authority of Parliament for all future proclamations.

III

This picture of Cromwell as a moderate whose ideas in the last resort derived from his training in the common law and in Parliament, is supported by some evidence of more theoretical views. Twice during his ministry Cromwell was closely associated with the publication of treatises on the State. The lesser instance is Thomas Starkey's *Exhortation to the people instructynge theym to unitie and obedience* (1535), a book which has been identified as the first exposition of the Anglican *via media*.[2] Starkey was promptly criticized for attacking both extremes, for being 'of nother parte but betwyx both indyfferent'.[3] Cromwell thought otherwise: to him the author had to apologize because 'thys mean ys not put out at large wych you requyre'. Starkey acknowledged the fault but doubted his capacity:

for this mean in al thyng ys a strange stryng, hard to stryke apon & wysely to touch, for by thys the armony of thys hole world ys conteynyd in hys natural course & bewty.

Cromwell, who thought Starkey more of a philosopher than a theologian,[4] may have been more interested in a *via media* in England than in the harmony of the universe, but it is highly significant that he should have insisted on it before the book was written, and that when all men faulted a book for taking its stand in the middle he should have thought the middle position insufficiently stressed. We have already noticed his moderation in practice, which now looks to have been based on a theoretical belief in a 'middle way'. So far from being the violent revolutionary radical of tradition Cromwell now

---

[1] Merriman, i. 409 f. This letter has been taken to prove that Cromwell wished to use proclamations in order to avoid statutes; it seems to me to prove just about the opposite. [For the Act of Proclamations, cf. above, no. 19.]

[2] Zeeveld, 'Thomas Starkey and the Cromwellian Polity,' *Journ. of Mod. Hist.* 15 (1943), 177 ff. (repr., with some cuts, in *Foundations*, 128 ff.).

[3] *Starkey's England*, p. lxxi.

[4] Ibid. p. xliii: 'you juge me more to be traynyd in phylosophye than in the trade of scripture'.

appears as the promoter of a successful compromise – the first exponent and perhaps the maker of that specific compromise on which the Church of England rests.[1]

A greater thinker than Starkey was also called upon to support the Henrician Reformation. This was Marsiglio of Padua, the fourteenth-century protagonist of the secular State against the papal claim to *plenitudo potestatis*. Starkey himself derived some of his most striking ideas from Marsiglio.[2] More significant for the present purpose is the publication, in 1535, of a translation of Marsiglio's *Defensor Pacis* by William Marshall. Marshall was one of Cromwell's team of propagandists, and Cromwell advanced him the money for this particular publication, a debt he seems later to have cancelled.[3] He welcomed this ready-made piece of propaganda which he encouraged Starkey to use on Pole and Marshall on the recalcitrant Carthusians, in neither case with any success.[4] In other words, he sponsored the book, and it is a reasonable conclusion that he read it. The immediate usefulness of a work which attacked the papal position on the ground that 'in . . . regno unico esse oportet unicum tantummodo principatum'[5] needs no underlining; but it is worth recalling that one of the sentiments ascribed to Cromwell by Pole concerned the monstrosity of two heads in one realm.[6] Pole never mentions Marsiglio, a fact which suggests that he may have been unconscious of the source of the saying and really for once quoting Cromwell correctly. Another tenuous link is provided by Cromwell's enquiry after Aristotle's views on the State; it is at least not impossible that this question should have been suggested to him by a study of Marsiglio, 'un aristotélicien positiviste'.[7]

Certainly there are some points to suggest that Marsiglio directly influenced Cromwell's thought. Marsiglio held that the State is autono-

---

[1] On the whole subject cf. Zeeveld's article, p. 227, n. 2. It is interesting to remark that Henry VIII could say about the *Exhortation* only that it was insufficiently drawn from Scripture (ibid. p. 187). [Despite Zeeveld, not about the *Exhortation*, cf. *Reform and Renewal*, 51.] This throws much light on the king's indifference to 'philosophy' and preference for theology – which again indicates where we must look for the leadership in the political revolution.

[2] Baumer, 'Thomas Starkey and Marsiglio of Padua,' *Politica*, 2 (1936), 188 ff. Mr Baumer displays much wonderment at Starkey's courage and revolutionary wisdom in putting forward constitutionalist notions 'at a time when Tudor despotism was at its peak'. The truth is that no one at the time put forward absolutist theories: constitutionalism was the thing.

[3] *LP* vii. 422–3; xi. 1355.   [4] *LP* viii. 1156; ix. 523.

[5] *Defensor Pacis* (ed. C. W. Previté-Orton, Cambridge, 1928), I. 17. 1.

[6] 'Apologia', 121.

[7] G. de Lagarde, *La Naissance de l'esprit laïque au declin du moyen âge*, ii. 155. On this point cf. also Previté-Orton's ed. of the *Defensor Pacis*, p. xiv.

mous and the Church subject to it; it has rightly been pointed out that the nearest realization of his views was achieved in the established Protestant Churches – that is, in Cromwell's Anglican Church.[1] Marsiglio, declaring the divine law irrelevant and ignoring the law of nature, held that only the positive law of the realm matters in human affairs;[2] we recall Cromwell's casual dismissal of the law of God in his letter to Fisher. On the positive law Marsiglio has much to say; his most lucid definition of it is 'regula . . . praeceptiva et transgressorum coactiva',[3] a view to which Cromwell, the maker of much penal legislation and the believer in statute, gave frequent practical expression. Marsiglio saw the essence of the State in its legislative activity, so that more than any other pre-Reformation thinker he approached the full modern notion of sovereignty;[4] as we shall see, legislative sovereignty was at the heart of Cromwell's thought. Though perfect proof is necessarily lacking, it does not seem too much to claim that as far as Cromwell was a theorist he was a conscious follower of Marsiglio.

As a practical statesman, however, Cromwell would have had to admit that Marsiglio's teaching, derived from observation of an Italian city-state, could not simply be applied to the kingdom of England. In this connection Marshall's translation deserves attention. The translator made some omissions and additions which, since he published under Cromwell's patronage, may safely be taken as consonant with Cromwell's views. For his omissions he has had much blame and scorn.[5] It is true that he transformed Marsiglio's preference for an elective monarchy into praise of one based on inheritance, that he omitted his author's insistence on the powers of the community to control and correct the ruler, and that he toned down Marsiglio's ascription of all ecclesiastical authority to the *legislator humanus*. But these changes were all demanded by the English conditions for which he wrote. That Marshall had no intention of doctoring Marsiglio's thought for the benefit of despotic theories is evident from the striking way in which his explanatory notes insist on bringing in Parliament. Marsiglio, the Italian, stressed the practice of the commune where the whole body of citizens, or at least its greater part (in quantity or

---

[1] Ewart Lewis, *Medieval Political Ideas* (1954), 543.
[2] Lagarde, *Naissance*, ii. 167 f.   [3] *Defensor Pacis*, II. 8. 5.
[4] Lewis, *Med. Pol. Ideas*, 256. Lagarde (*Naissance*, ii. 265) argues that Marsiglio came nearer a theory of sovereignty than Mrs Lewis will admit.
[5] P. Janelle, *L'Angleterre catholique à la veille du schism* (1935), 252 ff.; Hughes, *Reformation*, i. 332. The omissions are listed in Previté-Orton's edition of the *Defensor Pacis*, p. xl.

quality), made the laws, a repetition of the impossible (for England) that drove Marshall to distraction. The notes abound: 'He meaneth here of those lawes which do passe by acte of parlyament'; 'In all this longe tale he speaketh not of the rascall multytude but of the parlyament'; 'where soeuer he speketh of such multytude he meneth when it is assembled in yᵉ perlyamente, remember this to auoyde captyousness'.[1] He inserted Parliament in the text in a manner highly reprehensible in a translator, but also highly significant in one of Cromwell's propagandists.[2] The book confirms that Cromwell's mind was concentrating on the law-making power of Parliament, seeing here the essential core of the State demanded by Marsiglio.

Cromwell, then, was a common lawyer and parliamentarian who believed in moderation and the middle way, trusted in statute, and is likely to have learned from Marsiglio certain theoretical views on the character of the independent State and the nature of legislative supremacy within it. These last two points underlie the acts of Parliament in which the reconstruction of the English State was embodied.

IV

It is because the preambles of the Reformation statutes were propaganda that they offer a clue to the political doctrines held by the government. That the acts exemplify Cromwell's policy and thought is patent from his work on them; especially is this true of the fundamental statute, the Act in Restraint of Appeals to Rome, which contained the clearest piece of political theory.[3] At the same time, there are fewer such theoretical pronouncements than one could have wished; to the last, Cromwell's mind remains half-hidden behind the deeds to which it gave birth.

The proper starting-point is the preamble to the Act of Appeals.

Where by dyvers sundrie old autentike histories and cronicles it is manifestly declared and expressed that this Realm of Englond is an Impire . . . governed by oon Supreme heede and King having the Dignitie and Roiall Estate of the Imperiall Crowne of the same, unto whome a Body politike compacte of all sortes and degrees of people, devided in termes and by names of Spiritualtie

[1] *The Defence of Peace* (1535), fos. 27v, 28v, 45.
[2] E.g. in the fourth conclusion (ibid. fo. 138): the only law-maker is 'the prynce or his parlyament, or (where it is so vsed) hole vnyuersyte and congregacyon of Cytezens' – a paraphrase rather than a translation of the text. Also in I. 12. 5 (fo. 28) where 'valentiorem partem' is rendered as 'yᵉ bygger parte of them assembled in the parlyament'.
[3] Cf. above, no. 24, esp. pp. 86–7.

and Temporaltie, ben bounden and owen to bere nexte to God a naturall and humble obedience.[1]

These few words summarize the essence of the revolution. England, the act asserts, is a sovereign state, a political unit within which one authority only has the right to rule. The term used is 'empire' which here means simply national sovereignty: the king of England is an emperor, rules an empire, and wears an imperial crown because he has no superior on earth. The concept had a respectable and not unfamiliar history behind it. As early as 1208 the English canonist Alan stated that every prince owning no superior has as much power in his realm 'quantum imperator in imperio'.[2] Later, in the fourteenth century, French lawyers developed these gropings into the principle that 'rex superiorem non recognoscens est imperator in regno suo'. Cromwell may well have been familiar with this dictum, as Henry himself seems to have been when he said in 1516 that kings of England had never recognized any superiors on earth.[3] But in two ways the idea was here given a novel interpretation. While kings had called themselves emperors before, the Act of Appeals spoke of a sovereign territorial State, not only of a ruler with no superior. This change of a personal claim into a significant concept of political doctrine can, with some confidence, be ascribed to Cromwell, for the first mention of the term empire occurs in his corrections of the first draft of the 'Supplication against the Ordinaries', made in 1529, before he was even in the king's service.[4] Secondly, the notion of empire existing in all free monarchies had been developed against the claims of the Holy Roman Emperor; it had never been used to justify denial of the papal headship in the Church and the total subjection of matters spiritual to the lay ruler. Never before had the self-contained sovereignty of the national State been so fully realized or so bluntly stated.

Thus the basis of Cromwell's thought was a firm grasp of the principle of national sovereignty. He was clear, too, about the nature of the State so set apart. It was to be an organic unit consisting of the ruler and the body of subjects, both related to and dependent on each other. The apparent dualism of clergy and laity did not represent (as Mr Baumer has argued)[5] a revival of Gelasian doctrine; it simply

---

[1] 24 Henry VIII, c. 12 (*Stat. of the Realm*, iii. 427).
[2] Cited Schulz, *EHR* 40, 150, n. 8. The whole problem is well summarized in Lewis, *Med. Pol. Ideas*, 430 ff.
[3] Cf. J. Gairdner, *Lollardy and the Reformation* (1908), i. 283.
[4] PRO, SP1, 50, fo. 203. For the date cf. above, no. 25.
[5] *Kingship*, 28 f.

reflects the particular preoccupations of an act concerned with the administration of law, which had to take cognizance of the double system of law and courts actually in operation in the realm. This would have been clearer if motives of policy had not urged the government to abandon some rather extravagant theoretical claims: almost to the last, the act meant to allege that all jurisdiction, both lay and clerical, proceeded from the imperial crown of the realm, a claim which opposition from the Church forced out of the statute.[1] The unitary character of Cromwell's 'empire' was not affected by the existence of the Church courts with their canon law, any more than it was affected by the existence of other courts administering another law, such as Chancery with its equity.

However, this might suggest that the Cromwellian State was seen as a despotism centred in the 'Supreme heede and King'. In order to understand Cromwell's mind on this we must turn to the question of law. That Cromwell saw the essence of a state in its law is shown by the Act of Dispensations (1534) which implies such a legal criterion in the definition of a political organization when it states that England, 'recognysyng noo superior under God but only your Grace', is free from subjection to any laws except such 'as have been devysed made and ordyned within this Realme'.[2] It makes an exception for laws introduced from abroad which have received the consent of the people and the sufferance of the Crown, but of course the condition renders such foreign laws equivalent to native ones. By simply ignoring them, this view removes all those laws other than human – the law of God, the law of nature – of which both philosophy and jurisprudence were so fond, an interpretation expressly stressed in the Act for the Punishment of Heresy (1534) in which canonical sanctions are declared insufficient because they

be but humayne, being mere repugnaunte and contrarious to the prerogatyve of your ymperyall Crowne regal jurisdiccion lawes statutes and ordynaunces of this your Realme.[3]

The summary disposal of canon law as merely human can be linked with Cromwell not only because (as we have seen) he expressed similar views elsewhere, but also because the same denunciation of it as repugnant to the laws of the realm occurs in the draft of the 'Suppli-

---

[1] Cf. above, pp. 92f, 101. All the drafts, down to and including A and D, contained the claim, which was only abandoned after the conference on 5 Feb. 1533.
[2] 25 Henry VIII, c. 21 (*Stat. of the Realm*, iii. 464).
[3] 25 Henry VIII, c. 14 (ibid. 454).

cation' which he prepared for the 1532 session of Parliament.[1] His test for the validity of a law was thus not some extra-human body of rules, but the positive law of the realm, which means that he grasped the importance of legislative sovereignty within the sovereign State. A thoroughly Marsilian position, but it is likely that the views of a practising lawyer and statesman, concerned with this world only, simply found agreeable confirmation in the *Defensor Pacis*.

We now come to the crux of the matter: where, in Cromwell's view, lay the authority behind the positive law of the realm? Free enough though he was with deferential remarks about the imperial crown, it was not in a despotic king that he saw the law-giver. Once more we refer to the Dispensations Act:

In all and everey suche lawes humayne made within this Realme . . . your Royall Majestie and your Lordes Spirituall and temporall and Commons, representyng the holle state of your Realme in this your most high Courte of Parliament, have full power and auctoritie . . . the seid lawes . . . to abrogate adnull amplyfie or dymynyshe . . .

The legislative supremacy lies in the High Court of Parliament; it is exercised by king, Lords, and Commons, and therefore expresses itself in statute. This is precisely the doctrine which Cromwell's practice would lead one to expect, but it is gratifying to have it explicitly stated. The doctrine here expressed involves (in legal terms) the supremacy and omnicompetence of statute, or (in terms of political philosophy) the existence of constitutional or limited monarchy. There can be no talk of despotism while the highest expression of the State's activity is seen as the work of an assembly joining together the Head and the Body Politic of which the Empire of England is comprised. It was only after Cromwell had taught him this lesson that Henry could make his famous pronouncement of 1543, to the effect that 'we at no time stand so highly in our estate royal as in the time of Parliament' in which the king as head and the nation as members 'are conjoint and knit together'.[2]

As Cromwell freed the notion of empire from the encumbrances of the past and gave it full practical expression, so he freed statute from the limitations which had clung to it. That statute was the highest form of law-making in the realm had long been recognized. But so far all doctrine asserted the existence of a higher law with which statute must be consonant. Fortescue had seen this higher law in the law of nature: he held that statute could be unjust and would then be

[1] PRO, SP1/50, fo. 194.
[2] Tanner, *Tudor Constitutional Documents*, 582.

properly disregarded.[1] Even on the eve of the Reformation, St German, who ascribed overriding powers to statute, demanded that it should conform with the laws of God and of reason.[2] Though the judges of the fifteenth century admitted that statute could defeat canon law, they carefully excluded the field of *spiritualia*: statute could not make the king a parson, give laymen the rights of spiritual jurisdiction, or usurp the powers of the supreme head of the Church (that is, the pope).[3] Thus statute was not thought of as omnicompetent before the Reformation, simply because no human law was conceived of as possessing that quality. When the acts of the 1530s invaded the prohibited field of *spiritualia* (though statute did not in fact create but merely accepted the royal supremacy), they asserted the nullity of all those limitations. In the works of theorists, especially in Hooker, the law of nature was to stage a come-back, but some men grasped the point which Cromwell had made: as Burghley said, there was nothing that an act of Parliament could not do in England.[4] Thomas More showed that he understood the issue perfectly:

As this Inditement is grounded vpon an Acte of Parliament directly repugnant to the lawes of God and his holye Churche, the supreme Gouernment of which . . . may no temporall Prince presume by any lawe to take vpon him . . . it is therefore in lawe, amongest christen men, insufficient to charge any christian man.[5]

With the precision to be expected of a man of his stamp, he put his finger on the point that mattered; but his death demonstrated that in upholding a doctrine which certainly had age to recommend it he was wrong – wrong in law. However, his words will serve to remind us that the break with Rome and the emancipation of statute, which between them made up Cromwell's creation of true political and legislative sovereignty, did mark a break with the past that was revolutionary.

Thus, the sovereign nation state erected by Thomas Cromwell rested on the legislative supremacy of the king in Parliament, all imperfections and reservations disappearing as later developments subjected the Church, too, to that body instead of a personal royal

[1] Cf. Chrimes, *English Constitutional Ideas in the XV Century*, 201 ff.; E. F. Jacob, 'Sir John Fortescue and the Law of Nature,' *Essays in the Conciliar Epoch* (1943), 106 ff. (esp. p. 119).
[2] Chrimes, *Const. Ideas*, 209 ff.   [3] Ibid. 286.
[4] Quoted Holdsworth, *Hist. of Eng. Law*, iv. 186, n. 2.
[5] N. Harpsfield, *Life and Death of Sir Thomas Moore*, ed. E. V. Hitchcock and R. W. Chambers (E.E.T.S., 1932), 193.

supremacy. I suspect, though I cannot prove it, that Cromwell foresaw this change which the inevitable calling-in of Parliament was sure to bring about, but this whole question of the Henrician Church – vitally important though it is and often (as it seems to me) misinterpreted – cannot be discussed here. We merely wished to discover Cromwell's political ideas. We have seen that he had no intention of building a despotism. What he envisaged was the modern mixed sovereign, the king in Parliament, created by the deliberate infusion of the modern principle of sovereignty into those two great achievements of the middle ages – the assembly of king, Lords and Commons, and the common law of the realm. So far from attacking either, Cromwell gave greater authority to both by destroying the rivals who had limited them. Cold-blooded and ruthless though he was, he was also a constitutionalist who realized the potentialities of common law and Parliament, and who elaborated and employed the equipment of constitutional monarchy. There was no nemesis in the victorious struggle of the Commons in the seventeenth century, but only the lamentable failure of later statesmen and king's ministers to preserve the harmony between king and Parliament – natural or contrived – which Cromwell had made the basis of England's State and government.

32

REFORM BY STATUTE:
THOMAS STARKEY'S *DIALOGUE* AND
THOMAS CROMWELL'S POLICY*

Not so long ago it was generally held that with Thomas More's death
the light went out of English humanism and the intellectuals' share
ended in the government of their country. Of late, however, the
generation of younger humanists who started writing in the 1530s has
attracted much attention and much favourable comment. The names
of Elyot and Starkey, Morison and Taverner, if not yet quite household
words among students, have at least become newly familiar to Reformation scholars. Professor Zeeveld has demonstrated the share that
these men had in laying the intellectual foundations of the Church of
England.[1] Professor Ferguson has made a fine case for seeing in them a
first generation of practical thinkers who wished to use their training
in the cause of general reform.[2] And Mr McConica has termed them
Erasmians, whose influence he discovers in just about every thought
and deed of that decade.[3] It might be thought that these matters had
earned a rest, for a while at least. However, it seems to me that in this
discussion one distinctly central problem has been overlooked or at
least very inadequately treated. We know that these men thought
seriously and constructively about the nature of the state, that they
regarded participation in government – counselling the king – to be
the necessary duty of a scholar, and that they wished to reform the
commonwealth. What we have heard too little about are the specific
reforms they wished to promote, their positive purpose as councillors;
and we know nothing at all of their influence on legislation. Even Mr
McConica, whose interests were closest to this problem, tells us much
more about their lives and general ideas than about their specific
proposals. But until such questions are answered, it remains difficult
to judge these writers' true place and impossible to come to a proper
judgment of Thomas Cromwell's administration. The whole story is
very long and very complicated; on this occasion it will be possible to

---

* [Raleigh Lecture on History: *Proceedings of the British Academy*, 54 (1968), 165–88.]
[1] W. G. Zeeveld, *Foundations of Tudor Policy* (Cambridge, Mass., 1948).
[2] A. B. Ferguson, *The Articulate Citizen and the English Renaissance* (Durham, N.C., 1965).
[3] J. K. McConica, *English Humanists and Reformation Politics under Henry VIII and Edward VI* (Oxford, 1965).

attend only to what I believe must be the investigator's starting-point in the matter.

It has for some time been recognized that one piece of writing produced in that era attempted a comprehensive review of the needs of social reconstruction: Thomas Starkey's *Dialogue between Cardinal Pole and Thomas Lupset*, a title invented by the nineteenth-century editor of a tract found in manuscript. Historians have, however, been much more interested in Starkey's political ideas than in his programme of reform or in the possible connection between it and the government's actions. Another close look at Starkey's *Dialogue* is the more advisable because it is invariably used in its printed versions: and it has to be said that neither of the two editions we have is very satisfactory. They provide an accurate enough transcript – actual verbal errors are few[1] – but they hide all sorts of significant detail by making the treatise appear a complete and finished product, which it never was. This is the less surprising because the standard was set by the original editor, J. M. Cowper, who never saw the manuscript; he worked from a transcript provided by someone else.[2] Miss Kathleen Burton, on the other hand, who produced a handy version in modernized spelling, did look at the original, but she was too modest and preferred to follow Cowper's lead in his errors, inventions, and misleading opinions.[3]

The one known manuscript of the *Dialogue* is in fact a much corrected draft in the author's own hand.[4] There are a few deletions and very many additions. The division into chapters, the setting out of the two friends' speeches, and all the paragraphing that we find in the printed versions were introduced by the editors who thus hid the true appearance of the original. This is written continuously, without paragraphs of any sort, but does contain two breaks (not indicated in the editions) produced by the fact that on two occasions Starkey did not write down to the bottom of a page. Bound (now) with the treatise is a letter to Henry VIII, intended to accompany the book when it was sent as a present. This, too, is not in the least finished, as the editors and commentators might lead one to think. It is in the hand of a clerk who

---

[1] E.g. Lupset does not say that 'if a man consider lightly and judge them evenly' rather than think deeply he might jump to conclusions (ed. Burton, 110), but judge them 'overly', which makes better sense.

[2] He admitted this himself: S. J. Herrtage, *England in the Reign of Henry VIII* (E.E.T.S., 1878), p. cxxv.

[3] *A Dialogue between Reginald Pole and Thomas Lupset*, ed. K. M. Burton (1948). For purposes of reference, nevertheless, this readily accessible text in modernized spelling is the most convenient to use, and it shall be cited here as 'Burton'.

[4] PRO, SP 1/90, fos. 1 ff.

corrected a few small errors but also scribbled a number of doodles on the page; it lacks address or signature. This letter was never sent, though it looks like a fair copy rather than a draft. Despite the regular assertions to the contrary, it will therefore be seen that not only is there no evidence that Starkey presented the work to Henry VIII, but that the chances are strongly against his having done so. Obviously he had some intention to that effect, but the intention bore no fruit. The letter, drawn out fair, was nevertheless left abandoned; and the only version of the treatise to survive was in no state at all to be presented. Starkey certainly would not have dreamt of giving that rough draft to King Henry. The proper way of doing things was demonstrated by Richard Morison when he sent the king his proposals for codifying the law in Latin: he laboured hard over his draft, but what he delivered up is a handsomely bound and prettily written book, a simple though worthy gift to a monarch with intellectual pretensions.[1] Starkey's *Dialogue*, on the other hand, remained stuck at the draft stage, and there is no reason at all for thinking that Henry ever saw it.[2]

The state of the manuscript proves very clearly that Starkey did not write it at one time. In his draft letter to Henry VIII, he declared that the treatise consisted of three parts, the proper structure of a commonwealth, the ills of England, and the remedies for these; but he did not write it in these sections or indicate where the divisions were to come. The first break in composition came at the end of his part two, that which analysed what was wrong with England.[3] This is written in an ink that has badly faded but corrected in one which has remained much more legible. This better ink was used for the second piece to be written which begins with the curious passage in which Pole and Lupset go to hear mass before setting about the serious task of working out reforms; it terminates at what looks like having been the original final sentence.[4] There follows what is now the concluding section, which starts on a new page with the words 'So that, Master Lupset, now upon this point let us conclude'. When he added it, Starkey was moved to rearrange the passage just before it. There are several

---

[1] The draft is BM, Faustina C. ii, fos. 5 ff.; the presentation copy is BM, Royal MSS 18. A. l.

[2] This fact disposes of Mr Baumer's admiration for Starkey's 'audacity' in presenting Henry, 'at a time when Tudor despotism was at its peak', with a treatise that 'would have made the King almost a figurehead' (F. L. Baumer, 'Thomas Starkey and Marsilius of Padua,' *Politica*, 2 (1936), 188).

[3] Burton, down to p. 134.

[4] 'And so by this mean our politic body should be kept in order and rule, after the manner which we have before devised' (ibid. 183).

additions in the second part which, to judge from the ink, were made at some time other than the writing of the text itself.

When was the *Dialogue* written? The date is, naturally, important for assessing what influence the treatise may have had. Miss Burton rightly rejected Cowper's late date of 1538; while she sees that the book was certainly started not later than 1533 she puts its composition mainly into 1535,[1] which I think is still too late. True, the short last part was not written before the middle of 1535 or later because it refers to Erasmus's *Ecclesiastes*, which appeared that year, as published 'now, of late': the reference is in the original text, not inserted.[2] But the bulk of the treatise, the first two parts, must have been written much earlier because in both of them Starkey spoke of the pope in terms not possible after 1534. He attacked papal dispensing powers and wished to confine appeals to Rome to 'causes of schism in the faith',[3] matters which in England had been settled by the legislation of 1533–4, so that it would have been quite pointless for Starkey to talk the way he did. In the intended covering letter to the king he showed himself aware of current events, for there he praised Henry for having 'plucked up the root of all abuses, the outward power and intolerable tyranny of Rome'. Exactly when the main parts were written is not easy to say, for in 1533–4 Starkey was in Padua and it would be quite a while before news from England would reach him. The second part contains a further point to date it, a reference to Sadoleto's book on education, published in Venice in 1533, which – calling it 'of late days...put forth' – uses much the same phrase as that employed for Erasmus's book on preaching, so that a similar distance of a few months at most is suggested.[4] A date in late 1532 or early 1533 for the first section to be written and one in late 1533 for the second would seem the most probable.

It may therefore be conjectured with a good deal of confidence that Starkey wrote the parts of his *Dialogue* in which he expounded the true nature of a polity and described the deficiencies of England in this respect at one sitting, probably not later than early in 1533. As he went, he revised a little, as most of us would. He put it aside, but later that year he took it up again and having, on re-reading, made some changes in what he had written he went on to compose the part that

[1] Ibid. 193 ff.
[2] Ibid. 187. This point misled Mr Zeeveld into supposing that the whole treatise was written in 1535 (*Foundations*, 144, n. 48).
[3] Burton, 158, 178–9.   [4] Ibid. 182, 194.

prescribed remedies. This draft (done in Italy, a fact which may explain such things as that Starkey is frequently found asking for legislation that already existed) he brought with him when he returned to England in early 1535 and applied to Cromwell for employment. In reply to the minister's request for a sample of his skill he sent a paper on the Aristotelian doctrine of the commonwealth which turns out to be, in effect, a fair copy of part one of the *Dialogue*.[1] Very probably the sample pleased; Cromwell certainly took Starkey under his wing and may have encouraged him to attract the King's attention by completing his *magnum opus* and dedicating it to Henry. Starkey therefore once more revised his manuscript, adding a new concluding passage which switches very markedly from the discussion of particular reforms to general and rather elevated reflections. He also, in a few places, added to the earlier parts, and two of the additions deserve notice. Where he had followed Marsiglio in preferring an elective to a hereditary monarchy, he sought to make the text more palatable by prefacing his remarks with a fulsome encomium on Henry VIII's sterling qualities.[2] And where he advocated the establishment of new schools, he added the words 'to this use turn both Westminster and St Albans, and many other'.[3] The purpose of the first addition is self-evident; it confirms that the idea of making the treatise into a present for the king came as an afterthought. The second confirms that some additions to the 1533 text were made later, for it recognizes the coming end of the monasteries. It must surely have been made when the attack had begun, some time in the first half of 1536; for in his main text Starkey called firmly for the reform and not the abolition of religious houses.[4]

As Miss Burton recognized, every word now surviving must have been written before the summer of 1536 when the whole plan to bring Pole into the king's service collapsed – the plan in which Starkey had been the government's chief agent – and when it ceased to be possible to send Henry a treatise praising 'the king's traitor'. However, that disaster did supervene: the revision was never completed. Treatise and covering letter remained in draft; and there is no sign that Starkey ever looked at his cherished manuscript again in the two years that remained of his life. But now that we know how Starkey wrote his book we can

---

[1] Cf. Zeeveld, *Foundations*, 143 f. This paper ('What is policy after the sentence of Aristotle') cannot have been, as Mr Zeeveld supposed, the 'germ' of the *Dialogue*, written much earlier, but was clearly a piece from Starkey's big book worked over for the occasion.

[2] Burton, 154. 'But here you must remember ... some remedy. Wherein' is an addition inserted later.   [3] Burton, 169.   [4] Ibid. 145.

dispose of one question quickly: the views expressed in it must be his, and the use of Pole and Lupset was a literary device, no more. Though Starkey may have known Lupset, whose benefice he acquired, he joined Pole's household after Lupset had died there, so that he can never have heard the two of them converse. And while even those who have supposed that Starkey was really presenting his own views have also thought that very possibly he had heard Pole say some of the things here ascribed to him, it now seems clear that these frequent corrections and revisions at different times show an author at work on a manuscript in which he was developing his own ideas. We are fully entitled to use the *Dialogue* to prove the ideas of Thomas Starkey.[1]

Next we must consider how widely the manuscript might have become known. Its state fully explains why it was never published: the book was simply not ready for the printer. Years ago, Mr Baumer offered a different explanation, and if he were right the relations between Starkey and others would have to be judged very differently. He held that Starkey's thought was, as he put it, so much ahead of his time 'that he would scarcely have been understood in 1535 even if his writings had been circulated by royal command'.[2] Even Mr Baumer's maturer reflection still saw deep significance in the fact that the treatise remained unprinted until 1871: Starkey was a radical constitutionalist badly out of step with a despotic age.[3] And though the labours of the scholars whom I quoted at the start have done much to explain how ready the age was for many of Starkey's views, it may be necessary once again to emphasize that when he wrote Starkey's constitutionalism was much nearer to the conventional than the impossibly radical. After all, Professor Hurstfield has recently revived the thesis that early-Tudor government was at heart despotic, not constitutionalist, and that Cromwell, in particular, looking for efficiency, had no time for a monarch limited by consent or a system which did not place the king above the law.[4] If that had been so (and I fear I cannot accept it) Baumer would have been right: Starkey could hardly have thought it wise in such a climate to make public his views that kings should be

---

[1] Cf. Ibid. 3 ff., 197. J. W. Allen (*History of Political Thought in the Sixteenth Century*, 2nd ed. [1941], 143 f.) used the book to identify Pole's opinion.

[2] *Politica*, 2 (1936), 188.

[3] *Early Tudor Theory of Kingship*, 119, 148. Yet at the end of his book (p. 210) he was forced to recognize that 'the political writers of the Reformation' advocated a limited and law-controlled monarchy.

[4] 'Was there a Tudor Despotism after all?,' *TRHS* (1967), 83 ff. [Cf. no. 14 above.]

elected by Parliament, that the power to dispense from statute should be taken away, and that the rule of kings must be controlled by their submission to a permanent council of ministers.[1]

The question is important because Mr Baumer deduced from his concept of Starkey's radicalism the inference that 'his ideas can scarcely have had much effect on his contemporaries'.[2] This was certainly not Starkey's own notion: he did everything he could to earn government employ by advertising his ideas. In all his place-hunting letters to Cromwell, his only claim to regard is that he had positive advice to offer, and when he wished to make an impression he sent, as we have seen, a summary of his highly constitutionalist views on the nature of the commonwealth. Nor is there any doubt about Cromwell's part in this agreeable exchange of scholarly enquiry. He called forth the summary by asking his suitor 'what thing it is after the sentence of Aristotle and the ancient peripatetics that commonly among them is called policy', and he reacted to the gift by securing advancement for Starkey. Of course, he had reasons of his own: he wanted the use of Starkey's pen. But after their dealings he could have had no illusions about the man he was proposing to employ, and the thought of Cromwell showing favour to a man a hundred years ahead of his time – a man, according to Mr Baumer who speaks vaguely of the Civil War, more suitable to Oliver than Thomas – need not, perhaps, detain us. Cromwell knew what he was getting, and he would not have had his doubts about it, either. This was the man who kept among his papers one of the most tedious edifying tracts ever written in praise of conventional good kingship: not only kept it but read it, for at the top of a late page in that manuscript he scribbled 'what a king, what a tyrant [might be]'.[3] Perhaps Cromwell the Machiavellian, the ruthless promoter of an efficient despotism, looks to some a more impressive figure than the Cromwell who, wanting to do the right thing, laboured his way through these twenty-odd pages of tired wisdom and noted that there was a difference between a true king and a tyrant; but the latter is, I fear, the real Cromwell.[4]

There was nothing, then, in Starkey's political thinking that stood in the way of place and influence, and Starkey himself judged the situation better than some modern commentators have done. Nor was he a coward: the man who could explain to Henry VIII late in 1536

---

[1] Burton, 100, 102, 154, 156.   [2] *Politica*, 2 (1936), 188.
[3] PRO, SP 1/242, fos. 166–76v; Cromwell's note is on fo. 174.
[4] I have argued the case at greater length in no. 31 above.

that until Anne Boleyn's execution people could not be expected to believe that the king's doings proceeded from sound motives,[1] would not have felt any hesitation about publishing his Marsilian doctrine of kingship. He certainly did not tamper with any of the constitutionalist statements in the *Dialogue* when he prepared it for presentation to the king. But whether Starkey realized it or not, we cannot doubt that after the appearance of Pole's *De Unitate*, with its savage attack on Henry VIII, Cromwell would not have permitted the publication of a book in which Pole was depicted as setting the world to rights. His feelings emerge clearly enough in the quite hysterical and violent letter which he drafted, and perhaps sent, to Michael Throckmorton, Pole's secretary, who had tricked the lord privy seal into a false conviction that Pole would prove amenable.[2] However, Starkey himself did not suffer, even though he had been the most active and most sanguine promoter of all those approaches to his Paduan friend and mentor. He continued to enjoy Cromwell's favour and even got further preferment, six months after the Pole disaster.[3] But his book remained unrevised and unpublished.

Was it, then, true that it exercised no influence? Publication was certainly not, at the time, necessary to get a book a hearing; the notion that no one wrote in the modern manner, except to get into print, is anachronistic, and Cromwell used the printing press for a different purpose – to publish propaganda, not to subsidize the learning in which his relations with Starkey show him to have been keenly interested. Pole's own *De Unitate* first reached England in manuscript, and for a while it remained uncertain whether he would have the nerve to send his invective to the printer; in the autumn of 1536, Richard Morison offered to interrupt the writing of his *Apomaxis* 'and turn Cochlaeus in Polum' if Pole 'would be so mad to put forth' his book – provided Cromwell approved, that was.[4] Manuscripts were read, even manuscripts as unfinished in form as Starkey's *Dialogue*. And Starkey, as we have learned in recent years, was one of a group of men who believed that the duty of intellectuals lay in analysing practical problems of politics and advising on their solution: the *Dialogue* is about nothing else. Before we dismiss it as a work of no

---

[1] Herrtage, op. cit., p. li.
[2] Merriman, ii. 86 ff.   [3] Burton, 201.
[4] PRO, SP 1/113, fo. 210 (*LP*, xi. 1481). Morison never got round to answering Pole specifically; late in 1536 his talents were diverted by the Pilgrimage of Grace into writings against rebellion. His *Apomaxis*, delayed by these events, was an answer to Cochlaeus's attack on the King's doings (Zeeveld, *Foundations*, 158).

influence at the time, a closer look at this fundamental purpose seems advisable.

Starkey provided an important clue at the beginning of the second section of his draft, that section in which he offered his remedy for the ills that beset England. Pole has been enlarging on the need for better technical education among the people, and Lupset very fairly comments that his words were 'a very short remedy'; 'you must', he adds, 'show somewhat more at large how the youth should be brought up in arts and crafts more particularly.' But Starkey makes the point only to reject it and to justify his concise outline treatment: 'That is not my purpose,' he has Pole say, 'here now to do, for it were need then of every cure almost for to write a whole book. I will only touch . . . the most general points and the rest leave for the cure of them which in every cause have order and rule.'[1] The theorist was to confine himself to throwing out general ideas: the proper detailed development must be left to the experts. Pole is made to repeat the point a little later in the treatise: those who 'have authority and rule' are to have the course of their actions suggested to them by Starkey's 'general things'.[2] It thus becomes sensible to ask whether we can find any sign that any one, with or without 'rule', set about working up any of these brief suggestions into the practical form of 'a whole book'.

In the first place, there is very good evidence to show that others read the *Dialogue* and revolved its proposals. This evidence consists of three mainly abortive projects on the grand scale which took up hints in the book and worked them out at length, two of them significantly using the form of acts of Parliament, to this group (as to Cromwell) the natural and only instrument for achieving reforms. These two projects are the comprehensive poor law and the scheme for a centralized enforcement agency which have been previously discussed by myself and Professor Plucknett respectively.[3] The third is Richard Morison's suggested codification of the laws of England, something that neither could be, nor required to be, embodied in statute.

Starkey had a number of things to say on the problems of poverty and unemployment. He believed that sheer idleness had something to do with it, but on the whole he regarded this idleness – the upper classes' devotion to useless occupations and the lower classes' lack of employment – as a product of pointless ostentation on the one hand

---

[1] Burton, 143. [2] Ibid. 149.

[3] Above, no. 26; T. F. T. Plucknett, 'Some Proposed Legislation of Henry VIII,' *TRHS* (1936), 119 ff. (to which cf. my remarks, above, pp. 69–71, showing that this was not an official draft).

and economic dislocation on the other; and the two were linked in his mind. Though in the main he inclined to the toughness of the un-involved academic, he recognized also that ill fortune could contribute towards a man's poverty.[1] His remedies may seem obvious, but they were not then part of the law: provide work for those able to work and relief for the sick and helpless. He drew attention to the relief ordinance recently (1531) issued at Ypres.[2] In another place he suggested that convicts should be used 'in some common work', in the rebuilding of towns or 'some other magnifical work' organized by the govern-ment; and in yet another, he introduced the term overseers to describe local officials whom he wished to charge with the supervision of town buildings and public health, just after he had spoken of another set of allied officials whom he compared to the Roman censors.[3]

If, with these points in mind, we look at the draft poor law (which I have suggested was the work of William Marshall, another of Cromwell's pamphleteers) some interesting links emerge. Marshall, for one thing, published a translation of the Ypres ordinance in 1535, some two years later than Starkey had shown himself aware of its existence, but in the very year that Starkey's ideas could have become known to him. In his draft, he carefully elaborated the distinction between impotent, misfortunate, and merely idle poor towards which Starkey had been groping, and one of his most striking proposals concerned the undertaking of large public works to relieve unemploy-ment. And when he wished to invent a name for local officers respon-sible for the control of poverty he called them 'censors or overseers of poverty'. There are many things in his draft, the original of the new departure marked by the poor law of 1536, of which no trace is found in the *Dialogue*, but that is not the point. What matters is that some brief hints in the *Dialogue* appear in the draft in a thoroughly developed and worked over form, definite links being provided by the common presence of Ypres and of censors. It would be strange if all this were pure coincidence: rather, it looks very much as though Marshall had read the treatise or discussed such matters with its author.

Next there is the striking proposal to create a new court, presided over by six 'conservators of the commonweal', permanently estab-lished at Westminster, assisted by a regular police force of sergeants of the commonweal, and charged with the enforcement of penal statutes. Years ago I tried to show that this was not a strictly official draft – not

[1] Burton, 90 f., 93, 142, 148.
[2] Ibid. 160. [3] Ibid. 177, 183.

a piece of the government's actual legislative programme – but rather a proposal worked out privately for submission to Cromwell which got no further.[1] For one thing, it is not quite finished: the conservators' oath remains undrafted, the proposed seal is described in terms quite unsuitable to an act of Parliament, and the phrasing is not correct in all respects in that individual clauses do not repeat, as by this time they always did, that each new section was also enacted by the authority of Parliament. But the main body of the draft is complete, well worked out, and full of touches – like the reference to earlier legislation[2] – which show the draftsman to have been reasonably well informed and no crank. It therefore looks like a provisional draft prepared by someone who had reason to think that he could get his ideas listened to by the government. As Plucknett recognized, it cannot have been written before 1534, but how much later it was cannot be said at all.

The main ill to be remedied here – law enforcement – was one which exercised Starkey, too. He was aware of the problems posed by penal statutes, though he concentrated on the fact that they were regularly evaded by dispensations, not on the absence of reliable investigation and trial.[3] The crucial link is purely verbal: right at the end of his book, remembering that he had meant to suggest new officials responsible for the supervision of the whole administrative machine, he names them – 'conservators of the commonweal'.[4] His conservators were to do quite other things from those appointed in the draft, and the ideas in the draft are in no way Starkey's, but this identity of title cannot just be coincidence. 'Conservators of the commonweal' is not an obvious name to invent; so far as I know, the term never recurs again. It looks rather as though someone in the Starkey circle, taking up the problem of law-enforcement which certainly was not forgotten in the *Dialogue*, picked up the name which Starkey had dreamed up. This is the more likely because the title fitted the general supervisory function intended by Starkey much better than the very particular and specialized court function assigned by the draft. It seems to me unlikely that someone wishing to give a name to a new court responsible for trying breaches of penal statutes would, out of the blue, have hit on this form of words.

Lastly, there is Starkey's attack on the state of the common law, made famous by Maitland who used it in his argument – his unhappily very misleading argument – that in the early sixteenth century the

---

[1] Above, pp. 72–7. [2] *TRHS* (1936), 137.
[3] Burton, 100. [4] Ibid. 183.

common law was seriously threatened by a possible 'reception' of the law civil.[1] Starkey is usually supposed to have advocated the simple replacement of the common law by the civil law of Rome.[2] This is not what he says. He has Pole exclaim at length at the crudities and insufficiencies of the law, starting with its uncertainty.[3] There are too many and divers laws: 'wherefore I would wish that all those laws should be brought into small number, and to be written also in our mother tongue, or else put into Latin, to cause them that study the civil law of our realm [i.e. the common law] first to begin of the Latin tongue, wherein they might also afterwards learn many things to help this profession.' But then it occurs to Pole that worse things are wrong with the law of England than the use of 'this barbarous tongue, Old French', and that there is one obvious good remedy for it all: these troubles of 'tyrannical and barbarous institutions' could be 'wiped away by the receiving of this which we call the very civil law', that is the law of Rome.

Starkey therefore proposed the codification of the common law, in either English or Latin, but threw out the suggestion that its total replacement by the civil law would be an even more satisfactory radical solution. He allows Pole to ride over Lupset's sensible objection that after all those centuries of living under the old law such a reform would be extremely difficult, by asserting rather airily that if only the prince would put his authority behind the transformation it would come to pass very easily. However, Starkey himself may not have been very happy with this cavalier argument, for he has Pole concede that, since Lupset thinks total substitution too hard, they had best consider particular amendments. From the idea, however, that the law should be codified he does not retreat.

And this is precisely what Richard Morison set out to do. Of his scheme only two things survive: the first part of a Latin treatise on the law of real property, and the long English letter which accompanied this treatise on its journey to Henry VIII.[4] When he wrote these is

---

[1] F. W. Maitland, 'English Law and the Renaissance,' *Selected Historical Essays*, ed. H. M. Cam (Cambridge, 1957), esp. 137, 149. For the demolition of his argument cf. my remarks above, p. 223, and authorities cited there. The full recognition that the common law was in no danger and that it is wrong to think of a political conflict of laws and courts in the sixteenth century underlies the whole analysis of two important recent books: J. P. Dawson, *A History of Lay Judges* (Cambridge, Mass., 1960), and W. J. Jones, *The Elizabethan Court of Chancery* (Oxford, 1967).

[2] E.g. Baumer, *Kingship*, 135. On the other hand, Mr Zeeveld (*Foundations*, 130 ff.) and Mr Ferguson (*Articulate Citizen*, 323) see more accurately.

[3] Burton, 173 ff.   [4] BM, Royal MSS 18. A. l and II. A. xvi.

difficult to say. The editors of *Letters and Papers*, for no obvious reason, chose the year 1542,[1] but this seems much too late to me. The only topical reference occurs in the draft of the letter: when attacking the inability of English lawyers to make a properly constructed speech (a consequence of their lack of humanist training) Morison interlined the words 'Mr Cholmley excepted' but crossed them out again. Roger Cholmley was recorder of London from 1536 to 1544, being then appointed king's serjeant and, a year later, baron of the Exchequer; he had been of the order of the coif since 1531. The remark would surely come more suitably touching a man well known as a pleader rather than as a judge, and its insertion and removal suggest that Morison was working on the book round about 1535 or 1536, the date that seems increasingly crucial in the history of Starkey's influence. Morison followed Starkey to England out of Pole's household not later than the end of 1535; he, for one, could have become acquainted with the ideas of the *Dialogue* in Padua.

Morison, though a markedly less original mind than Starkey, was a much better and wittier writer, and his long letter is a splendid piece of work – full of vigour, shrewdness, and eloquence. But what he actually has to say – excepting a long attack on the pope which he admits is off the point – amounts to very little more than an elaboration of the ideas thrown out in the *Dialogue*. The health of any body politic depends on its law, 'the pillar that sustaineth and holdeth up any commonwealth'. This should be easily learned and taught; its prac- titioners should be able to teach others, 'not still to be scholars ever learning, never learned, ever doubtful, never certain, ever pleading, seldom determining controversies'. Exactly the point from which Starkey had started: English law is 'infinite and without order or end', and all this weighing up of cases makes the law far too uncertain.[2] Hence 'innumerable suits', says Morison; 'this causeth suits to be long in decision', says Starkey. 'Long suits', adds Morison, 'require much and often counsel, counsel requireth money, no penny no plea.' That it is only the greed of lawyers which leads to protracted litigation is Starkey's opinion in another place.[3] Morison rides off on the examples of Athens and Rome: Athens, Sparta, and Rome are Starkey's examples of well-governed communities using laws in their own language.[4] At this point Morison recollects himself: 'But what', he says to the king, 'do I cumber your grace's ears with ethnic histories?' He

---

[1] *LP* xvii, App. A, 2.
[2] Burton, 173 f.
[3] Ibid. 113.
[4] Ibid. 131.

promptly goes on to expatiate on Moses and the reception of the Decalogue.

Next he explains his real purpose. The laws of England are a linguistic mingle-mangle – 'some words Saxon, some British, some Latin, some French, some English, yea and some Greek, and some none of all these'. This leads to needless argument over 'the etymology and the interpretation'. He considers the use of English, and here he changed his mind. Perhaps first guided by Starkey's suggestion that English might do, he first wrote of it with modified praise, but this he crossed out, and his final version is highly condemnatory of the language as a vehicle for learning. Latin is best: it has the necessary technical terms, and past legal records are often 'in a tongue that smelleth of the Latinity, but indeed barbarous and far from it'. And thus he launches into a long defence of the need for better education among lawyers who should be trained in philosophy and logic and the law of God, whereas at present they want to learn nothing that does not bring immediate profit. Put the laws into Latin, and lawyers will have to get the right training even to understand the laws; and in consequence they will become much better able to serve the king in politics too: to analyse the needs of the commonwealth, and to become ambassadors abroad (where at present the king uses bishops and doctors 'who be chiefly ordained to preach and teach God's Word'). The plea for diplomatic employment may well be Morison's own who was later to be an able ambassador, but the stress on the services of lawyers as political advisers reminds one of the whole powerful argument about the counselling duties of intellectuals which underlies the *Dialogue* and seems to have found so ready a response in Cromwell's mind. Morison's lengthy exposition of it does no more than elaborate Starkey's brief remark that a knowledge of Latin would assist lawyers to learn many things helpful in their profession.

To judge by the sample which Morison provided, it is a very good thing that the codification of the common law was not undertaken by him or in Latin, but allowed to wait a century for Sir Edward Coke's English prose. Morison's attempt to reduce the law of tenures and inheritance to order suffers from two rather fatal defects: a devotion to vapoury philosophising and an uncertain grasp of the law. What he provides is not a code but a kind of elevated undergraduate essay. However, that is not the point: which is, rather, that we have here a manifest example of the way in which a general suggestion in Starkey's *Dialogue* could be worked up into a device of its own. Taken together with the other deposits of Starkeian notions in detailed, though in part very different, proposals, it shows that the *Dialogue* was read in the circle of pamphleteers whom Cromwell gathered around him, and that its ideas proved fruitful in stimulating thought and planning. Yet the writings so far discussed came to nothing; did the blueprint of reform, which Starkey brought with him from Italy, leave any mark on the real makers of policy and on that policy itself?

There are many statutes, proclamations, and half-done proposals surviving from the years 1535–40 with which Starkey's suggestions can be compared, but several difficulties stand in the way of straight-forward deductions. In the first place, Starkey was certainly not the only man around with ideas; we remember Clement Armstrong and his treatises of the commonwealth who, dead by May 1536, can assuredly not have sat at Starkey's feet.[1] And contemporary thinkers, reflecting upon the same problems, are always likely to produce very similar answers. Next, one of the chief targets of would-be reformers was, naturally, the Church, its courts and its faith, and on this Starkey, concentrating on the ills of the commonwealth, had little enough to say. He did advocate the bible and religious services in the vernacular,[2] but that does not make him the father of the English bible. One would dearly like to know what mind gave birth to the most interesting proposals concerning heresy trials which the age produced: the setting up of a lay commission of six, charged with assisting, and in effect controlling, the bishops in their dealings with heretics. The idea was first adumbrated in a general memorandum on various projected reforms which also contained the first hint of Marshall's great poor law draft;[3] at this time the commissioners were to have investigatory powers only, without the right to arrest or punish. This paragraph of the memorandum was then worked up into a draft statute to repeal Richard's II's heresy act on the grounds that new arrangements had been made: these, recited at length in the preamble, turn out to be the appointment of the commission, treated as accomplished fact, which now was to have also executive functions.[4] The memorandum clearly formed a rough outline of reform proposals, and such points as the

[1] S. T. Bindoff, 'Clement Armstrong and his Treatises of the Commonwealth,' *Economic History Review*, 1st ser., 14 (1944–5), 64 ff.
[2] Burton, 128, 184.
[3] PRO, SP 6/7, p. 55. Cf. *BIHR*, 27 (1954), 198 ff. The date assigned by *LP* v. 50 – 1532 – is completely conjectural and entirely improbable.
[4] PRO SP 1/151, 132–9.

poor law and an attempt to reform church services link it loosely with the Starkey group; Starkey was no bigot, admitting that 'heretics be not in all things heretics', and the chief purpose of the proposed commission was to make sure that this fact should be remembered by the spiritual judges.[1] Still, this is insufficient ground on which to build, especially as other men, anxious to restrain the bishops, have left sufficient evidence of their concern in the record.

The main trouble about tracing Starkey's influence really arises from the character of his 'remedies'. They fall into two sorts – the very commonplace and the quite out of the way. Some are so obvious that laws of the sort he asked for had long been in existence; others are so recondite that no sensible statesman could have thought them practicable. As an example of the sort of fantasy of which he was capable, take his attempt to prevent tyranny: he proposed to revive (as he thought) the office of constable of England, putting its power into commission in order to avoid excess of it in one man, and charging this 'council' with the tasks of keeping the prince to the law and appointing his permanent council.[2] He seriously supposed that good government would be assured by a body consisting of the constable, the earl marshal, the lords steward and great chamberlain, four judges, four citizens of London, and the two archbishops, a body acting as 'a little parliament' permanently vigilant in reviewing the actions of the Crown. Shades of the Provisions of Oxford. However much Cromwell may have in general respected intellectuals, he must at times have had his doubts about their understanding of reality.

However, Starkey did not always elaborate pipe dreams, and the proposals that I have called commonplace deserve attention. It would be quite wrong to suppose him necessarily ignorant of legislation which, in turn, he was putting forward afresh. The sixteenth century knew that good laws cannot be enacted too often; it held that the best way of driving home the present reality of a point long since made is to re-enact the earlier statute, preferably in an improved form. Laws, said Starkey, are needed because centuries of experience have shown that men will not be brought to perfection by 'instruction and gentle exhortation' alone.[3] Their 'imbecility' and 'weakness of mind' require tougher measures, and when he suggests a law he by no means need be taken to suppose that it would be the first on a given subject. If, therefore, we want to know whether Starkey exercised any influence on those who conducted affairs, we must look not only at new legislation but also at the possibility that activity and pressure increased in matters which had already received legislative attention.

Let me therefore review some of Starkey's pet notions. Like others, he was worried by the problem of depopulation, but he had a special affection for direct remedies designed to allure 'man to his natural procreation, after a civil order and politic fashion'. Thus he proposed to allow secular priests to marry, to prohibit the keeping of serving-men beyond the number that could be 'set forward to some honest fashion of living and lawful matrimony', and to penalize bachelors by excluding them from civic office and taxing them for the benefit of married men overburdened with children.[1] This is Starkey the fanciful, but not everybody thought so: the attempt to intervene in marriage habits crops up in a paper sent to Cromwell which suggested legislation to prevent young men from marrying till they are 'of potent age' and strong men from marrying widows.[2] The rest of that paper also has echoes of Starkey. An act is asked for 'for restraint and utter extinction of abuses of lawyers', as Starkey demanded that the effects of 'the avaricious minds and covetous of proctors and advocates' be dealt with;[3] and this point in the memorial impressed Cromwell sufficiently to make him include in a list of forthcoming legislation (much of which was enacted) an act for reducing the numbers of lawyers in all counties, 'which persons', he added in his own hand to the fair copy made from his own draft, 'be the cause of great plea and dissension'.[4] In these matters of matrimony as a prop to population and restraints on lawyers to cut down on burdensome litigation we do, I think, see Starkey at least putting ideas into heads in government circles.

None of this became law. Starkey was perhaps a little more successful with another of his foibles. He believed that England's farmers paid insufficient heed to the scientific breeding of animals, and he may have persuaded Cromwell to do something at least about horses. The act of 1536, which was of Cromwell's promotion, for improving the supply, expressly concentrated on points of breeding, prohibiting the use of mares and stallions of insufficient height and encouraging the use of deer-parks for controlled experimentation. Cromwell returned to the matter in 1540, in an amending act which among other things per-mitted the destruction of inadequate animals found in the open.[5] So far as horses were concerned, Starkey's concern could rest satisfied.

---

[1] Ibid. 138 ff.   [2] *LP* ix. 725 (ii).   [3] Burton, 172 f.
[4] PRO, SP 1/102 fo. 5. Cromwell's original draft is ibid. fo. 7.
[5] Burton, 96, 159; PRO, SP 1/102, fo. 5; 27 Henry VIII, c. 6; 32 Henry VIII, c. 13.

He also urged action in areas where, though Parliament had spoken before, little pressure was applied till the later 1530s, the era of Cromwellian reform in the commonwealth. Thus he was particularly troubled by the prevalence of idle games of chance and of amusements which were taking people from better employment, especially – but not exclusively – from keeping up their archery. Now, of course, the law on this point already fully agreed with him, though it should be noted that the earlier Henrician laws concentrated more on the need to maintain defence while Starkey stressed more heavily the evils of gambling.[1] Is it, then, pure coincidence that the first thorough proclamation for the enforcement of the older acts appeared in February 1537, that specific orders for enforcement to the officers responsible were not issued until the same year, that a proclamation of September 1538 confined itself to reciting the laws against games and made no mention of the archery statutes, and that a very much more comprehensive act on the whole subject emerged in 1541, in the clearing-up process after Cromwell's fall which embodied ideas of his for which he had not been given time?[2] Perhaps, though, it was as well that Starkey also did not live to see this act, for whereas he had particularly lambasted the nobility and their servants for wasting their time in idleness, an amendment in Parliament explicitly permitted all with incomes over £100 per annum to engage in the unlawful games in their own houses. No one would pretend that Starkey drafted the Cromwellian legislation and proclamations, but the sudden revival of interest in this topic at the very least goes well with what Starkey emphasized among the ills of England in the treatise brought to notice just before action got going.

Starkey's bonnet also harboured a bee about English towns which he thought decayed and filthy, as no doubt they were, especially compared with the Italian cities that served him as a model.[3] He wanted civic officers to supervise beautification and sanitation, but this he did not get. He also stressed the need for rebuilding, a matter in hand before ever Cromwell heard of him, at least in Norwich and Lynn, towns which apparently themselves promoted the necessary

---

[1] 3 Henry VIII, c. 3, 6 Henry VIII, c. 2; Burton, 148.
[2] *Tudor Royal Proclamations*, vol. 1, nos. 138, 163, 183; 33 Henry VIII, c. 9. Proclamation no. 138 is dated by Hughes and Larkin to ?1533, for no reason except that R. R. Steele placed it there; as they themselves note, it was not actually proclaimed until March 1537. Some earlier proclamations (ibid. nos. 63, 108, 118) cover much the same ground but very briefly and inadequately by comparison with Cromwell's.
[3] Burton, 75, 92, 161.

bills.[1] However, in 1536 and 1540 three acts created wide powers in superior lords and municipal corporations over negligent occupiers and owners in no less than sixty towns, most of the leading ones amongst them.[2] The question of towns links Starkey with other men working on reforms. A draft act which proposed to solve municipal impoverishment by confining all sales of goods to fairs and markets and by compelling all artisans to reside within borough limits, was probably the work of Thomas Gibson, an obscure pamphleteer known, however to Clement Armstrong, whose will he witnessed.[3] We note that Starkey favoured a system of control over entry into all crafts, that an anonymous tract wished to confine cloth-making to towns long decayed, and that Armstrong also wanted to see artisans confined to towns.[4] I have already said that different people would come to similar conclusions on similar problems, and Gibson probably got his ideas from Armstrong who owed nothing to Starkey. But this is not to forget that Starkey also wrote on these themes, and if the sudden spurt of governmental energy owed anything to any writer, Starkey, whom Cromwell promoted, is a better candidate than Armstrong whom he ignored. Cromwell preferred reform by statute, a point which seemed obvious to Starkey; but Armstrong, we must remember, did not trust Parliament and did not believe in statute.[5]

The most complex issue, and one far too long to be fully discussed here, in which Starkey's *Dialogue* involved him touched the crucial economic question of the time, the manufacture of woollen cloth and the most profitable way of selling it. On this topic Cromwell, who in any case had personal experience to guide him as well as important friends among the leading merchants of London, received unsolicited advice from every sort of quarter. He was told how a profit of £33,000 could be made for the Crown by transferring the staple of cloth from Antwerp to London,[6] a point also made rather differently by Armstrong who, in the course of his interminable papers, thought of ways of doing down the merchant adventurers as well as everybody else.[7]

[1] 26 Henry VIII, cc. 8, 9 (1534).
[2] 26 Henry VIII, c. 1, 32 Henry VIII, cc. 18, 19.
[3] Cf. above, pp. 69, 73 n. 1.
[4] Burton, 147; *LP Add.* 1382 (1); *Tudor Economic Documents* iii. 117. Professor Bindoff inclines to the view that the anonymous tract, too, is at least in part Armstrong's (*Econ. Hist. Rev.* 14 (1944–5), 65 f.), but after inspecting the manuscript I am not sure that I agree.   [5] *Tudor Econ. Doc.* iii. 121 f.
[6] *LP Add.* 918 (1–3). There is no reason for the *LP* dating to 1533. The documents were certainly received by Cromwell because Ralph Sadler endorsed them to that effect.
[7] *Tudor Econ. Doc.* iii. 119.

The first writer attacked the Calais Staple on the grounds that its existence encouraged men to invest their savings there with a minimum of risk, which prevented them (allegedly) from using their capital to expand the native cloth industry. The argument that English capitalists needed only some inducement to pour the golden waters of life over the manufacture of woollens also occurs in Starkey's book: the Staplers' export of raw wool, he said, removed the raw material to the advantage of foreign clothiers, but if that trade were stopped and the Staple broken 'there be marchand men that by the help of the prince will undertake in few years to bring clothing to as great perfection as it is in other parts'.[1] It is worth remembering that all of Starkey's remarks predate the likely production of all except Armstrong's treatises, and the anonymous piece just referred to thus has echoes of Starkey's thought which set it apart from Armstrong's commonplace; for the mere idea that English cloth be sold to all comers in England is found often enough in economic discussions at the time.

However, the destruction of the Calais Staple was one piece of advice which Cromwell did not take, nor did he ever directly attempt to transfer the cloth staple to England. He probably knew better than the pamphleteers that the bulk of English wool was already being manufactured in England, and he knew that England could not retreat from Antwerp as simply as that. Unlike Starkey, he apparently saw no virtue in the puritan proposal to stop the import of luxuries like wine,[2] a measure which would have depended on doing without a market for raw wool altogether and therefore ill accorded with Starkey's other trading schemes. Instead Cromwell adapted the counsel he received to produce two measures which Schanz described as 'a true masterpiece'.[3] They consisted of a proclamation of February 1539 and an act of 1540. The proclamation[4] reduced the customs payable by foreigners to the level of those paid by native merchants; the statute,[5] the first really well worked out navigation act, among other things reserved the benefit of the concession to foreigners who exported English manufactures acquired in England in English vessels only. Thus those foreigners who were willing to support English shipping would also in effect create something like Armstrong's cloth staple in England and were encouraged to do so by a reduction in costs which would very seriously affect the trade in English cloth exported to Antwerp for

[1] Burton, 158.   [2] Burton, 144.
[3] Schanz, *Handelspolitik*, i. 86 f., 372.
[4] *Proclamations*, i. 281 ff.   [5] 32 Henry VIII, c. 14.

purchase by continental merchants there, while yet no one could say that Cromwell had crudely intervened in the established London–Antwerp trade.

The experiment, timed for seven years in the first instance and never renewed, nevertheless ran into hot opposition from both the Antwerp interests and the Merchant Adventurers, opposition which Cromwell's successors, faced with the renewal of expensive war, were to find it impossible to resist. This does not deprive it of the distinction of being a bold scheme, with a fair chance of success, for achieving the advantages which all the theorists said could be obtained from concentrating the sale of cloth in England. And, once again, Starkey's *Dialogue* contains remarks in which the germ of the scheme may possibly be discerned. Starkey advocated the abatement of excessive cutoms dues but this was to be for reducing the price of essential imports, a policy not seriously taken up till the age of Huskisson. And with this he linked a strong recommendation that English merchants should use only English ships. There had been navigation acts before, but even re-enacting them in 1536 had proved of little avail; Starkey's demand was not for an innovation but for more effective measures than those in use. The great act of 1540 was just that – or it would have been if Henry VIII's policy in the 1540s had not forced the government to abandon these efforts to back English industry and shipping.

In all these matters, therefore, there are signs of much the same interrelationship. It can never be said outright that Cromwell adopted a proposal of Thomas Starkey's for legislative enactment, and it would indeed have been strange if he had done so. Starkey's own remarks were, purposely, only hints for a possible policy; he wrote away from England and a long way away from the reality of affairs; what he and others had to do, once Cromwell employed them, was to turn germs of ideas into possible statutes. What emerged was sometimes too grandiose to be used. On the other hand, it goes without saying that Cromwell's considerable legislative programme needed draftsmen and advisers; that Starkey was among the latter may be fairly inferred from the fact that some of the main areas of reformist action were those on which his analysis had concentrated. There are odd scraps of evidence to suggest how things happened. For instance, we have two draft preambles for statutes seemingly worked out by themselves for attachment to an act to be separately drafted; both are heavily corrected by Cromwell. One was intended for a depopulation statute: after rehearsing earlier acts, it comments on the decay of tillage, ruin of houses, and needs of poor people in terms which recall Starkey's remarks on the waste of ground 'before time occupied and tilled' and his suggestion that the poor be settled on new holdings carved out of the waste.[1] The other considers rural unemployment which it is hoped to solve by encouraging linen-weaving in the country-side, thereby in a way combining two of Starkey's preoccupations – the need to increase the rural population and the need to encourage all crafts.[2] Here reform legislation, inspired by 'commonwealth' ideas, was worked out for Cromwell's careful revision, so that the co-operation of minister and planners comes across very clearly.

However tenuous the specific links between the *Dialogue* and official policy may, therefore, appear, they are real and fit in well with everything we know about this government's doings. And Starkey's *Dialogue* is the only general statement of the day on social and economic reform which is anything like as diverse as the reforms which were planned or carried by Cromwell's administration. Some of the things done reflect the attitudes and even on occasion the specific demands of the treatise, and a few things, which it did not prove practicable to adopt, were drawn directly out of it. It does not, therefore, seem to me too much to claim that for Cromwell's advisers, and thus for Cromwell himself, this work of Cromwell's ablest tame pamphleteer provided something like a reservoir of ideas, certainly of ills and up to a point of remedies. Some of his most striking thoughts could find no welcoming reception. This is particularly true of his political devices – his proposals for an elective kingship, for a privy council appointed in Parliament, and for a supervisory council of ephors presided over by that antique officer, the constable of England.[3] But both the general radical tenor of his thought and the particular lines of attack are closely related to what was done.

Of course, no one can tell whether the government needed the stimulus of reading the *Dialogue* – or of having its author among the group of advisers – before deciding what needed doing. We should certainly not think of Cromwell as humbly carrying out a programme devised by a bunch of humanists. But neither, on this and other evidence, should we think of him as a pure pragmatist, a hand-to-mouth man, or a mere co-ordinator of the pressures applied by lobbyists. He thought about the needs of the realm in a systematic

---

[1] PRO, SP 1/69, fos. 17–19 (*LP* v. 721 [12]); Burton, 73 f., 140 f. The *LP* dates of all these drafts are entirely conjectural and rarely correct or even probable.

[2] PRO, SP 1/151, fos. 122–3 (*LP* xiv. I. 872).

[3] Burton, 150 ff., 156, 165 ff.

manner, listening to theorists, reading their proposals, and revising their drafts. They in turn clearly felt that in him they had a minister worth writing to and for. As Morison put it in a letter to Cromwell whose flattery was quite sincere: 'I am a graft of your lordship's own setting; if I bring forth any fruits I know who may claim them.'[1] Or again: 'Sed animus tuus in Christi Evangelium, studium illud tuum in veritatem, much more move me than all that ever I look to have of your lordship.'[2] The policy of the Tudor revolution and its programme of reform were steered by a man to whom statute offered the opportunity of bringing about that betterment of the commonwealth which the educated minds of the day were clamouring for. Neither were all their ideas sensible nor all his measures successful, but the parties to this discussion were in earnest and tried sincerely.

[1] PRO, SP 1/113, fo. 210 (*LP* xi. 1481).
[2] PRO, SP 1/133, fo. 253 (*LP* xiii. I. 1297).

GENERAL INDEX

Abbot, George (archbishop of Canterbury), 166

Abbot, Charles, Lord Colchester (Speaker), 175 n. 2

Abergavenny, lord, *see* Neville G.

Accursius, 206

Alan, 231

Aldridge, Robert, 99

Alesius, Alexander, 221 n. 6

Alvarde, Thomas, 98

Anne (queen of England), 158, 162 n. 1

Anne of Cleves, 73 n. 5

Antwerp, 254

Apologia (Pole), 217

Apology and Satisfaction (1604), 169–82

Apomaxis (Morison), 243 n. 4

Arches, court of, *see* Church of England, courts of

Aristotle, 217, 228, 240, 242

Armstrong, Clement, 63–4, 69, 71–3, 250, 254–5

Aston, Thomas, 178

Athens, 248

Audley, Thomas, drafts acts, 64, 79, 81, 85, 105 and n. 4, 109, 115, 118, 131 n. 2; lord chancellor, 99, 223; Speaker, 111, 128

Augsburg, 137

Austin, John, 204–8

Aylmer, John (bishop of London), 34

Bacon, Francis (lord chancellor), 165, 175, 177–8

Bacon, Nathaniel, 177, 179

Bancroft, Richard (archbishop of Canterbury), 166

Bangor, bishop of, *see* Salcot

Barton, Elizabeth, 57, 73 n. 5

Bate's Case, 210

Beaumont, Henry, 175

Beaumont, Thomas, 177

Bedford, earl of, *see* Russell F.

Bedyll, Thomas, 99

Beeston, Hugh, 178

Benet, William, 99

Bentham, Jeremy, 197

Berwick, 74 n. 1, 76

Bible, 66, 80, 250

Bodin, Jean, 31, 56, 205, 207 n. 2, 213

Bohemia, 120

Boleyn, Anne, 100, 152, 243

Boleyn, Thomas, earl of Wiltshire, 135

Boniface VIII (pope), 201

Bonner, Edmund (bishop of London), 99

Boston, William (abbot of Burton), 99–100

Bosworth, 3

Bracton, Henry de, 211, 224

Bristol, bishop of, *see* Thornborough J.

Buckingham, duke of, *see* Villiers G.

Buckinghamshire election, *see* Goodwin's Case

Burghley, lord, *see* Cecil W.

Burgo, Nicholas del, 99–100

Burlacy, William, 177

Burton, abbot of, *see* Boston W.

Calais, 51, 222, 226, 255

Calvin, Jean, 198, 203

Cambridge, *see* Universities; King's College, 54 n. 3

Canterbury, archbishop of, *see* Abbot G., Bancroft R., Cranmer, T., Laud W., Pole R., Warham W., Winchelsea R.; election at, 75; prerogative court of, 97 n. 2

Carleton, Dudley, 175

Carlisle, 76

Carmelites, provincial of (? John—), 99–100

Carr, Robert, 178

Cartwright, Thomas, 198

Castiglione, Baldassare, 220

Catherine of Aragon, 85–6, 93 n. 4, 99, 101

Cavendish, George, 225

Cecil, Robert, 179, 180, 181

Cecil, William, lord Burghley, 61, 234

Centeners, court of, 72–4

Century of Revolution, The (Hill), 155

259

Index

Index

Earlier Stuarts, The (Davies), 156
Edgehill, battle of, 189
Education, 240, 249
Edward I (king of England), 14, 20-2, 29, 31, 37, 105
Edward II (king of England), 22, 46
Edward III (king of England), 22-4, 44-5, 105
Edward IV (king of England), 30, 38, 47, 56
Edward V (king of England), 33
Edward VI (king of England), 138, 149, 225
Eliot, John, 168, 179, 186
Elizabeth I (queen of England), attitude to Parliament, 166, 170, 172, 174, 181; legislation in reign of, 56, 137-8, 141, 149, 225-6, monarchy of, 201; Parliament in reign of, 4, 6, 8, 36, 44, 52-3, 57-60, 128 n. 4, 159, 162, 171, 180, 182; also 157, 161, 198
Elsynge, Henry, senior, 10, 16
Ely, bishop of, see Goodrich T., Thirlby T.
Elyot, Thomas, 236
Enclosure, 138
Erasmus, Desiderius, 236, 239
Evolution of Parliament, The (Pollard), 7
Exchequer, baron of, 248; chamberlain of, 178; chief baron of, 28, and see Fleming T.; hand, 64 n. 4
Exhortation to the People, An (Starkey), 227

Fiennes, William, lord Say and Sele, 186
Filmer, Robert, 204 n. 1
First Fruits, 66, 79-81
Fisher, John (bishop of Rochester), 120-1, 127, 131 n. 1, 216, 217 n. 1, 222
Fitzgerald, family, 65
Fitzjames, James (lord chief justice), 226
Fitzwilliam, William, 135
Fleming, Thomas (chief baron), 210
Forma Subventionis Pauperum (Ypres), 151-2
Fortescue, John (lord chief justice), 28-9, 30, 32-3, 35, 57
Foxe, Edward (bishop of Hereford), 99-100, 134, 223
Foxe, John, 88 n. 1
France, monarchy of, 161, 199-200, 212, 231, representative institutions in, 21, 27-8, 30 n. 3, 31, 39-42, 48-9, 52, 56
Fuller, Nicholas, 175

Gardiner, Stephen (bishop of Winchester), 99-100, 219-20, 223-4

Germany, 188; representative institutions in, 32
Gibson, Richard, 68
Gigson, Thomas, 72-3, 74 n. 2, 77, 254
Gladstone, William Ewart, 196
Godfray, Thomas, 151
Goodrich, Thomas (bishop of Ely), 99
Goodwin's Case, 171, 173, 177-8
Gray's Inn, 224
Gwent, Richard, 99-100

Hakewill, William, 10, 16, 169 n. 3
Hale, Matthew, 169 n. 3, 181
Hales, John, 63, 71
Hall, Edward, 87 n. 4, 88 n. 2, 104 n. 1, 110, 112, 114, 116-17, 120-2, 128-9, 134, 135 n. 1
Hare, John, 177
Hastings, Francis, 173 n. 1, 177
Hatton, Richard, 54
Henry III (emperor), 200
Henry III (king of England), 20, 22
Henry VI (king of England), 24, 26, 45-7, 105
Henry V (king of England), 25
Henry VI (king of England), 25, 43, 46
Henry VII (king of England), 69 n. 5, 135; his queen, 54 n. 1; Parliament under, 29, 35, 54, 56-7
Henry VIII (king of England), and Church, 127, 130-2, 134-6; and Starkey, 237-40, 242-3; and Supplication, 112, 114, 129; attitude to Parliament, 32-3, 37, 57, 62; divorce of, 52, 85-6, 88, 93, 99-105, 113, 124; drafting of acts, 66, 84, 90-1, 105, 138 n. 4, 153; government of, 35, 74, 75-6, 223; legislation of, 56, 138-9, 225; monarchy of, 201-2, 215, 219, 231; Parliament in reign of, 4, 26 n. 1, 38, 41, 59, 182; wives of, see Anne of Cleves, Boleyn A., Catherine of Aragon; also, 217, 222 n. 8, 228 n. 1, 247-8
Henry, prince, 178
Herbert, John, 178
Hereford, bishop of, see Foxe E.
Heresy, 68, 80, 93-4, 120, 127, 130-1, 232
History of Parliament Trust, 5-6
Hitler, Adolf, 208
Hobbes, Thomas, 213
Hoby, Edward, 178
Hollis, John, 178
Homily of Obedience, 203
Hooker, John (alias Vowell), 10

261

Index

INDEX OF AUTHORS CITED

Includes only passages in which writers' views are discussed or assessed; writers contemporary with the events with which they deal are listed in the General Index.

Index

McIlwain, C. H., 198, 204 n. 1, 207
Mackie, J. B., 215 n. 1
Maitland, F. W., 63, 74, 92 n. 3, 195, 223, 246–7
Marchant, R. A., 164 n. 2
Merriman, R. B., 108, 109 n. 2, 125 n. 4, 215 n. 1
Miller, E., 20 n. 1
Mitchell, W. M., 176 n. 2, 179 n. 3
Moir, T. L., 4, 16 n. 1
Morgan, I., 164 n. 2
Mosse, G. L., 207 n. 3
Myers, A. R., 30 n. 3

Namier, L. B., 4–8, 162
Neale, J. E., 4–10, 57, 59, 83 n.*, 128 n. 4, 159, 166
Notestein, Wallace, 6–8, 15, 128 n. 4

Ogilvie, C. 165 n. 3
Ogle, A., 108–9, 110 n. 1, 123 n. 3, 129 n. 1

Parker, T. M., 215–16, 217 n. 1, 220–1, 224 n. 3
Pearson, A. F. S., 198
Pennington, D. H., 4 n. 7
Pickthorn, K. W. M., 108 n. 2, 117 n. 1, 215 n. 1
Plucknett, T. F. T., 67, 69–70, 244, 246
Pollard, A. F., 7, 10, 108, 119, 215
Post, G., 207 n. 1
Prestwich, Menna, 185 n. 1
Prothero, G. W., 169 n. 3, 171 n. 1

Rabb, T. K., 161 n. 1, 175 n. 1, 176–7, 179 n. 2
Ranke, L. von, 156, 196
Rapin-Thoyras, Paul de, 156, 170
Relf, Frances, 6, 15

Reynolds, Beatrice, 207 n. 2
Roskell, J. S., 3, 5, 27, 30 n. 2, 43 n. 1, 46

Schanz, G., 139 n. 2
Sedgwick, R., 5
Selley, J., 196 n. 1
Simpson, H., 15
Smith, H. M., 108 n. 2, 224 n. 3
Spufford, P., 20 n. 1
Steele, R. R., 253 n. 2
Stone, L., 67, 72–7
Strateman, Catherine (Mrs C. S. Sims), 10
Strype, J., 117, 119, 133 n. 4
Stubbs, W., 3, 43, 97 n. 1, 103 n. 2, 197

Taft, A. I., 121 n. 2
Tanner, J. R., 169 and n. 3, 171 n. 2, 173–4
Tawney, R. H., 138
Thorne, S. E., 57 n. 4
Tierney, B., 206 n. 3
Trevelyan, G. M., 156–7
Trevor-Roper, H. R., 4 n. 6, 165
Tucker, M. G., 194 n. 1

Ullmann, W., 210

Walzer, M., 165 n. 1, 188
Weisberger, L. A., 220
Wilks, M. J., 206 n. 1, 207 n. 1, 208
Williams, O. C., 11
Williams, P. H., 55 n. 2
Willson, D. H., 166 n. 1, 171 n. 1, 179 n. 3, 180 n. 5
Wormald, B. H. G., 167 n. 2

Zagorin, P., 4, 164 n. 1, 184–7
Zeeveld, W. G., 151 n. 3, 152 n. 3, 220, 228 n. 1, 236, 239 n. 2, 240 n. 1, 247 n. 2

267